SOCIAL NETWORKS AND SOCIAL SUPPORT

Sage Studies in Community Mental Health 4

SAGE STUDIES IN COMMUNITY MENTAL HEALTH

Series Editor: **Richard H. Price**
Community Psychology Program,
University of Michigan

SAGE STUDIES IN COMMUNITY MENTAL HEALTH is a book series consisting of both single-authored and co-authored monographs and concisely edited collections of original articles which deal with issues and themes of current concern in the community mental health and related fields. Drawing from research in a variety of disciplines, the series seeks to link the work of the scholar and practitioner in this field, as well as advance the state of current knowledge in community mental health.

Volumes in this series:
1. Gary VandenBos (Editor): *PSYCHOTHERAPY: Practice, Research, Policy*
2. Cary Cherniss: *STAFF BURNOUT: Job Stress in the Human Services*
3. Richard F. Ketterer: *CONSULTATION AND EDUCATION IN MENTAL HEALTH: Problems and Prospects*
4. Benjamin H. Gottlieb (Editor): *SOCIAL NETWORKS AND SOCIAL SUPPORT*

Additional Volumes in Preparation

social networks and social support

edited by
BENJAMIN H. GOTTLIEB

Volume 4, Sage Studies in Community Mental Health

SAGE PUBLICATIONS　　Beverly Hills　　London

For Lois and Evan

For information address:

SAGE Publications, Inc.
275 South Beverly Drive
Beverly Hills, California 90212

SAGE Publications Ltd
28 Banner Street
London EC1Y 8QE, England

Printed in the United States of America

Library of Congress Cataloging in Publication Data
Main entry under title:

Social networks and social support.

(Sage studies in community mental health : 4)
Includes bibliographies.
Contents: Social networks and social support in community mental health / Benjamin H. Gottlieb — Stressful events and social supports / John Eckenrode and Susan Gore — Social support in the adjustment of pregnant adolescents / Manuel Barrera, Jr. — [etc.]
1. Community mental health services — Social aspects. 2. Self-help groups. 3. Voluntarism. I. Gottlieb, Benjamin H. II. Series.
RA790.S612   362.2′042   81-9351
                AACR2

ISBN 0-8039-1669-8
ISBN 0-8039-1670-1 (pbk.)

THIRD PRINTING, 1983

CONTENTS

SERIES EDITOR'S PREFACE

When we use the term "mental health care," most of us immediately think of large bureaucratized hospitals, clinics, or other similar agencies staffed by professionals delivering "episodes of care." It is easy to overlook the fact that this represents only a tiny fraction of the total amount of health and mental health care provided in North America every year. Because of the images conjured up by professional discussions of "health care systems," there is a temptation to neglect the largest of all forms of health care. This form of care is not provided by professionals, no elaborate plans have been developed for its service delivery, and seldom if ever is money exchanged for an episode of care.

The form of health care to which I am referring consists of social networks and systems of social support among kin, neighbors, and members of voluntary associations. In Gottlieb's words, this book deals with "the manner in which human attachments are structured as systems of support and the resources that are exchanged among the members of these systems." Despite the complexity and importance of these structured human attachments for health and psychological well-being, we have given them only passing attention. Now in a time when our culture seems increasingly preoccupied with social fragmentation and separateness, the idea of social networks and social support suddenly has become attractive.

The present volume records current progress in research and action concerning the nature and impact of social support. In this book, Gottlieb has gathered together a group of conceptually incisive contributors who have developed detailed and critical conceptions of social support and social networks. The critical scholarly perspective

7

is complemented by a sensitivity to the nuances of value and diversity among social groups they study.

Gottlieb first anchors us in the history of the concept of social support and reviews the early works of pioneers who first explored the health-protective effects of human attachment. He also provides conceptual groundwork that prepares us for what is to come. We are then introduced to a series of contributions examining the moderating effects of social support on the stresses that result from major life transitions. This research prepares us to consider then the next series of papers, which are concerned with the structure and function of social networks and their role in promoting social support. We are given an opportunity to examine the relationship between formal health care systems and the informal system I described earlier, consisting of lay groups concerned with mutual aid and support.

This last set of concerns is of particular importance to mental health and health care professionals. We are only now coming to recognize the benefits that can accrue from a collaboration between formal systems of health care and the much larger but more diffuse system of social support that may exist in the community.

This is a volume for many audiences. It is for researchers who are in search of sharper distinctions, new conceptions, and innovative applications. It is for administrators and evaluators concerned with service design that is responsive to community needs. And it is a book for clinicians and program developers who are interested in providing care that mobilizes and encourages the natural support systems which so profoundly affect the quality of their clients' lives.

– Richard H. Price

ACKNOWLEDGMENTS

The essays appearing in this volume bring to bear a variety of perspectives on the role of social support in the coping process and on the contribution of laypersons to the provision of human services in our communities. Collectively, these chapters summarize and integrate our current knowledge about the impact of the social environment on health and well-being, and they offer an agenda for future research and action initiatives that explore ways of optimizing social support in people's lives. In soliciting papers for this volume, I hoped, in addition, to obtain a set of empirical studies that would clarify the meaning and measurement of the terms "social support" and "social network," terms that are ubiquitous in recent social science literature, yet often vaguely understood. I also undertook the preparation of this volume out of my own interest in further elaborating an ecological and naturalistic viewpoint on the process of social adaptation. This book is unified by its focus on the health consequences arising from the interplay between people and the social orbits in which they participate.

Certain persons and institutions provided the encouragement and resources necessary for the completion of this project. The contributors have made my first book-editing venture a very satisfying experience, and I thank them collectively for their prompt and effective revisions of early chapter drafts. Rick Price, the editor of this series of studies in community mental health, was ever enthusiastic about the volume's significance and provided sound editorial guidance throughout its preparation. Three of my colleagues in particular — Tony D'Augelli, Bart Hirsch, and Roger Mitchell — provided important feedback about the plan of the book and about the ideas contained in my own chapters. I also wish to acknowledge, with thanks, the support provided by the Social Sciences and Humanities Research Council of Canada in the form of a leave fellowship that supplemented the assistance rendered by the University of Guelph during the sabbatical I was granted. I am also grateful to Cynthia Nighswander for her competent work in preparing the final book manuscript for submission and for her attention to the minutiae associated with this task.

I have dedicated the volume to my wife, Lois, and to my son, Evan. Each of them sustained me in special ways during the course of my work on this book. Lois took precious time off from her beginning law studies in order to provide the sort of human dialogue I needed at the project's outset, and at crucial times she helped me to keep my priorities in perspective. Evan, who had just entered kindergarten, somehow seemed able to gauge the times when I needed to be left alone and when I needed to be lured away to his land of Shrinky-Dinks and Lego. I treasure the companionship and support we three share.

Chapter 1

SOCIAL NETWORKS AND SOCIAL SUPPORT IN COMMUNITY MENTAL HEALTH

BENJAMIN H. GOTTLIEB

During the past decade researchers from a number of social science and health-related disciplines have turned their attention to the study of social forces in the natural environment that contribute to the maintenance and promotion of people's health. While these investigators bring to bear methods of research that are favored by their disciplines and speak in an idiom not easily understood by outsiders, their inquiries converge on a phenomenon of fundamental importance to human welfare: the manner in which human attachments are structured as systems of support and the resources that are exchanged among the members of these systems. Sociologists have this phenomenon in mind when they speak about the role of voluntary associations in fostering social integration, and when they document, in Durkheim's fashion, the adverse health consequences experienced by those who occupy socially marginal or minority statuses, or by those who have "lost" their communities. Urban anthropologists reference this phenomenon in terms of a more distinct unit of social structure, seeking to analyze how the morphology of people's social networks and the characteristics of their ties affect the level of support to which they have access. Researchers in social work and in urban studies have investigated neighborhood-based "natural helping networks," viewing them as expressions of the social interdependence that can arise from a shared living environment, while social psychiatrists and allied mental health professionals have concentrated on mutual-help groups, the most visible and highly organized form of lay helping arrangements. In short, at this historical moment there exist a variety of perspectives on the phenomenon of social support and an equally rich data base. Our present need is to draw together these varied perspectives, to facilitate greater communication as a basis for collaboration among the disciplines pursuing this research, and to consider how our current knowledge base can inform the design of preventive interventions that mobilize social support. This volume is directed toward these three tasks.

In this chapter my primary purpose is to trace several historical themes in the field of community mental health and in closely related fields that have adumbrated current multidisciplinary interest in the topic of social support. I will also identify certain contemporary forces in the academic sphere and in society which I believe have spurred inquiry into the nature and effects of social support. I conclude with an overview of the contributions I have selected for this book, contributions that collectively epitomize the range of policy issues, programmatic initiatives, and research directions that are currently being pursued in the study of social support.

THEMES CONVERGING ON THE STUDY OF SOCIAL SUPPORT

While it would be presumptuous to make the claim that current research and action on the topic of social support are a direct outgrowth of prior developments in the field of community mental health, it is possible to identify certain recurrent themes of the past forty years that have at least foreshadowed the attention now being drawn to the role of informal helping networks in health maintenance. It is only for the sake of parsimony that I have organized these historical themes into two categories. In fact, these themes are closely interwoven and their relation to one another will become clear once I outline how contemporary developments have drawn them together.

The Social Environment and Health: Early Ecological Investigations

Approximately four decades ago, Faris and Dunham (1939) published their classic treatise on the ecological correlates of mental disorder in Chicago. Examining the spatial and temporal distribution of psychoses in that city, they documented two significant trends: the highest incidence of schizophrenia was concentrated in the most disorganized central zone of the city, and high rates of schizophrenia occurred consistently in the ethnic minority enclaves throughout the city. While the former finding was eventually explained via the adverse health consequences of conditions of social isolation and social disorganization prevailing in the central city, Dunham (1959: 240) implicated "breaks in or barriers to communication between persons in a given population" in the genesis of schizophrenia among ethnic group members who lived in minority settlements. Some two decades later, Alexander Leighton and his colleagues conducted a series of epidemiological surveys within several Canadian maritime communities that differed in their degree of social disintegration (Hughes et al., 1960; Leighton, 1959). Here, too, a set of ecological hypotheses were generated from the associations that obtained between the prevalence of psychiatric disorders and such psychological markers of local social disorganization as a sense of anomie, a sense of confusion about appropriate standards for behavior and for moral conduct, and a sense of futility about one's ability to gain nurturance and recognition.

We can identify a second strand in the fabric of ecological research that related conditions of social disorganization to the genesis of disorders in the work of Hinkle and Wolff who, in 1954, established the Human Ecology Study Program at Cornell University. In collaboration with researchers from several health and social sciences, these investigators sought to assess the extent to which cultural, geographic, and interpersonal changes in people's lives were associated with increased vulnerability to periods of physical illness. Their pioneering methods of exploring these relationships involved the collection of extensive data about the respondents' entire medical histories, their current health statuses, their personality structures, the meaning they attached to recent outstanding life experiences, and their accounts of their current life situations in relation to their immediate and past social environments. Further, their research is notable not simply because their careful methods of investigation added credence to the general proposition that people's relation to their social environment has a major influence on their health; it also generated a series of novel ideas about specific situational and personality factors that differentially affected people's success in adapting to similar and often harsh environmental conditions. Their formulations about the factors that seem to be health-protective among certain individuals and populations drew attention to the importance of certain coping styles and of access to compensatory social ties in explaining differential vulnerability to environmental stressors. In the following quotation from Hinkle's (1974: 40-41) summary of some of the findings from the Human Ecology Study Program, I have emphasized material that points to these two sets of moderating variables.

> Some people who remain free from illness in the face of major life changes appear to have *psychological characteristics which help to "insulate" them from the effects of some of their life experiences.* . . .
> The loss of a husband or wife, the separation from one's family, the isolation from one's friends, community, or country, the frustration of apparently important desires, or the failure to attain apparently important goals produced no profound or lasting reaction. They . . . *readily shifted to other relationships* when established relationships were disrupted.

Holmes and Rahe (1967) subsequently built on this legacy from medical ecology and, in addition, drew heavily on the psychobiological work of Adolf Meyer (1951) in developing the Social Readjustment Rating Scale, an instrument that has allowed investigators systematically to survey and quantify the social readjustment or adaptive challenge associated with a great variety of changes in people's accustomed life patterns. Items on this rating scale have been ranked and assigned weights according to the readjustment they require, with "death of spouse" accorded the highest mean value of 100 units and "minor violations of the law" accorded the lowest value of 11 units (Holmes & Rahe, 1967: 216). While today there is much controversy surrounding the most meaningful strategies of assigning weights to the items and much discussion of the underlying dimensions and psychometric properties of the scale itself (Rabkin & Struening, 1976), there is no doubt that this research tool has offered greater precision to ecological investigations of the relation between disturbances and adversity in the environment and the onset, severity, and course of illnesses, both psychiatric and medical. Equally important, the development of the Social Readjustment Rating Scale has stimulated a great deal of research focusing on the circumstances, both psychological and situational, under which life events are capable of producing adverse health consequences. In particular, the same two sets of factors originally identified by Hinkle and Wolff (1958) — personal variables such as psychological defenses, past experience, and cognitive processes, and situational variables such as access to social resources — have been proposed as critical mediators or moderating variables in the relationships between life events and health outcomes (Dohrenwend & Dohrenwend, 1978).

Another noteworthy but often overlooked link in the chain of ecological research relating social factors and life events to health was forged by a team of organizational researchers drawn from the Survey Research Center and and the Research Center for Group Dynamics at the University of Michigan. Together, they planned a systematic program of research devoted to unraveling the mutual interactions between, on the one hand, the motives, self-identity, and personality of workers, and, on the other hand, the objective conditions existing in the workplace. Through a series of empirical inquiries carried out in diverse industrial settings in the 1950s, they obtained converging evidence pointing to four major sets of variables whose interaction jointly determined worker health: properties of the objective social environment, including both intra- and extraorganizational role relations; characteristics of the psychological environment, which together reflect the individual's own perception and experience of the objective social environment; characteristics of the person, including psychological states, physiological states, and self-identity; and characteristics of the individual's behavior, including the coping techniques and defensive styles expressed in the process of adjustment to the environment (French & Kahn, 1962).

The theoretical yield of this ambitious program of research has only recently been fully acknowledged (Cobb, 1974). First, it drew attention to the process whereby objective organizational conditions are translated into personal psychological meanings which, in turn, condition the "goodness of fit" of the employee in the work milieu. As we shall see, subsequent research initiated by Rudolph Moos has enlarged our understanding of the dimensions along which the external environment is evaluated and experienced by people, and which are differentially associated with their morale and health states. Second, the metatheoretical model propounded by French and Kahn (1962) also gave explicit recognition to variables that may intervene between objectively and subjectively experienced environmental stress, with the effect of enhancing or decreasing susceptibility to adverse health. They showed, for example, that greater immunity could result from the employment of certain psychological defenses that intervene between objective and subjective stress and that prior experience with a similar stressor might also be capable of moderating adverse subjective reactions. Similarly, the immediate social context in which workers participate, and, in particular, its adequacy in satisfying the individual's needs, could intervene between objective and subjective stress, thus also conditioning health outcomes. This latter finding thus represents the most succinct statement of the ecological thesis I have been tracing, namely, that people's relation to their social environment has a critical influence on their health. Indeed, French's (1974) studies, aimed at assessing the moderating effects of social support on the job, have led him to conclude that "supportive relations with other people can often act as an effective buffer between job stress and strain, particularly physiological strain, within the person" (1974: 19).

As I have just noted, Moos's (1974a, 1974b) contemporary explorations of the properties of human milieux have led to the identification of several dimensions common to a great many social environments. He has organized these dimensions into three well-known classes of variables reflecting people's perceptions of (1) the interpersonal sphere; (2) the personal development sphere; and (3) the sphere that concerns the extent of order, control, and change in the milieu. In a paper coauthored with Kiritz, Moos set out to review the literature relating these social-climate dimensions to the health of setting occupants (Kiritz & Moos, 1974). Their findings echo the proposition French voiced regarding the role of supportive social ties in the workplace, and which earlier ecological researchers had expressed in more global terms and in the context of epidemiological studies relating general conditions of social disorganization to vulnerability to illness:

> The social stimuli associated with the relationship dimensions of
> *support, cohesion,* and *affiliation* generally have positive effects —
> enhancing normal development and reducing recovery time from
> illness, for example [Kiritz & Moos, 1974: 109].

The connection between these several lines of ecological inquiry and contemporary research and intervention involving social networks and support systems, can be succinctly explained in two ways. On the one hand, a set of ecological guidelines can be generated for the purpose of creating or redesigning human milieux so as to ensure that adequate levels of support are available to all the setting's occupants. This strategy is well exemplified in Moos's (1974) efforts to effect changes in the size and staffing patterns of hospital wards, changes which altered people's perceptions of several aspects of the social climate of the wards, including a shift toward more favorable assessments of the relationship dimensions. Interventions of this sort are properly conceived of as primary-preventive in nature, since they are directed toward engineering social milieux in which people are firmly anchored and emotionally sustained.

On the other hand, social support can be mobilized as a secondary preventive strategy on behalf of persons who are vulnerable due to the threat engendered by acute or chronic turbulence in their broader social environment. Here I am referring to programs that attempt to bring people facing specific adversities and transitions into meaningful contact with a peer group, hoping in this way to effect some moderation in their subjective experience of stress (Gottlieb, forthcoming). A classic example of this strategy is the creation of support groups among couples experiencing the transition to parenthood (Mc Guire & Gottlieb, 1979; Wandersman, 1978; 1980). These groups, sometimes referred to as "situation-transition groups" (Schwartz, 1975), encourage participants to compare notes with one another about the emotional quality of their common experiences and about coping strategies they are newly practicing, and they often result in the formation of new friendships that endure beyond the last structured group meeting (Barrett, 1978).

Lay Resources in Mental Health

A second historical theme adumbrating contemporary interest in the topic of social support touches on the importance of a diversity of informal helping resources that are ubiquitous in the community and that ought to be drawn into any comprehensive plan to meet the mental health needs of citizens. The lay resources that have figured importantly in the community mental health literature range from ordinary citizens who have been especially attentive and responsive to emotional distress within the confines of their neighborhood, to representatives of the major socializing institutions of the community, whose work roles have naturally spilled over to include certain informal counseling activities. In addition, mutual-help associations populated by persons who share a problem in living or who wish to be advocates on behalf of others with such a problem have always been among the most visible lay helping resources.

I am drawn again to Warren Dunham's early work pertaining to the ecological study of mental disorders, since his attention to the community dynamics associated with the emotional adjustment of citizens led him to an equal concern about the health-enhancing and health-preserving forces in the environment. In a paper appearing in *Mental Hygiene* in 1940, he directed his attention to the design of aftercare services that ought to be available to the returning mental patient (Dunham, 1959). In his conviction that any such program ought to be "functionally related to the local community" (1959: 246), not only did he argue in favor of involving indigenous community leaders in the formulation of policy and in the organization and administration of the program, but he also strongly endorsed the educational work of a mutual-aid organization composed of ex-mental patients, describing it as "the outstanding mental hygiene achievement of the decade" (1959: 246). In the following excerpt from an address he presented to the Illinois Psychiatric Society in 1939, Dunham (1959: 246) voices a philosophy strikingly similar to present-day thinking about ways of bringing informal resources to bear on the task of reintegrating the mentally ill in the community:

> The Association of Former Patients has taken the lead in reminding us again that it is to the community that the patient returns after he has recovered from his mental illness. In a real preventive program, the community would provide for the recovered patient resources to which he could turn for help in making the necessary readjustment to the community life.

Twenty years later, the social psychiatrist Leonard Duhl addressed a meeting of the American Psychiatric Association and expanded on his understanding of the role a range of informal "caretakers" plays in fielding the emotional problems and attenuating the stress experienced by a large segment of the population. Generalizing from a small-scale study revealing that college students tended to turn for help to religious counselors, residence staff, and academic offices rather than to the psychiatric services on campus, Duhl (1963: 70) argued that psychiatrists needed to shift their focus to ways of "helping people to help others" and to "developing a network of resources that a community uses and can use when its members are under stress." Most important, in discussing the prospects for a new consulting relationship between psychiatry and the informal caregiving sector of the community, Duhl sounded a warning which has since been frequently repeated, namely, that the process of interaction between the parties must be carefully modulated so as to reinforce and support the care lay helpers extend, not to refashion it through an apprenticeship in psychiatry.

Indeed, during the period just prior to passage of the Community Mental Health Centers Act, a great deal of attention was devoted to the difficulties associated with delivering comprehensive mental health services to urban populations in general and to poor and minority communities in particular. It was during this epoch that Gerald Caplan (1964) developed his seminal papers outlining the principles of preventive psychiatry and, in collaboration with his colleagues at Harvard, outlined a program of consultation that could be mounted among diverse community gatekeepers such as teachers, family physicians, and public health nurses. A productive group of researchers at the Mental Health Study Center of the National Institute of Mental Health were equally active in formulating ideas and policy initiatives concerning ways professionals might enlarge and buttress the role of informal resources in the urban community. Klein (1959), for example, called attention to the unique role of the clergy in matters of mental health, while Kelly's (1966) insightful essay, "The Mental Health Agent in the Urban Community," alerted professionals to the fact that "urban agents" such as apartment house managers, hairdressers, and local merchants are not only the first line of defense when emotional problems arise among working-class people, but they also mediate between the local culture and the formal system of health services in metropolitan areas. Furthermore, Kelly wove these ideas about the informal helping and referral functions of urban agents into a broader fabric of research, which aimed to delineate how local social structures and social processes influenced people's access to resources, including mental health services, and how this relationship in turn conditioned personal adaptation.

The publication of two monographs prepared by President Kennedy's Joint Commission on Mental Health and Illness brought to bear national data and lent more formal authority to these several perspectives on the importance of lay resources in mental health. In *Americans View Their Mental Health,* Gurin et al. (1960) documented the extensive reliance the public placed on informal caregivers as well as on family members and friends when "periods of unhappiness" and personal problems overtaxed self-help efforts. Similarly, the volume titled, *Community Resources in Mental Health*

(Robinson et al., 1960) gave explicit recognition to a broad field of social forces and institutional resources that appeared to promote mental health but that the professional service sector had not accommodated. These and other studies calling for changes in the traditional treatment system to make it more appropriate and accessible to lower socioeconomic groups and minority populations (Albee, 1959; Riessman et al., 1964), and more closely articulated with the informal resources and primary institutions of the community, provided the rationale for the development of new outreach programs of mental health consultation and new manpower programs intended better to serve the needs of the poor and the disadvantaged. The New Careers movement, the antipoverty movement, and the community mental health movement, while emphasizing somewhat different intentions, all emphasized the need to recruit nonprofessionals for diverse tasks associated with the delivery of human services. They have indeed been extensively deployed in virtually every sphere of interpersonal helping and, while there remain serious problems related to their conditions of work and relations with professional practitioners and administrators (Alley et al., 1979), there is much evidence testifying to their clinical effectiveness (Durlak, 1979; Karlsruher, 1974) and their ability to serve a bridging function between those in need and agencies with the resources to meet those needs (Alley et al., 1979). In their insightful social history of the paraprofessional movement of the 1960s, Levine et al. (1979: 65) conclude with the following statement concerning the bases of paraprofessional effectiveness:

> Looked at from an historical and cross-cultural perspective, paraprofessionals were not simply cheaper, less thoroughly trained professionals; rather, they were individuals who contributed unique skills, perspectives, affiliations, and/or motivations that resulted in the development and delivery of more relevant and accessible services.

The relationship between these various lines of research and action centering on the role of lay resources in the field of community mental health and contemporary developments in the study and promotion of social support systems is self-evident. The number of mutual-help groups is ever expanding, and increasingly professionals are helping to initiate and sponsor such groups among their own clientele. Programs of consultation for a diversity of informal community caregivers, such as extension agents and hairdressers, and for institutionally based gatekeepers, such as lawyers, teachers, and members of the clergy, are also widespread. Paraprofessionals and volunteers are preferred as staff members in psychosocial rehabilitation programs for "deinstitutionalized" mental patients, such as Fountain House in New York and The Club at Rutgers Community Mental Health Center in New Jersey (Lanoil & Turner, 1979). In addition, the historical emphasis placed on mobilizing an informal network of support on behalf of vulnerable populations is beginning to find expression in research (Cohen & Sokolovsky, 1978) and intervention strategies (Hammer, forthcoming) that explore the effects of altering the more intimate primary group structures in which these populations are embedded. Their formulations about the ways in which people's personal networks of social ties can be restructured or reoriented so as to provide more adequate support (see Wellman's and Hirsch's chapters in this volume) represent an important new development in the study of the health-protective effects of lay helping resources.

THE EMERGENT FOCUS ON
SOCIAL SUPPORT

In my characterization of prior investigations of the relationship between health and the social environment, and in my review of the historic importance of incorporating lay resources in the provision of mental health services, I have attempted to illuminate the seeds of present-day interest in the topic of social support. We can now better appreciate how these early developments in community mental health theory and practice foreshadowed the field's modern investments in those social interventions that strengthen the community's natural helping resources and in research concerning the adaptive consequences arising from the interplay between people and the informal social structures in which they are embedded. Yet the link between the past and contemporary formulations about the role of social support in health protection is still hazy, since it only received its full articulation in the early 1970s when the epidemiologist, John Cassel, and the social psychiatrist, Gerald Caplan, each contributed seminal papers on the nature and public health implications of social support. In what follows I briefly outline their contributions, which gave such great impetus to current inquiries and interventions on this topic.

The Epidemiological Formulations
of John Cassel

Cassel's early thinking about the relationship between "psychosocial processes" and stress is best reflected in a paper devoted to untangling the ambiguous and contradictory research findings on the health consequences of urban life (Cassel, 1974). As an epidemiologist, Cassel was fundamentally concerned with the process whereby environmental conditions such as crowding, inadequate housing, and deteriorating neighborhoods exercised an ill effect on people, as demonstrated by a series of studies linking such conditions to higher infant mortality rates, higher incidence of tuberculosis and digestive diseases, and, in the mental health field, to a higher prevalence of diagnoses of psychosis. This familiar ecological inquiry led to the classic epidemiological problem of accounting for the fact that, while some persons fell victim to the noxious environment, others were unaffected. In unraveling this problem he called upon Rene Dubos's (1965) work on the origins of microbial diseases and also tapped a body of animal research linking certain forms of social disorganization, and changes in these patterns, to biological changes, which in turn affected the animal's vulnerability to disease.

His synthesis of these two bodies of knowledge culminated in a proposition we have encountered before, namely, that changes in the immediate social environment are capable of altering people's resistance to disease, via the metabolic effects they trigger. In explicating the way certain psychosocial processes enhance susceptibility to disease, Cassel (1974) argued that at the height of social disorganization people or animals appear to suffer from confusing or insufficient signals from their social milieu, and sometimes they suffer from the absence of any feedback. In short, Cassel maintained that ill health is predicated on a loss of equilibrium due to disordered signs and signals from significant others or due to the lack of information necessary to correct deviations from course. As I will show later, Gerald Caplan's disquisitions on the topic of support systems took these notions of social feedback as their theoretical cornerstones. Turning now to the evidence he had uncovered that some people (and animals) were apparently unaffected by the social upheavals and discontinuities to which they were exposed, Cassel (1974) identified a second, general category of psychosocial processes, which he designated as health-protective. He loosely referred to these processes as involving "the strength of the social supports provided by the primary groups of most importance to the individual" (Cassel, 1974: 478). Here, I emphasize the fact that Cassel did not operationalize the social support construct, but instead cited a diverse series of studies intended to illustrate his meaning. Hence, much of the work subsequent to Cassel's writings, and several of the chapters in this volume (those by Barrera, DiMatteo and Hays, and by Hirsch), are bent on the task of identifying the precise meaning and measurement of the social support construct. To sum up, Cassel's main legacy rests on the two lines of ecological inquiry he spurred: inquiries devoted to analyzing how people's interactions with the social environment conspire to augment their vulnerability to illness and disease, and how social forces can be mobilized in these situations for the sake of health protection. Cassel (1974: 479) strongly advocated work on the latter topic, since he believed it offered a more practical avenue toward primary prevention:

> Of the two sets of factors, it would seem more immediately feasible to attempt to improve and strengthen the social supports rather than reduce the exposure to the stressors.

Functions and Types of Support Systems in the Community: Gerald Caplan's Contribution

Caplan picked up the threads of Cassel's (1974) theoretical formulations, notably the evidence suggesting that the harmful effects of social disorganization stem from confusing or absent feedback from the social environment, and wove them into the fabric of social psychiatry he had produced ten years earlier in his *Principles of Preventive Psychiatry* (1964). For example, his own understanding of the social forces influencing the course and outcome of developmental and situational crises converged with Cassel's (1974) statements implicating primary-group ties in the amelioration of stress. In his paper, "Support Systems," Caplan (1974) set himself to the task of illuminating the nature of the social support radiated within the primary group, detailing its importance for the health and welfare of citizens. Equally important, he elaborated a scheme for classifying types of support systems and outlined a variety of activities that community mental health workers could pursue both to initiate and to stimulate the development of supportive attachments in local catchment areas.

Caplan's statements about the helping functions of support systems are much clearer than his understanding of their structure. In an often cited quotation, he identifies their three major contributions to people's well-being:

> The significant others help the individual mobilize his psychological resources and master his emotional burdens; they share his tasks; and they supply him with extra supplies of money, materials, tools, skills, and cognitive guidance to improve his handling of his situation [Caplan, 1974: 6].

While he uses the term "system" in referring to these supportive aggregates, he does not elaborate on any of the structural properties that others familiar with systems-centered thinking might consider, nor does he comment on how such systems germinate and evolve. Instead, he briefly comments on the importance of relationship durability as one hallmark of a *system* of supportive social ties, and then mainly concentrates on the task of depicting three forms of support systems he has encountered. Here again, I highlight the omission of information about the structural properties and boundaries of support systems and about their formation and development in Caplan's writings, so that the reader can better understand other aspects of the current controversy surrounding basic definitional issues in the study of social support.

The labels Caplan (1974) attaches to the three types of support systems he describes have generally not been adopted by subsequent investigators, but it is usually acknowledged that he was comprehensive in his coverage of their protean character. From his discussion, one can discern emphases on mutual-help groups; neighborhood-based, informal arrangements for the delivery of helping services; primary-group networks composed of kith, blood, and pseudo-family ties; and his long-standing interest in the informal help extended by community gatekeepers such as physicians and members of the clergy. His most valuable bequest to the field of community mental health is, as always, his ideas about the roles professionals can assume in preventive interventions involving these support systems. He shows, for example, how traditional mental health consultation can be extended to the creation of support groups among gatekeepers in the same occupation; he exhorts professionals to play a part both in launching mutual-aid groups on behalf of people undergoing major life transitions and developmental crises, and in lending their research and training skills to existing groups; and he suggests that similar organizing and buttressing activities can be undertaken at the neighborhood level, where professionals can work with key citizens who are at the center of local helping networks, assisting them to expand the reach of these networks and to clarify their understanding of human relations and social needs. Each of these action initiatives has since been more fully developed in contemporary community mental health programs, and several are described in this volume by Froland and his colleagues, by Mitchell and Hurley, and in a second chapter which I have authored.

SOURCES OF CONTEMPORARY INTEREST IN NETWORKS OF INFORMAL SUPPORT

Cassel's theoretical disquisition implicating the social environment in the origins and amelioration of stress, and Caplan's practical strategies for mobilizing social support systems, have drawn a great deal of attention only in part because they were able concisely to integrate and articulate the implications of the early research I have reviewed concerning the role of social-ecological factors and informal helping resources in community mental health. In addition, their ideas provoked much discussion and stimulated a great deal of research because they suited the values and the research paradigms to which a great many practitioners and researchers subscribed, and because their ideas resonated to consumer criticisms of the health care system in America. In what follows I elaborate on each of these themes, and in so doing I hope to inform the reader's understanding of the forces fueling contemporary inquiries into the nature and effects of social support.

In all that Caplan (1974) has to say about the manner of working with support systems, it is evident that he places a premium on the *collaborative* nature of the relationship between the professional and local citizens, and that he believes that successful collaboration is in large part determined by the professional's ability to appreciate and respect the *cultural diversity* of communities. Caplan explicitly cautions community mental health workers about the dangers of making others over in the professional mold and thereby supplanting indigenous forms of lay help. Further, his examples of diverse types of support systems suggest that differing local conditions call for different pathways for promoting social support. Both of these values were consonant with sentiments that prevailed among practitioners and academics in the community mental health field at that time. On the one hand, there were increasing pressures on mental health centers to address the needs of ethnic populations, rural communities, and other historically underserved populations, and to do so in a manner that did not force these people into the limited options offered by the traditional, professionally dominated service system. On the other hand, there was a growing recognition of the fact that the paraprofessional movement had been derailed from its original goals of identifying the needs of, and building a bridge to, the residents of these underserved communities, and that this had occurred because of the professional system's tendency to *incorporate* rather than to *collaborate with* indigenous leaders and talented local residents. In short, as Mitchell and Hurley point out in Chapter 11 of this volume, experience gained from the paraprofessional movement taught that citizens should be mobilized for the sake of mental health without colonizing them and that the influence of nonprofessionals ought to rest on their connection to their host communities, not on the credentialing they receive from professionals.

The study or development of natural support systems has offered a way of realizing the values placed on collaboration and cultural diversity. It allows for an appreciation of how people in contrasting subcultures take hold of indigenous resources and organize themselves into social aggregates that are capable of withstanding threats to their members' well-being. It offers insights into the manner in which local sociocultural patterns, belief systems, and environmental forces condition definitions of social support and the preferences that people express for certain sources of social support. Two examples may help to clarify how these values are expressed in action.

There is little question that the sort of "natural helping network" that Collins (1973) discovered in a neighborhood in Portland, Oregon, which proved so effective as an informal day-care system, was an expression of local norms about reciprocity between neighbors, an outgrowth of the spatial configuration of the neighborhood itself and its effects on patterns of social interaction, and a reflection of the common values local residents held about the care of their children. Similarly, when Leutz (1976) attempted to identify a set of lay referral agents in East Harlem, New York, he first identified the informal social settings in which local residents participated. His search took him to local spiritualists, merchants, and the owners of social clubs who proved to be critical sources of support and advice for local residents because they were members of numerous social networks and had access to much information about jobs, social services, and local social affairs. Recognizing their centrality in the life of the community, Leutz educated them about local drug treatment services and, with their consent, tried to improve the accuracy of their referral practices. In both of these examples, the authors first attempted to understand local configurations of interpersonal ties associated with the expression of help; only subsequently did they attempt to optimize local helping functions by establishing a coordinate, peer relationship with key influentials.

Caplan's and Cassel's ideas about the role of social support in health protection were favorably received also because they dovetailed with recent formulations about the epidemiology of mental disorder, and because they suggested an agenda for research on stress and coping that could best be accomplished via the sort of naturalistic and "ecologically valid" methods of inquiry to which a growing number of applied social scientists had become committed.

Bloom (1979) has recently spelled out how Cassel's and Caplan's ideas about social support can be integrated within a revised epidemiological framework providing a new focus for preventive interventions in community mental health. Bloom opens his discussion with a general summary of the research on the relation between stressful life events and diverse illness episodes, and draws two conclusions from this work: (a) physical and/or mental illness is induced by triggering or precipitating events in a person's current environment, not necessarily by long-standing predispositions; and (b) these stressful life events and transitions seem to increase general vulnerability to disease, not susceptibility to specific diseases. He then brings these two conclusions to bear in his revision of the traditional public health formulation of prevention, arguing that, while the accepted epidemiological model begins by identifying a specific disease and proceeds to pinpoint and eradicate its causes, his conclusions suggest that one should instead begin by identifying those life events with harmful *general* consequences and then seek to reduce or eradicate those consequences. In short, Bloom maintains that, at least in the mental health sphere, we should turn our efforts toward designing preventive interventions on behalf of populations experiencing those stressful life events known to generate adverse emotional outcomes. Calling on Cassel's (1974) work, Bloom suggests that social support offers one important avenue for neutralizing these consequences. Here I might add that it is particularly advisable to take this avenue when people face life events that entail or threaten the loss of significant social ties. Events involving potentially great social losses include divorce and separation (see, for example, Wilcox's chapter), death of a social intimate, job loss, retirement, and geographic moves. Other events requiring reorientation to or rearrangement of the social environment include first-time parenthood (see, for example, Barrera's chapter on this topic), school and college entrance, and job changes. The more general implication of Bloom's "new paradigm" for primary prevention is that social support is a key resource for health promotion because of its "generally salutary but unspecifiable effect on health" (1979: 181).

The topic of social support also provided a new focus for naturalistic and ecologically valid methods of inquiry into life-span development and social adaptation. It offered another means of gaining a richer contextual understanding of coping behavior and human development, since its study requires consideration of the complex interplay between the attributes of individuals, attributes of the social aggregate in which they are embedded, and attributes of the situational and sociocultural environment influencing the structure and the behavioral patterns of these social aggregates. Indeed, it is increasingly clear that such variables as social competence, need for affiliation, locus of control, and "network orientation" (Tolsdorf, 1976) distinguish between persons who have high versus low access to social support. Social network analyses, such as those reviewed by Wellman and by Hirsch in this volume, also reveal that support is predicated on certain patterns of social interdependence that arise from structural characteristics of people's social worlds. Thus, differences in the size, density, composition, and stability of people's "personal communities" have implications for the quality, diversity, and reliability of the support available to them. Similarly, factors in the broader environment appear to constrain or encourage the formation of social networks. In one townhouse community I have studied (Gottlieb, 1981), I found that the physical spacing of the units, the location of the children's playground, and even weather conditions affected the formation of local social ties. It was also clear that high population turnover and the absence of any common settings or regular communitywide social events combined to fashion a highly anomic milieu. Finally, in the study of environmental forces that influence the character of social support, we must attend to the sociocultural milieu, since it shapes the meanings people attach to symptoms of disequilibrium and conditions their help-seeking and help-giving behavior. As Garrison (1977) has shown in her compelling studies of the support systems used by Puerto Rican women, dominant cultural beliefs about the causes and cures of maladies dictate the sort of indigenous helping pathways and lay referral practices that people follow. To sum up, a holistic and ecologically sound understanding of the role of social support in coping and social adaptation thus requires study of the interactions between broad sociocultural factors such as these, the proximal social and physical environments that form the context for coping, and the personality and competencies people bring to the life demands they face.

A third source of influence that I believe has spurred much contemporary action-research on the topic of social support originates outside the academic and agency spheres and pertains generally to consumer criticisms of the manner in which health services are being delivered and public alarm about the gaps existing in that delivery system. The litany of grievances includes objections to the impersonal manner in which patients or clients are treated at the hands of efficiency-minded professional practitioners; frustrations encountered in their attempts to find their way through a health care bureaucracy that has become so specialized as to mystify the average consumer, and so fragmented as to render most services either incomplete or redundant; criticisms of a system of care that, in its awe of high technology and sophisticated interventions, tends to downplay the patient's role in effecting change and to entirely overlook the role his or her family members and close friends can play in the course of treatment; and, finally, vexations in the face of a health care enterprise committed neither to the preventive tasks of identifying and neutralizing psychosocial stressors in the environment, nor to the work of promoting health through environmental action.

Aside from voicing these complaints, consumer groups have also taken action on their own to redress some of their grievances. For example, self-help groups have proliferated and continue to attract great numbers of people whose personal problems, exceptional statuses, or physical disabilities have been ignored or, at least, incompletely addressed by the professional system. People are choosing to stay out of hospitals and to give birth at home, or to face death in the homelike environment of a hospice. People are taking their health into their own hands by thinking more about the way they eat and exercise, and by reading more about self-care and wellness. Granted, not everyone is doing these things, but my point is that the research community has heard the protests, it has noted consumer-led changes in health practices, and these signs have, in part, prompted investigators to assess further how natural social forces and informal caregiving arrangements can contribute to health promotion.

Problems of Terminology and Measurement in the Contemporary Study of Social Support

Readers interested in familiarizing themselves with the research terrain designated by the term "natural support system" will find that it is marked by a series of contours, not by any single outline. The term itself has taken on numerous connotations and now stands for such diverse types of lay helping arrangements as mutual-help groups (a type of support system that hardly qualifies for the adjective "natural"); neighborhood-based associations whose members exchange goods, services, information, and friendly visits; and the kith and kin network, a social structure unit that encompasses all of an individual's primary-group ties. One need not be a clinician to recognize that family members and friends do not always merit the appellation "support system," and the fact that this sort of labeling is widespread in the literature reveals something about the romanticism or myopia that has seeped into research on the topic of social support. In short, all sorts of resource exchanges among citizens untrained in helping skills are being given the same label, thus rendering it meaningless. We should give more precision to our definition of the term "natural support system," or we should abandon it and talk separately about the supportive functions of mutual-help groups, neighborhood-based helping arrangements, and social networks. I favor the latter option for two reasons. First, because I believe that we can best understand what the three have in common, and what definitional term can therefore be applied to all three, by first separately investigating their supportive functions. Second, because I believe that preventive interventions which mobilize social support can involve any one of these three social systems, and that separate examination of the functioning of each can therefore best inform the planning of these interventions.

Two other notes on terminology are necessary here. The term "support system" has recently been used to designate a combination of formal and informal resources organized by professionals on behalf of psychiatric populations being treated or receiving aftercare services in the community (Turner & Ten Hoor, 1978). While I cannot discern the reasons for substituting this new phrase for activities formerly known as community-based treatment and aftercare, suffice to say that this volume has little to do with that topic. The only point of convergence between the study of the social resources available to clinically diagnosed populations and the study of social support is reflected in several recent studies analyzing the structure and composition of the social orbit in which psychiatric populations participate (e.g., Hammer et al., 1978; Sokolovsky et al., 1978) and assessing the factors that determine their patterns of social participation (Mitchell, forthcoming; Mitchell & Trickett, forthcoming). For the most part, this volume discusses the nature, sources, and health consequences of naturally occurring forms of social support in the everyday life of ordinary citizens. Second, in this volume, as in all dictionaries, the word "network" is treated as a noun, not as a verb (i.e., "networking"). I have seen it treated as a verb by certain clinicians (e.g., Rueveni, 1979) who practice a form of treatment called network therapy, and by some of my agency colleagues, who refer to the age-old process of coordinating their activities with other agency workers as "networking." Neither of these topics is addressed in this book; instead, following Wellman's definition in his chapter, the social network represents a unit of social structure that includes "a set of nodes and a set of ties connecting these nodes — where the nodes may be persons, groups, corporate entities, or other institutions."

The nature, meaning, and measurement of the social support construct itself are still being intensely debated in the literature as well, and this lack of agreement about operational and conceptual definitions contributes to our present inability to compare and summarize studies that investigate the empirical effects of social support on health. The contributions to this book, and in particular the chapters by Barrera, Eckenrode and Gore, Hirsch, DiMatteo and Hays, and Wilcox, epitomize the methodological differences and uncertainties that beset current inquiry into the nature and consequences of social support. While their ideas, and those presented by other prom-

inent investigators, cannot be adequately summarized in this intro-
ductory chapter, it is nevertheless possible to distill from their work
three meanings and measures that have become attached to the social
support construct: (a) social support defined in terms of people's
levels of social integration/participation; (b) social support defined as
a by-product of people's interactions in a social network with particular structural properties; and (c) social support defined in terms of
people's access to a set of resources typically present in their more
intimate peer relationships.

These three categories of meanings also reflect three levels of
analyzing the relations between the individual and the social environment. At the *macro* level of analysis, the social integration/
participation approach concerns itself with people's involvement
with the institutions, voluntary associations, and informal social life
of their communities. A recent epidemiological study by Berkman
and Syme (1979), and the work carried out by Lin, Simeone, Ensel,
and Kuo (1979) on the role of social support in moderating the impact
of life events on the health of Oriental persons, are good examples of
this macro approach. In the former study, social support was operationalized via items inquiring about the respondent's marital status,
church membership, level of participation in group associations, and
level of contact (high, medium, or low) with family members and
friends. In the latter study it was tapped via questions about involvement with Chinese people, organizations, and activities; sentiments
toward and participation in the neighborhood; job satisfaction; and a
count of the number of close friends in the broader geographical area.

At the *mezzo* level of analysis, the social network approach nar-
rows the interactional focus to the pattern of relations that people
maintain within a distinct social aggregate. Here, analysis centers on
structural differences among people's social worlds and the ways
these differences determine differential access to resources needed in
the process of coping and adaptation. Hirsch's (1979, 1980) analyses
of network density and of the character of the ties among network
members (analyses that he reviews in a chapter of this volume)
exemplify how network assessment can inform our understanding of
social-structural factors conditioning people's access to social support. Guidelines for future applications of network analysis to the
study of social support have also been summarized in this volume by
Wellman, while Barrera's chapter describes his initial efforts to reconcile data generated via network analysis with other methods of
investigating social support. At present the major virtues of the

network approach are that it offers a set of properties that can be analyzed to obtain a fine-grained portrait of the adaptive consequences arising from people's interactions in a finite social orbit; it represents a single unit of analysis including persons from the full range of social settings in which people participate; and it considers the effect of interactions among these people on the well-being of the person who is the subject of study.

Finally, the *micro* level of analyzing social support is represented by a group of studies that inquire into people's access to intimate relationships, and seek to identify the resources available in such confiding social ties. These studies tend to be more qualitative than quantitative and more processually oriented than structurally oriented. They tend to focus on what Weiss (1974) has called "the provisions of social relationships," what Henderson et al. (1978) refer to as "the affectional adequacy of primary-group relationships," and on the "informal helping behaviors" (Gottlieb, 1978) that may lie at the heart of social support. Henderson et al. (1980) have drawn heavily on both Weiss's (1974) typology of relational provisions and Bowlby's (1969, 1973) disquisitions about the importance of attachment in healthy human development, to create an instrument which reveals the extent and adequacy of social support in primary groups. The "Interview Schedule for Social Interaction" begins by identifying the respondents' common associates and then delves extensively into the quality of the respondents' relationships with persons to whom they feel most attached. A recent report by Henderson (forthcoming) and earlier micro-level studies that mark social support in terms of people's access to a *single* confiding relationship (Bunch, 1972; Lowenthal & Haven, 1968; Miller & Ingham, 1976), conclude that such detailed, subjective measures of social support yield empirical results documenting its ability to "buffer" the impact of psychosocial stress on physical and mental health.

Others may certainly disagree with the distinctions I have drawn among these three approaches to defining the meaning of and operationalizing the social support construct. As I have said, measurement in this area is still in its chrysalis state, and until more progress is made toward reconciling contrasting measures and developing valid and reliable instruments, little can be confidently said about the role of social support in moderating the impact of stress on health. The contributions to this book signal that progress is being made in these domains and in others that have more to do with the manner in which lay resources can be combined with professional services in the field of community mental health. Indeed, I hope that this book will contribute both to our understanding of issues requiring greater attention in the empirical study of social support and to the planning of preventive interventions mobilizing support on behalf of those undergoing significant social readjustment in our communities.

ABOUT THE VOLUME

I have organized this volume into three sections. Part I is composed of four chapters devoted to empirical investigations of the role of social support in moderating the stress of life events. I have encouraged the authors of these chapters to spare no details about the manner in which they set about the task of operationalizing the social support construct, or about the theoretical assumptions guiding this work. In each case, they have effectively illuminated certain aspects of the present controversy surrounding the measurement of social support, and collectively their work has culminated in a series of guidelines for work needed in this area.

Eckenrode and Gore's chapter begins Part I with an exceptionally probing analysis of recent trends in the study of the relation between stressful life events and illness. Their critique of past research highlights its failure to consider the mutual relations between stress and support processes and the impact of these processes on the social field in which people are embedded. They cogently argue that life events exert a significant impact not only on the focal individual but also on his or her network of ties, and they maintain that any assessment of social support must therefore consider how such "network stress" constrains the process of mobilizing support. Calling on preliminary data from a study of women who utilize a neighborhood health clinic, Eckenrode and Gore illustrate the additional information about support processes yielded by analyzing the consequences of stress at the individual *and* the aggregate (network) levels.

In Chapter 3, Barrera discusses his work on the development of two complementary measures of social support: the Inventory of Socially Supportive Behaviors, composed of 40 items that reflect the diversity of ways social support is expressed, and the Arizona Social Support Interview Schedule, which taps people's perceptions of the social field from which they obtain support and of the adequacy of that support. Following a brief overview of his preliminary efforts to assess the psychometric properties of these instruments, Barrera describes their application in a study of the adjustment of pregnant adolescents. Here, he finds that the qualitative indices of support, having to do with the respondents' satisfaction with and need for support, are the strongest predictors of their levels of symptomatology. He creatively uses the information derived from his other measures of social support to generate hypotheses about the factors conditioning the respondents' subjective reports. Above all, his paper convincingly demonstrates the importance of applying multiple measures to the study of social support, and it offers two promising approaches to measurement, both of which emphasize the multidimensional character of the support construct. Wilcox's chapter presents a method of measuring social support that bears a strong resemblance to Barrera's Social Support Interview Schedule. He too elicits members of the respondents' "support networks" by asking them to identify persons who provide them with certain types of help for certain types of tasks/needs they face. These data are collected at two points in time, however, since his investigation concerns the effects of marital disruption on the stability and composition, and on certain aspects of the density of his respondents' networks. In particular, he uses these data to test his hypotheses that women whose support networks were markedly reduced in size following separation from their spouses, and women whose preseparation networks overlapped a great deal with their former spouses', would experience the greatest difficulty in adjusting to the separation. His results support the latter hypothesis, not the former. Indeed, several subanalyses he conducted point to the superiority of low-density networks in aiding the adjustment of his respondents. Wilcox blends qualitative data drawn from his interviews with the respondents into his discussion of the reasons this feature of network structure proves adaptive.

Chapter 5 concludes Part I with DiMatteo and Hays's review of the literature pertaining to the role of social support in coping with and recovering from serious illness. These authors also outline the support requirements of the family members and the staff attending to the needs of the ill. Throughout their discussion they highlight the importance of distinguishing between objective and subjective measures of support, and they repeatedly call for greater precision in measuring the outcomes — physical, emotional, and role-related — of interventions intended to optimize social support on behalf of the ill and those who care for them. They cite as among the most salient weaknesses of the existing research in this area of health psychology, the lack of attention paid to cultural differences affecting patients' reactions to illness and perceptions of medical care, and the tendency to ignore issues associated with the "goodness of fit" of social support interventions with the patient's personality and accustomed modes of defense; and they comment on the absence of any discussion about the potentially adverse consequences (for the patient's self-esteem and feelings of dependence, for example) experienced by those who find themselves exclusively in the role of the recipient of support.

Part II of the volume is wholly dedicated to exploring the utility and practical applications of network analysis in the study and promotion of social support. The principal aim of this section is to illuminate the complex relationships existing between the structural properties of people's social worlds, the nature of their ties to the members of these networks, and the access to resources that are generated by these social aggregates. As I noted earlier in this chapter, the network-analytic approach to the study of social support is only in a rudimentary stage of development. The work carried out to date, however, suggests that the form and character of people's social orbits and the norms governing the behavior of the constituent members play a critical part in determining how successfully people are able to cope with life's challenges and how effectively they can balance their own needs for independence and attachment.

Chapters 6 and 7 have each been authored by a prominent network researcher. Hirsch begins with a useful overview and integration of three keystone studies that have explored the application of social network analysis to the study of coping behavior. He then proceeds to describe how social networks, as "personal communities," provide a variety of resources that help to anchor and confirm people's social identities and that, during times of stress and transition, help people to establish more satisfying social identities. With this conceptual groundwork in mind, Hirsch enlarges on his views about the nature of those interactions between people and their social networks that can result in enhanced psychosocial well-being as well as those that can diminish personal well-being. He also addresses the implications of these theoretical formulations for the design and evaluation of interventions in the field of community mental health. In Chapter 7, Wellman briefly surveys the uses of network-analytic approaches in several social science disciplines and updates our knowledge of their most recent applications in the field of sociology. He then presents a penetrating criticism of the application of network analysis to the study of social support systems. Wellman shows how the work to date has tended both to overlook certain critical dimensions of the structure and content of people's social ties and to distort other aspects of social organization that bear on people's access to social support. In particular, he asserts that inquiries into structural variables associated with the expression of social support must attend more closely to the separate strands that define the content of social ties and to the analysis of clustering and resource control within networks. In addition, he argues that greater attention should be directed to issues of symmetry and voluntarism in dyadic exchanges.

I wrote Chapter 8 for this book out of a conviction that community mental health workers needed a better understanding of the ways in which social support could be mobilized in preventive interventions. I describe several specific programs of this kind and organize them into two categories: those that focus on improving the supportive quality of network contacts and those that attempt to bring people into contact with similar peers during times of transition and stress. In each case I try to show how considerations of network structure and composition might have better informed the design of these interventions, and I identify a set of variables — both personal and situational — that program planners ought to consider more closely when they make decisions about the targets and occasions for interventions centering on the optimization of social support.

Part III of the volume probes the prospects for creating a mutually beneficial partnership between lay and professional helping resources in the human services. Lenrow and Burch open this section with a provocative and incisive analysis of the attitudes that members of mutual-aid networks and professionals hold about one another and that account for the tensions surrounding their mutual relations. They discuss the two parties' failure to reach an accommodation in terms of the overarching concept of interdependence. Further, they hold that when professionals are able to surrender the belief that they alone possess the resources to stimulate change, and instead share with their clients the responsibility for effecting change, then their stance toward the helping relationship will converge with the character of mutual aid practiced by ordinary citizens. Their masterful analysis of the values impeding meaningful interdependence between professional and client indicts aspects of professional training, childhood socialization, and the broader society. Their observations of social forces that are working to reduce the obstacles to change in these relationships are equally insightful.

Chapter 10, by Froland et al., reports also on some of the forces that are both driving and resisting efforts to interlace professional and lay sources of manpower in the delivery of human services. Moreover, their discussion draws on the information collected from a national sample of ongoing programs that have experimented with this sort of innovative alliance. They have been able to classify the various approaches used by agencies in working with lay resources, and each of the five approaches entails a different strategy for organizing and supporting the work of citizens. Hence, the generalizations they are able to make about the process and struggles involved in blending the informal with the professional arise from the direct experience of agency personnel and from the authors' own observations during their site visits to each program. The guidelines they offer to professionals who hope to take program initiatives featuring the involvement of lay people in service delivery represent an especially useful contribution.

The final chapter, by Mitchell and Hurley, contrasts past strategies of involving laypersons in community mental health activities with present opportunities to do so. In particular, they point to some of the past problems in defining the paraprofessional's role, some of the myths about nonprofessional helpers, and some of the strains created by the organizational context in which the paraprofessional has been placed, in order to alert policy makers and practitioners to the fact that the same issues are likely to surface once again in present programs involving collaboration with natural helping networks. Finally, they make a well-reasoned and well-supported plea to mental health workers to be more precise in specifying the processes and desired outcomes of such collaboration, to attend more closely to the influence of neighborhood context on support system functioning, and to take steps which ensure that they do not impose their own values about the helping enterprise on local citizens.

REFERENCES

ALBEE, G. W. *Mental health manpower trends.* New York: Basic Books, 1959.

ALLEY, S. R., BLANTON, J., & FELDMAN, R. E. *Paraprofessionals in mental health.* New York: Human Sciences Press, 1979.

ALLEY, S. R., BLANTON, J., FELDMAN, R. E., HUNTER, G. D., & ROLFSON, M. *Case studies of mental health paraprofessionals.* New York: Human Sciences Press, 1979.

BARRETT, C. J. Effectiveness of widows' groups in facilitating change. *Journal of Consulting and Clinical Psychology,* 1978, *46,* 20-31.

BERKMAN, L. F., & SYME, S. L. Social networks, host resistance, and mortality: A nine-year followup study of Alameda County residents. *American Journal of Epidemiology,* 1979, *109,* 186-204.

BLOOM, B. L. Prevention of mental disorders: Recent advances in theory and practise. *Community Mental Health Journal,* 1979, *15,* 179-191.

BOWLBY, J. *Attachment and loss, Volume 1: Attachment.* London: Hogarth Press, 1969.

BOWLBY, J. *Attachment and loss, Volume 2: Separation, anxiety and anger.* London: Hogarth Press, 1973.

BUNCH, J. Recent bereavement in relation to suicide. *Journal of Psychosomatic Research,* 1972, *16,* 361-366.

CAPLAN, G. *Principles of preventive psychiatry.* New York: Basic Books, 1964.

CAPLAN, G. Support systems. In G. Caplan (Ed.), *Support systems and community mental health.* New York: Basic Books, 1974.

CASSEL, J. Psychosocial processes and "stress": Theoretical formulations. *International Journal of Health Services,* 1974, *4,* 471-482.

COBB, S. A model for life events and their consequences. In B. S. Dohrenwend & B. P. Dohrenwend (Eds.), *Stressful life events.* New York: John Wiley, 1974.

COHEN, C., & SOKOLOVSKY, J. Schizophrenia and social networks: Ex-patients in the inner city. *Schizophrenia Bulletin,* 1978, *4,* 546-560.

COLLINS, A. H. Natural delivery systems: Accessible sources of power for mental health. *American Journal of Orthopsychiatry,* 1973, *43,* 46-52.

DOHRENWEND, B. S., & DOHRENWEND, B. P. Some issues in research on stressful life events. *Journal of Nervous and Mental Disease,* 1978, *166,* 7-15.

DUBOS, R. *Man adapting.* New Haven, CT: Yale University Press, 1965.

DUHL, L. J. The changing face of mental health. In L. J. Duhl (Ed.), *The urban condition: People and policy in the metropolis.* New York: Basic Books, 1963.

DUNHAM, W. H. *Sociological theory and mental disorder.* Detroit: Wayne State University Press, 1959.

DURLAK, J. Comparative effectiveness of professional and paraprofessional helpers. *Psychological Bulletin,* 1979, *86,* 80-92.

FARIS, R. E., & DUNHAM, W. H. *Mental disorders in urban areas.* Chicago: University of Chicago Press, 1939.

FRENCH, J. R. P., Jr. Person-role fit. In A. McLean (Ed.), *Occupational stress.* Springfield, IL: Charles C Thomas, 1974.

FRENCH, J. R. P., Jr., & KAHN, R. L. A programmatic approach to studying the industrial environment and mental health. *Journal of Social Issues,* 1962, *18,* 1-47.

GARRISON, V. The "Puerto Rican Syndrome" in psychiatry and *espiritismo.* In V. Crapanzano & V. Garrison (Eds.), *Case studies in spirit possession.* New York: John Wiley, 1977.

GOTTLIEB, B. H. The development and application of a classification scheme of informal helping behaviours. *Canadian Journal of Behavioural Science,* 1978, *10,* 105-115.

GOTTLIEB, B. H. Social support and social participation among residents of a married student housing complex. *Journal of College Student Personnel,* 1981, *22,* 46-52.

GURIN, G., VEROFF, J., & FELD, S. *Americans view their mental health.* New York: Basic Books, 1960.

HAMMER, M., MAKIESKY-BARROW, S., & GUTWIRTH, L. Social networks and schizophrenia. *Schizophrenia Bulletin,* 1978, *4,* 522-545.

HAMMER, M. Social networks and the long term patient. In S. Budson & M. Barofsky (Eds.), *The chronic psychiatric patient in the community: Principles of treatment.* New York: Spectrum, forthcoming.

HENDERSON, S. Social relationships, adversity, and neurosis: An analysis of prospective observations. *British Journal of Psychiatry,* forthcoming.

HENDERSON, S., DUNCAN-JONES, P., BYRNE, D., & SCOTT, R. Measuring social relationships: The interview schedule for social interaction. *Psychological Medicine,* 1980, *10,* 1-12.

HENDERSON, S., DUNCAN-JONES, P., McAULEY, H., & RITCHIE, K. The patient's primary group. *British Journal of Psychiatry,* 1978, *132,* 74-86.

HINKLE, L. E., Jr. The effect of exposure to culture change, social change, and changes in interpersonal relationships on health. In B. S. Dohrenwend & B. P. Dohrenwend (Eds.), *Stressful life events.* New York: John Wiley, 1974.

HINKLE, L. E., Jr., & WOLFF, H. G. Ecologic investigations of the relations between illness, life experiences and the social environment. *Annals of Internal Medicine,* 1958, *49,* 1373-1388.

HIRSCH, B. J. Psychological dimensions of social networks: A multimethod analysis. *American Journal of Community Psychology,* 1979, *7,* 263-278.

HIRSCH, B. J. Natural support systems and coping with major life changes. *American Journal of Community Psychology,* 1980, *8,* 159-172.

HOLMES, T. H., & RAHE, R. H. The social readjustment rating scale. *Journal of Psychosomatic Research,* 1967, *11,* 213-218.

HUGHES, C. C., TREMBLY, M. A., RAPOPORT, R. N., & LEIGHTON, A. H. *People of cove and woodlot.* New York: Basic Books, 1960.

KARLSRUHER, A. E. The nonprofessional as a psychotherapeutic agent: A review of the empirical evidence pertaining to his effectiveness. *American Journal of Community Psychology*, 1974, *2*, 61-77.

KELLY, J. G. The mental health agent in the urban community. *American Psychologist*, 1966, *21*, 535-539.

KIRITZ, S., & MOOS, R. H. Physiological effects of social environments. *Psychosomatic Medicine*, 1974, *36*, 96-114.

KLEIN, D. C. The minister and mental health: An evaluation. *Journal of Pastoral Care*, 1959, *13*, 230-236.

LANOIL, J., & TURNER, J. C. Paraprofessionals in psychosocial rehabilitation programs: A resource for developing community support systems for the "deinstitutionalized" mentally disabled. In S. Alley, J. Blanton, & R. E. Feldman (Eds.), *Paraprofessionals in mental health*. New York: Human Sciences Press, 1979.

LEIGHTON, A. H. *My name is legion*. New York: Basic Books, 1959.

LEUTZ, W. The informal community caregiver: A link between the health care system and local residents. *American Journal of Orthopsychiatry*, 1976, *46*, 678-688.

LEVINE, M., TULKIN, S., INTAGLIATA, J., PERRY, J., & WHITSON, E. The paraprofessional: A brief social history. In S. Alley, J. Blanton, & R. E. Feldman (Eds.), *Paraprofessionals in mental health*. New York: Human Sciences Press, 1979.

LIN, N., SIMEONE, R. S., ENSEL, W. M., & KUO, W. Social support, stressful life events, and illness: A model and an empirical test. *Journal of Health and Social Behavior*, 1979, *20*, 108-119.

LOWENTHAL, M., & HAVEN, C. Interaction and adaptation: Intimacy as a critical variable. *American Sociological Review*, 1968, *33*, 20-30.

McGUIRE, J. C., & GOTTLIEB, B. H. Social support groups among new parents: An experimental study in primary prevention. *Journal of Clinical Child Psychology*, 1979, *8*, 111-116.

MEYER, A. The life chart and the obligation of specifying positive data in psychopathology. In E. E. Winters (Ed.), *The collected papers of Adolf Meyer, Volume III, Medical Teaching*. Baltimore: Johns Hopkins Press, 1951.

MILLER, P., & INGHAM, J. G. Friends, confidants and symptoms. *Social Psychiatry*, 1976, *11*, 51-58.

MITCHELL, R. Social networks and psychiatric clients: The personal and environmental context. *American Journal of Community Psychology*, forthcoming.

MITCHELL, R. E., & TRICKETT, E. J. Social network research and psychosocial adaptation: Implications for community mental health practice. In P. Insel (Ed.), *Environmental variables in the prevention of mental illness*. Lexington, MA: D. C. Heath, forthcoming.

MOOS, R. H. *The social climate scales: An overview*. Palo Alto, CA: Consulting Psychologists Press, 1974. (a)

MOOS, R. H. *Evaluating treatment environments*. New York: John Wiley, 1974. (b)

RABKIN, J. G., & STRUENING, E. L. Life events, stress, and illness. *Science,* 1976, *194,* 1013-1020.

RIESSMAN, F., COHEN, J., & PEARL, A. *Mental health of the poor.* New York: Free Press, 1964.

ROBINSON, R., de MARCHE, D. F., & WAGLE, M. K. *Community resources in mental health.* New York: Basic Books, 1960.

RUEVENI, U. *Networking families in crisis.* New York: Human Sciences Press, 1979.

SCHWARTZ, M. D. Situation/transition groups: A conceptualization and review. *American Journal of Orthopsychiatry,* 1975, *45,* 744-755.

SOKOLOVSKY, J., COHEN, C., BERGER, D., & GEIGER, J. Personal networks of ex-mental patients in the inner city. *Human Organization,* 1978, *37,* 5-15.

TOLSDORF, C. Social networks, support, and coping: An exploratory study. *Family Process,* 1976, *15,* 407-418.

TURNER, J. C., & TEN HOOR, W. J. The NIMH community support program: Pilot approach to a needed social reform. *Schizophrenia Bulletin,* 1978, *4,* 319-344.

WANDERSMAN, L. P. Parenting groups to support the adjustment to parenthood. *Family Perspectives,* 1978, *12,* 117-128.

WANDERSMAN, L. P. The adjustment of fathers to their first baby. *Birth and the Family Journal,* 1980, *7,* 18-26.

WEISS, R. S. The provisions of social relationships. In Z. Rubin (Ed.), *Doing unto others.* Englewood Cliffs, NJ: Prentice-Hall, 1974.

Chapter 2

STRESSFUL EVENTS AND SOCIAL SUPPORTS
The Significance of Context

JOHN ECKENRODE and SUSAN GORE

There is no question that the concept of psychosocial stress continues to occupy a central role in current theoretical approaches to psychological health and disorder. Since the mid-1960s, the predominant research approach to stress and its relation to physical and mental health has been the study of discrete life events or life changes occurring over a relatively short time period. The measurement of these life events was formalized by the development of the Schedule of Recent Experiences (SRE) by Holmes and Rahe (1967), and the popularity of this assessment tool is evidenced in the hundreds of research studies that have adopted this method of assessing stress. These studies have investigated the relation of life events stress to a wide variety of physical and psychological outcomes (see Dohrenwend & Dohrenwend, 1974, and Rabkin & Struening, 1976, for reviews). While this research is not universally supportive of a causal link between life events and health outcomes, enough research has been reported to support the idea that life events, particularly if accumulated over a relatively brief time period, represent some risk to physical and mental health.

Authors' Note: The work reported here was supported by a grant from the National Center for Health Services Research (HS 0302901). We would like to thank Joan Liem and Robert J. Haggerty for comments on an earlier version of this chapter.

There are several reasons for the popularity of the life events approach to stress. First, the measurement tool itself is short and easy to administer, requiring no special training on the part of the researchers. This feature opened the way to the study of a complex phenomenon in a wide variety of research and clinical settings. Second, and more substantive, the events lists are made up of situations commonly occurring in a given population (e.g., marriage, divorce, residential moves, job changes), as opposed to cataclysmic but infrequent occurrences, such as war and natural disasters. The frequency of these events grounded the notion of stress in the everyday lives of individuals, making the stress concept more recognizable and understandable to professional and layperson alike. Third, by defining stress in terms of discrete, time-limited events, cause-effect relationships can be readily established. Through prospective study of life events that can be more accurately placed in time, researchers can be fairly confident that such events preceded the onset of an acute illness, a depressive episode, or a hospitalization.

Since the original development of the SRE and the studies that followed, many questions have been raised with regard to the psychometric properties of the scale and the adequacy of the research employing it (e.g., Brown & Harris, 1978; Mechanic, 1974; Rabkin & Struening, 1976). This, in turn, has resulted in multiple revisions of the original technique and a reassessment of the nature of the stress-illness relationship.

We will now review some of the major trends in current research on life events, taking the perspective that these trends reflect a general effort to incorporate contextual variables and approaches into stress research. We will also suggest ways a fuller treatment of context would advance our knowledge of stress and social support processes. We begin our discussion by examining the implicit and explicit assumptions of the life events model, since these assumptions in many ways still guide research on stress, and, as we will argue, also guide inquiries into the relationship between stress and social support.

LIFE EVENTS RESEARCH

In its original form, the life events model contains at least the following explicit and somewhat related set of assumptions:

(1) that change per se is the critical (and only) property of life events that defines their stressfulness;

(2) that a given life event (e.g., a job change) requires the same amount of adjustment for different individuals;

(3) that different types of events can be considered together in terms of the adjustment they collectively demand (i.e., stress "scores" can be equated regardless of the particular constellation of events from which they are derived); and

(4) that normative ratings (established by judges) of the amount of adjustment required by an individual could be substituted for measurement of adjustment on an individual-by-individual basis.

These assumptions, in turn, have influenced the types of research questions that have been asked (as well as ignored) by researchers adopting this method of stress assessment, and they have also influenced the development of theory in the field. While there are some widely accepted theoretical underpinnings to the development of the SRE and related instruments (e.g., Selye's notion of the General Adaptation Syndrome, 1956), the often uncritical use of this measurement tool has, as Mechanic (1974) points out, tended to influence and perhaps constrain stress theory rather than inform it.

The theoretical model of stress under which the assumptions reviewed above are embedded has several important features. First, stress is defined as an environmental demand on the organism, with these "stressors" conceptually and analytically separated from the person experiencing the events or the circumstances surrounding the events. This definition has had a particular appeal to researchers who have attempted to assess the role of stress in the onset of psychological disorder. The significance or meaning of the events is presumed to lie in the properties of the events themselves, rather than in the dynamic interaction between an individual and the particular event(s) under study. Lazarus and his colleagues (Lazarus & Cohen, 1977; Lazarus & Launier, forthcoming) have referred to this model as reflecting a pure stimulus-response (S-R) model of stress. The approach explicitly ignores individual differences in the stressfulness of particular events.

Second, there is an assumed direct link between life events and the outcomes under study. Psychological or social processes that could possibly occur between the events and the appearance of illness symptoms (or other outcomes) are not typically included in such research. For this reason, the current concern with how people cope with stressful life events is not evident in early events research.

Third, the analysis of stress is confined to the level of the individual, and questions regarding the relation of events to broader societal structures and processes do not typically enter into events research.[1] Also, since events are implicitly viewed as largely fortuitous happenings, the role of individual choice or responsibility in the exposure to certain events does not receive much consideration.

We have outlined these assumptions and implications of the original life events model of stress because many of the recent criticisms of and additions to the events model center on these major features. Recent studies often contain modifications in the original SRE instrument, in the scoring of events in terms of stressfulness, in the range of variables included in a single study, or in the research designs employed. These developments, discussed in more detail below, have led to some new and exciting types of research. We perceive some commonalities in these efforts, which if recognized could not only serve as a framework for understanding these trends, but also as a source of new ideas.

The Contextual Analysis of Life Events and Their Stressfulness

While the early phase of stress research had a characteristic emphasis on the *prediction* of illness rates from knowledge of stressful life events, research now emphasizes *explanation* of these correlations between events and illness. Thus, a common research focus on issues of *context* is emerging. By "context" we mean the embeddedness of life events within temporal, psychological, and social situations that determine both the meaning of the events and the individual and group capacities for dealing with them. Attention to the major ways in which researchers have attempted to place stress in context should reveal the problems and prospects for contextual approaches.

The significance of context underlies most research on the construction and scoring of life events lists. These scales have been useful predictive instruments because they embody the lowest common denominator of stress: occurrences of sufficient magnitude to bring about change in the usual activities of most individuals. The principal definitional and methodological problems that researchers have had to address concern (1) the selection of occurrences that affect most people, and (2) the determination of the stressfulness of those events. Contextual information has been utilized in a variety of ways to address both of these issues.

The first problem above is an issue of sampling events, and raises questions about the distribution of events in different sociocultural settings and, within these, about the diversity of events over the life course. The selection or sampling of standard events to make up life events lists presupposes a constancy of context across settings and people, an assumption that is now being questioned. Dohrenwend (1974), for example, has reported that when community residents (New Yorkers) were asked about the "last major event in your life that, for better or for worse, interrupted or changed your usual activities," their responses showed surprisingly little overlap with a life events checklist. One result of such research has been the explicit consideration of context for the development of population-specific, or setting-specific, events lists, such as for children (Coddington, 1972), college students (Sarason et al., 1979), or persons in specific occupations (e.g., for air traffic controllers; see Hurst et al., 1978).

Another trend in stress research has been the consideration of context in determining the stressfulness of life events. In early events research stressfulness was equated with the degree of readjustment or change required by each event on the SRE, with degree of change being fixed for each event and based on normative estimates (i.e., weights based on the perceptions of judges who do not actually experience the events they are rating). Thus, the determinations of stressfulness are established a priori and collected separately from data on persons actually exposed to life events. Despite evidence cited by Holmes and Masuda (1974) regarding the generalization of these stress values or weights, many recent events instruments allow for individual ratings of stressfulness in an attempt to recognize individual variability with regard to the personal meaning of life events.

A more fundamental revision of the original life events model, however, has been a shift away from defining stressfulness in terms of amount of change, per se, to a consideration of other properties of life events or other aspects of context that may be more useful in explaining the meaning and impact of events. Most attention, for example, has been given to the commonsense expectation that events with undesirable implications are more stressful than those with desirable implications (e.g., Paykel et al., 1969; Vinokur & Selzer, 1975). Similarly, researchers are now examining other contextual features of events, such as their "controllability" or degree of "anticipation" (e.g., McFarlane et al., 1980) in an effort to uncover their most fundamental properties. The question, however, is whether these properties are inherent in the nature of the events and can be understood apart from the broader personal and social context in which the events occur.

We may, from the face value of events, derive some crude ordering of events based on certain properties (e.g., a car accident as less controllable or anticipated than starting a new job); but many other events (e.g., job loss) will fall into the "ambiguous" category without a consideration of other contextual data that define personal meaning. With change per se no longer universally considered as the property of life events that makes them stressful, it also becomes increasingly difficult to conceive of life events lists as "objective" measures of stress, reflecting demands originating solely from the environment. In addition, these attempts to explore such contextual factors bring into focus two other limitations of the life events model. The first concerns the implicit assumption that events are fortuitous in nature and that they are discrete or time-bound occurrences. The second is that any *single* dimension or property of life events (change, desirability, control, anticipation, and so on) will be sufficient to define degree of stressfulness and the impact of life events on health status.

Researchers now agree that many events are not truly chance or random experiences, that several are themselves the consequences of mental health status, and that others are to a degree self-initiated. Once we accept the notion of nonrandom occurrence, we begin to question under what conditions events occur, and whether knowing these conditions tells us more about life stress than does knowing the various stress eruptions that may only be symptomatic of these conditions. For example, based on their research on precursors of psychological disorders in children, Gersten and her colleagues (1977) maintain that stressful events only play an *indirect* etiological role in psychological disorder, and that they most probably are reflections of more long-standing, causally more significant, life difficulties. Ongoing life conditions (of the children who constituted their study population), such as impoverished economic standing, quarreling and unhappy parents, or punitive parents and a chronically ill mother, thus set the stage for the occurrence of discrete events.

While we need not go so far as to reject the significance of life events in illness processes, their context, meaning, duration, and cumulative impact must be better addressed. Toward such investigations, Surtees and Ingham (1980) have presented a formulation that recognizes the complexity of life adversity, takes into account both life events and life conditions, and incorporates a temporal perspective. They argue that the threat inherent in each life event dissipates over time, but that the clustering of several events and their occurrence within a context of long-term adverse conditions entails additive and interactive stress processes that determine both degree of stress and the overall rate of threat dissipation. We see this model as illustrative of a contextual perspective, as it focuses on the relationships *among* stress variables and locates clusters of variables within time frames that are significant in explaining psychological impact. In contrast, the study of discrete stress events has relied on the aggregation of events as a basis for inferences about severity, while ignoring the interrelation of specific stress events as they occur in meaningful temporal sequences.

The value of exploring several types of contextual data when attempting to define stress and stressfulness is clearly illustrated in the work of Brown and Harris (1978). Instead of avoiding issues of the personal meaning of events to individuals, they explicitly employed a methodology for measuring meaning that involved inquiring about several aspects of the context surrounding particular life events (including the degree to which the event was anticipated, the amount of social supports available, and the like). These data were then utilized in determining the stressfulness of events. Two contextual features emerged as particularly important to the onset of depression. The first is a temporal variable, defined in terms of the short- versus long-term threat implied by particular life events. Only events representing a severe, long-term threat to the women in the study were found to play a role in the onset of depression. In addition, the interesting feature of these more threatening events is that they usually entailed some experience of interpersonal loss, deprivation, or stress. These experiences included "separation or threat of it, such as death of a parent, or a husband saying he is going to leave home; an unpleasant revelation about someone close, forcing a major reassessment of the person and the relationship, such as finding out about a husband's unfaithfulness; a life-threatening illness to someone close" (Brown & Harris, 1978: 103). Other research (e.g., Paykel et al., 1969; and as reviewed by Dohrenwend & Egri, 1979) has also established that the most virulent life events tend to be those that disrupt or threaten to disrupt social ties.

Recent life events research has thus gone beyond many of the implicit or explicit assumptions regarding the definition and measurement of stress made in early life events research. These efforts are characterized by a consideration of various contextual features, including the social-relational context. *Contextual analysis,* however, means more than obtaining measures of *contextual variables*. It also implies a study of the *relationship among* contextual variables. This latter concern underlies the second major trend in stress research in recent years, namely, the search for factors that mediate and explain the stress-illness relationship.

In the following discussion, we will argue that the study of social supports as one set of mediating factors has not progressed in ways that have allowed for an adequate examination of their "stress-buffering" function, the greatest obstacle being an inattention to the processes through which social supports are mobilized and utilized. We will suggest modifying existing approaches to include broader contextual analyses of stress and supports in which the two are seen as interdependent. Finally, we will present some illustrative data bearing on these issues.

Support Systems as Contextual Resources

The diversity of social support definitions has been discussed elsewhere (Gore, 1980), but all have a common focus on the helping properties and processes of the social-relational systems in which persons are located. These support networks are hypothesized to provide resources for successfully dealing with both stressful life situations and the emotional disturbances related to them. If support is the key to enhanced coping capacity, this could explain the frequent observation that many individuals undergo very stressful life experiences but suffer no adverse health consequences.

Research on this stress-buffering mechanism of social support is contextual in two regards. First, social support resources are assumed to be rather stable and ongoing features of the life situation and thus are significant properties of the stress context. Other contextual variables include socioeconomic status, education, and religiosity. Kessler (1979) defines these factors and social supports as the components of a "vulnerability factor" that defines the psychological impact of stressful experiences.

A second, more specific meaning of context is inherent in the idea of a social support *system* whose boundaries and properties can be defined and characterized. In order to understand these systems or contexts, stress researchers have drawn on social network analysis. For the most part, the concept of network support has been assessed through summing the number of potential helpers as reported by survey respondents, and through characterizing these donors in terms of their reliability, proximity, intimacy, and so forth. Thus, a support network is an aggregate of potentially helpful affiliates.

Earlier we provided a review of stress research in which we noted several common features of the events paradigm, two of which are particularly relevant here. The first is the view of stress as a discrete event that is depersonalized and can be characterized as an objective feature of the environment. The second is the focus on the individual as the unit of analysis. These conceptions continue to underlie current approaches to the study of social support and its relationship to life stress (e.g., as is exemplified in the conception of support as a discrete resource or helping transaction).

As a whole, much of the research on the stress-buffering role of social supports can be placed within the following paradigm:

(1) A single or several health outcome variables are selected as criteria upon which to judge the impact of stress.
(2) Life stress is measured as an aggregate score from the SRE or a derived instrument.
(3) Social support is measured by proxy variables such as marital status (with the married hypothesized to be better supported), number of friendships, relatives nearby, or organizational involvements; or the degree of perceived trust or reliance on others, in the abstract.
(4) Social support is seen as orthogonal to stress; support and stress are thus seen as independent.
(5) Variance in illness as explained by life stress is calculated before and after controlling the support variable.
(6) The statistical finding that the correlation between stress and illness is reduced in the presence of support is taken as evidence that stress-buffering has occurred.

This way of investigating the stress-buffering role of social supports mirrors the static, "structural" approach to stress that the original life events model represented. Just as contextual factors were once considered unimportant in defining the meaning of stress, they are now largely ignored in investigations of social support. And while social support is viewed as an important contextual variable in stress research, it is assumed that stressors come from "out there" and that social support resources, if present, buffer these stressors in ways that are left largely unspecified. Thus, we have very little information about social support *processes,* and are left with a rather narrow view of both stress and social support as essentially "independent variables."

Some studies, however, have reported substantial correlations between stress and social support variables (e.g., Carveth & Gottlieb, 1979; Dean et al., 1980). While part of this association is probably due to a certain amount of redundancy in current stress and support measures, part could also reflect a true interdependence of stress and social support processes. If so, this poses clear methodological problems for testing the stress-buffering role of social supports in static cross-sectional research. In past life events research, similar problems of "confounding," such as the inclusion of events that are symptoms or consequences rather than causes of disorders, have been dealt with by excluding such events from the relevant analyses. Such an approach does not represent a real solution in the case of stress and social support, however, since the majority of events in such lists directly or indirectly involve social relationships. Removing such events (e.g., death of a spouse) from the lists when testing stress-support relationships would thus result in events lists of questionnable validity.

There are two other approaches to this issue, however, which will potentially be more useful. The first involves the "disaggregation" of stress and support indices, the overall goal being the linking of supportive behaviors more closely to the specific stresses they are hypothesized to affect (Gore, 1980). There is some indication that recent life events studies are beginning to do this by asking respondents to relate instances of support surrounding specific life events encountered. These stress-specific support measures may redress some of the more obvious measurement problems, such as substituting proxy measures (e.g., marital status, social participation) for measures of actual support exchanges. They also begin to reflect the multidimensional nature of individual social relationships, in that a specific individual (say, a husband) may appear in an event description as a source of stress ("increased arguments with spouse") and as a supporter in other instances.

The second approach is the explicit recognition of the *interdependence* of stress and support processes. The prevailing research models omit such considerations and focus on the complexity of the stress situation *or* of the support situation as if the parameters and processes were relatively independent. This assumption is fallacious on three counts:

(1) that sources of support differ from sources of stress;
(2) that perceptions of stress occur independently of perceptions of the availability of support; and
(3) that stress has no impact on support systems or, conversely, that support systems bear no causal relationship to stress occurrences.

With regard to the first proposition, it is not necessary to cite research in support of the idea that a given social relationship (or network) may involve both stress and support. The second proposition is at odds with any interactive definition of stress (e.g., Lazarus & Cohen, 1976; McGrath, 1970) that views stress as arising from the perception that demands exceed resources. Regarding the final proposition, it is evident that many stressors affect all members of a network (as in the death of a central figure), and some (as in mobility or interpersonal conflict) function to dissolve a network that cannot then be expected to act as a mediating agent. Both examples highlight the need to conceive of stress as often *internal to networks* or as *impacting on a network*. Stress therefore can be discussed on the individual level of analysis and on the level of the network, although stress researchers, by focusing on the individual, have failed to develop strategies for assessing "network stress." It also becomes apparent that stress constitutes an important aspect of context surrounding social support, just as social support is an important part of context surrounding stress.

TOWARD A CONTEXTUAL ANALYSIS OF SOCIAL SUPPORT

The primary reason social support must be considered a crucial aspect of the stress context is its stress-buffering qualities (although its "preventive" functions have been largely overlooked). Stress-buffering is ultimately an issue of process, with the most relevant processual questions having to do with support mobilization — that is, how *potential* supporters in a network become *actual* supporters, given a stressful situation.

The context within which such mobilization takes place must, therefore, not only include that set of individuals identified as potential supporters (however defined) in a variety of situations, but also those forces constraining the mobilization process. These constraints can take various forms: subjective and objective constraints; constraints rooted in the individual or the network. Subjective constraints would include such things as the values and beliefs individuals may hold with regard to when others should be called on for help, and who those persons should be. Objective constraints include not only such potential barriers to help as physical distance, but also the level of demands on those persons who are potentially available for support (whether or not these are clearly understood by the potential recipients of the aid). We propose that by measuring levels of stress in networks, we not only arrive at a better understanding of stress on the level of the individual, but also provide a more complete context for analyzing social support processes in social networks.

ILLUSTRATIVE FINDINGS

The Study Population and Questionnaire Instrument

In the preceding discussion we have outlined several ways in which a more complete analysis of context should advance current thinking with regard to stress and support processes. In order to illustrate some of these points further, we will present some preliminary findings from a study we are currently undertaking. This is a prospective study of 356 women randomly sampled from the registration list of a neighborhood health center in Boston that serves primarily working-class clients of diverse ethnic backgrounds. The overall purpose of the research is to investigate the role of stress and social supports in the utilization of primary-care health services. The research design calls for all participants to take part in an initial interview, to have their medical records reviewed for one year following that interview, and then to be reinterviewed. In addition, 100 women were asked to keep a daily health and stress diary for one month following the first interview. Finally, medical providers at the clinic are being asked to assess the role of psychosocial stress in any medical visit by participants or members of their families. The results presented below are confined to the data from the initial interviews.

These interviews provide information regarding stressful life events and longer-term stressful life conditions, social supports, self-evaluations of psychological and physical health status, certain aspects of health attitudes and beliefs (e.g., health locus of control; propensity to seek care), recent health and illness behaviors (e.g., use of medical services), and a number of issues related to the participants' relationships with the specific health centers under study (e.g., satisfaction with services).

As noted above, stress was measured both in terms of discrete life events and ongoing life conditions, although we will concentrate our discussion here on the life events results. The life events scale consists of items grouped into the areas of neighborhood/housing, personal relationships, work, health, and finances. Several items correspond to those used in the SRE (Holmes & Rahe, 1967), while others were designed specifically for this study. The time period assessed was one year prior to the interview. For each event that respondents said had occurred, they were asked when the event occurred and how stressful the event was for them. The most important feature of the scale for the present discussion, however, is that the focus of the questionning was not restricted to what happened directly to the respondent, but also included events affecting significant others (defined as someone in their immediate family or household, a relative, or a close friend). If a respondent's first response was that an event had affected herself, she was asked if that event had also affected someone else in her network.

The presence of supportive relationships was measured in two ways in this study, reflecting the distinction between "potential" and "actual" support. Potential supporters were defined as (1) that subset of family members, relatives, and friends whom the respondent said she could "count on" to help her deal with unspecified personal or family problems; (2) individuals the respondent said she could turn to for help with hypothetical problem situations (e.g., if she needed to borrow $200); and (3) individuals whom the respondent said she could have called on (but did not) for help with the most important situations she said she had to deal with in the previous year. Actual supporters were defined as those individuals who had, in fact, helped with these problems. This included "formal" (e.g., health professionals, police) as well as "informal" supporters, although we will restrict our discussion here to informal sources of help.

The data presented below highlight two related sets of issues raised in the preceding discussion of contextual approaches in stress and support research. First, while stress is conceived as an individual-level variable in life events research, the stressful events of significant others can impact on respondents in a number of ways. Because of this, we believe that there is a need to assess stress at the individual and aggregate (or network) levels of analysis within the same study. Toward this goal, we distinguish between stressful events happening to self and those happening to others and propose the utility of the concept of social network in describing stress and support processes at both levels and providing the necessary bridge.

Second, contextual analysis makes salient the fact that social relationships are the source of both stress and support in people's lives. Yet, as we have previously discussed, stress and support processes are usually considered to be independent phenomena. Rather than ignore this, we believe researchers should begin to describe and analyze this interdependence in its various forms.

Questions of both structure and process are relevant here. One means of characterizing network structure is in terms of a ratio of persons undergoing or causing stress to those potentially available as supporters. Variables of this nature address the interdependence of stress and support as they provide a means for characterizing person resources that takes into account person liabilities. The central processual question concerns the implications of variations in the amount of distribution of stress in the network for the process of support mobilization. We hope that the following illustrative data will serve to generate interest in both types of questions.

Network Stress and Its Individual Impact

In our research, respondents were asked about the occurrence of events without reference to the person involved (e.g., "had *a* home broken into" vs. "had *your* home broken into") and were then asked to whom the event had happened. We should point out that this procedure will necessarily result in some "misclassification" of events, since some events (e.g., moved to a new home) are likely to involve both the respondent and other persons directly, but only one person is coded. If the respondent was the central actor in the event (e.g., *they* moved rather than a friend moved), the event was coded as happening to the respondent, thus resulting in some underestimation of the event's effect on others involved in the respondent's move. Alternatively, some events coded as happening to others may have directly involved adjustments for the respondent (e.g., a child's hospitalization), thus resulting in some underestimation of events affecting the respondent. We offer these caveats primarily to suggest that other coding schemes are not only possible, but theoretically meaningful and, therefore, should be explored.

Although original life events instruments and subsequent revisions usually include a few items pertaining to other family members (e.g., "major change in the health or behavior of a family member"), to our knowledge, only three published studies employing life events as a measure of stress have systematically inquired about life events impacting on persons other than the respondent being questioned. These are the studies of Brown and Harris (1978) and Lin et al. (1979), which have examined antecedents and correlates of depression, and a study by B. S. Dohrenwend (1976) examining ethnic and sex differences in the degree to which life events are perceived to be controlled or anticipated. Brown and Harris (1978) report that only self-focused events of moderate severity were associated with the onset of depression, a result consistent with the findings of Lin et al. (1979). Dohrenwend (1976) reports that while levels of anticipation did not distinguish events occurring to the respondent as opposed to others, respondents did perceive having more control over events occurring to themselves. Women also tended to report proportionally more events that happened to others than did men, although the number of such events was rather small.

The rationale for including other-focused events in these studies was that these events may directly impact on the *amount of stress a particular individual was experiencing* at a given time. None of these studies, however, has examined these data on other-focused stress in terms of the *implications for social support processes,* which is the center of our discussion here.

In our sample, the mean number of events respondents reported experiencing personally was 4.4 or 30 percent of the total, while 10.5 or 70 percent of the total were events experienced by others. Table 2.1 displays these results by type of event. Two points are of interest here. First, inquiring about events affecting others adds a significant number of events to the total, with respondents reporting more than twice as many events affecting others as those affecting themselves. Second, events affecting others were reported in every category of event covered, although proportionally fewer such events related to finances were disclosed.

Events affecting persons other than the respondent were most frequently cited for friends (29 percent), followed by children (19

TABLE 2.1   Mean Number of Events to Respondent and Others by Type
of Event

| | Focus of Events | | |
Type	Respondents	Others	Total Events
Neighborhood/housing	.8	1.8	2.6
Relationships	.8	2.3	3.1
Work	.5	2.0	2.5
Health	1.5	3.5	5.0
Finances	.8	.9	1.7

percent), siblings (17 percent), other relatives (16 percent), parents (10 percent), and husbands or boyfriends (9 percent). Respondents, therefore, did not simply report events experienced by others in the household, such as children. This highlights the importance of the social network as the appropriate unit of analysis for such questions. If we had only inquired about family or household members, a significant number of events would have been overlooked.

The next question we addressed was how the reporting of life events experienced by self and others was related to demographic or background factors. Some of these results are shown in Table 2.2. The only characteristic that was related to the same degree and in the same way to the frequency of both types of events was the age of the respondent, possibly reflecting the often-discussed age bias in the types of events included in such scales. Several of the other respondent characteristics showed quite different relationships with reports of the two types of events. Having a low income, being young with young children at home, being unemployed, not living with a husband, and having lived in the community for a shorter length of time were all associated with reporting more events that directly affected the respondents. A different profile emerged for events affecting others, where being young and having a higher income, more education, and an English-speaking (versus a Spanish-speaking) background were associated with reporting more such events.

There are several possible explanations for these data. First, factors such as educational level or ethnic background may be related to the willingness of respondents to disclose information about them-

TABLE 2.2   Zero-Order Correlations Between the Number of Events and
             Selected Background Characteristics

Respondent Characteristics	_Focus of Events_	
	Respondents	_Others_
Family income	$-.10^*$	$.21^*$
Education	$.07$	$.33^*$
Age	$-.13^*$	$-.14^*$
Age of youngest child	$-.17^*$	$-.08$
English-speaking background	$-.06$	$.26^*$
Married	$-.19^*$	$.06$
Employed	$-.23^*$	$-.08$
Length of time in community	$-.20^*$	$.03$

$^*p < .05$

selves and others. While we cannot entirely rule out this possibility in
our data, we generally did not find a reluctance on the part of any
subgroup of respondents to disclose personal or sensitive information
to the interviewers, nor would such a general tendency explain why a
factor such as income would be related in different ways to the
reporting of events affecting self as opposed to others. A second
explanation centers on the occurrence of different numbers of events
affecting self versus others for different income, age, or ethnic groups.
For events affecting respondents, our data are consistent with observations of previous researchers (e.g., Dohrenwend & Dohrenwend,
1965), who have reported that individuals in lower social classes may
be exposed to proportionally more stressful life events or that the
occurrence of episodic stressful life events may be related to, or
simply reflect, underlying chronic stressful life conditions, such as
unemployment (Gersten et al., 1977; Liem & Liem, 1978), which are
unequally distributed among social classes.

On the other hand, the reported correlates of events affecting
others were somewhat puzzling at first, in that it was not clear why
respondents with higher incomes, for example, would report more
events affecting others, while reporting fewer affecting themselves. A
possible and perhaps straightforward explanation emerges, however,

when we consider the social network as the most relevant unit of analysis for interpreting such observed relationships. If certain network characteristics are related both to the reporting of events affecting others and to factors such as income or education, the observed relationships between these variables may be partially explained. A simple hypothesis in this regard would be that the size of the respondents' networks may vary with income or educational level, and since size per se should bear some relationship to the reported number of events affecting others (especially if all types of events are considered), respondents with higher incomes or education should report more such events. In our study we, in fact, observed significant positive correlations between the educational levels of respondents and both their reported number of friends and their reported number of relatives in the area, both used here as indicators of network size. The frequency of events affecting others was in turn related to both the number of relatives in the area and the number of friends, making the above hypothesis plausible. Our purpose here, however, is not to test such hypotheses, but rather to suggest that the frequency of stressful events in individuals' social networks may be related to the structure of those networks.

The significance of events affecting persons other than our respondents ultimately lies not in the numbers of such events or even in how those events are distributed among different age, sex, or ethnic groups. Rather, the importance of such events to questions of individual and community mental health lies in their relationship with (1) the experience of stress for individual respondents, (2) social support processes in respondents' social networks, and (3) the mental and physical well-being of the respondents. Clearly, if such events have no demonstrated impact on the respondents in terms of reported levels of distress or as they influence the social support processes in their networks, they will not be of much interest to health practitioners.

Our initial approach to these questions involved comparing the respondents' ratings of the stressfulness of the events they directly experienced versus those experienced by others. Using a 4-point scale, respondents rated the extent to which they were worried or upset when the event happened. Table 2.3 summarizes these results. While slightly more of the "extremely" upsetting events were experienced by respondents, this was not the case for events rated as "very"

TABLE 2.3 Stress Ratings of Events as a Function of the Person to whom they Occurred

Person	How Stressful			
	Not at All	Somewhat	Very	Extremely
Respondent	38%	21%	18%	22%
Child	53	17	14	15
Husband/boyfriend	43	25	16	16
Sibling	58	19	14	9
Parent	36	19	27	17
Other relative	59	20	12	9
Friend	58	23	13	6

or "somewhat" upsetting. Many events reported to other individuals were thus clearly not trivial from the viewpoints of our respondents.

The relationship of both types of events to several measures of health status and health behavior are shown in Table 2.4. An examination of this table reveals that, across all correlates, the measure of events to others probably contributes as much to the explained variance of these measures as the measure of self-focused events. Results for individual health-related variables also suggest that events to others may be a more important predictor of certain health outcomes. A closer examination of the types of events involved suggests some possible explanations. For example, for those events to others occurring with a relatively high frequency (over 100 observations), two that received some of the highest ratings of stressfulness were hospitalization and having a serious illness or health problem. As such, the observed relationship between events to others and the person's own health behaviors, such as having a physical exam, may partly reflect the meaning of these events for the respondent's personal sense of vulnerability to illness, a factor that has been shown to relate to preventive health behaviors (Rosenstock, 1966).

Network Stress and Support Mobilization Processes

We have presented data suggesting the utility of adopting the social network as a unit for sampling life events and for the analysis of

TABLE 2.4   Selected Health Status and Health Behavior Correlates of
Life Events to Respondents and Others

	Focus of Events	
Variable	Respondent	Others
Reported health status as poor	.11*	−.10*
Negative affect[a]	−.26*	.09*
Positive affect	−.03	.08
Described herself as unhappy	.19*	−.01
Reported an episode of being sick in last two months	.22*	.17*
Reported an episode of a child being sick in last two months	.06	.10*
Reported an illness-related medical visit in last two months	.22*	−.03
Reported a child had an illness-related medical visit in last two months	.09*	.08
Reported having a physical exam in the last year	−.04	.15*
Reported a child having a physical exam in the last year	.12*	.12*
Reported a dental visit in the last year	.08	.14*
Reported a dental visit for child in the last year	−.08	−.09*

a. The positive and negative affect scales were adopted from Bradburn (1969); lower scores
signify more affect.

*$p < .05$

stress effects. We have restricted ourselves to descriptive data regarding the frequency of life events to respondents and significant others in the respondents' lives, and we have presented some preliminary correlational analyses that point to the relative importance and differential impact of some of these types of events on the respondents' reported health status and health behavior. In our previous discussion, we proposed that a consideration of stress within the social network is an essential part of the context with regard to social support processes, in that it partly defines constraints that may be present on potentially supportive relationships. The nature and degree of constraints on supportive relationships has never to our knowledge been a focus in stress research, but, as indicated earlier, it is central to support mobilization processes. Furthermore, the problem of constraints emphasizes the benefits of moving between individual- and aggregate-level analyses in the same study.

The most general research hypothesis suggested by this discussion is that, as levels of stress in networks increase, the probability of individuals obtaining support from those networks decreases, which, in turn, should affect the ability of all individuals within those networks to cope successfully with stressful life events or chronically stressful life conditions. Testing this or more refined hypotheses, however, must be preceded by more descriptive research on support processes in social networks and by development of network concepts that describe the interrelationships between stress and support in networks. Toward the latter end, we have begun to develop measures that define the extent to which that subgroup of individuals experiencing life events (a crude measure of network stress) overlaps with the subgroup of individuals named as potential supporters (by the criteria outlined earlier). Hypothetically, the degree of overlap between the two sets of individuals could vary from complete overlap (thus resulting in one set of affiliates who are probably close ties) to no overlap.

The simplest measure of overlap is the absolute number of people who appear in both the events lists and as potential supporters. In our sample, the mean number of individuals experiencing events was 5.5, while the mean number of potential supporters was slightly more than 10. The number of overlapping pairs from the two sets of individuals ranged from 0 to 12, with a mean of 3.3. While these numbers would be expected to vary with different procedures for measuring stress and support, there appears to be sufficient variability in this measure to warrant its use in further analyses. A more sensitive measure of overlap than the total number of overlapping relationships may, in fact, be a proportion, such as the precentage of potential supporters who have also experienced stress events. This type of measure would take into account the varying sizes of networks. The potential meaning of different configurations of stress and support in social networks for the mobilization of social support resources must await future research and analysis of our own data, but we propose that it is at least theoretically reasonable to assume that networks characterized by a high degree of overlap will be different in important ways from those with the same amount of stress or network support, but with little or no overlap in those areas.

SUMMARY AND CONCLUSIONS

We have characterized a number of diverse research programs and studies as having a common emphasis on context. This emergent direction is marked by innovations in the conceptualization and measurement of life stress. Study of social supports is a second noteworthy facet of a contextual approach.

Toward building on these developments, we believe that research designs must now provide for (1) analyses at both the individual and the network levels, and (2) exploration of temporal relationships and processes within the stress or support context.

Regarding the first requirement, we have suggested that the concept of network is a useful vehicle for describing social stress as well as social support. The benefit of a network approach to stress assessment is twofold. First, taking the network as the locus of stressful occurrences provides insight into the social sources of distress (Pearlin & Lieberman, 1977). Giving explicit attention to the origin of events improves on the current practice of purging from events lists, on the basis of ad hoc impressions, those events seen to be nonfortuitous. In addition, assessments of network-based (and network-affected) stress offer a point of departure for determining the extent of network resources and the demands for them. Thus, as network support capability is a function of the existing level of demand and of available resources, aggregate-level measures of resource constraints are significant in the study of support processes.

Our data collection is at this time in progress and we cannot report on our efforts to study the second requirement for contextual study, namely, the sequencing of stress processes and support activities. What follows, however, is our argument for including a temporal dimension in stress research. To date, attention to issues of timing has been conspicuously absent.

The study of temporal relationships and processes includes historical analyses (on the personal and social levels), which define the context leading up to significant stressful junctures, as well as prospective study of periods subsequent to these events and terminating after observation of the coping process. Regarding the contexts that lead up to stress periods, we have noted the significance of research on the number, severity, and sequencing of life events, and on the etiological significance of longer-term stressful life conditions. In our opinion, without a broad scope of information on stress context the meaning of particular occurrences will be obscured. Also, questions of the relationship between stressful events and longer-term conditions can only be addressed through such temporal analyses. For example, at what point do stressful events erupt in a predictable fashion from adverse life conditions, or are events and conditions relatively independent? (Eaton, 1978, has raised similar questions.)

Turning to the support variables, we have argued that support context begins with consideration of the pool of potential supporters, which is then narrowed to possible supporters after constraints on these persons are taken into account. (This is where the extent of supporter resources and other demands on the supporter become evident and are evaluated.) This description of support context is based on a model of decision-making (Jones & Fischer, 1978) that may not fully or accurately account for the selection of supporters. However, we find it a useful paradigm, as it draws attention to the gulf between potential and actual supporters and to the significance of the means through which the former become the latter.

The second phase of temporal study includes attention to the actual instances of support mobilization that are understood to mediate stress processes. This is the heart of the coping process with regard to the use of social supports. The individual experiences that are the outcomes of support decision-making and mobilization are the data that describe the stress-buffering mechanism that is usually inferred from statistical analysis alone.

To conclude, we believe that contextual study best addresses the research problems discussed earlier concerning the measurement of stress and supports, and the documentation of how supports are mobilized and used in stress situations. Each of these goals has practical implications. First, our existing research tools are not effectively translated into useful clinical instruments. Broad measures of stress experiences and support resources will be adequate only as gross indicators of functioning, but are otherwise likely to be misleading. Instead, contextual study of support processes is the most productive means to practical ends, because such analysis will provide an understanding of the conditions under which supports are available and can be mobilized to deal with life problems. Such analyses are also likely to distinguish between those events that are significant in causing distress and disorder and those that are merely symptomatic or etiologically unimportant. Since the goals of community health programs are to foster coping at the individual level, and to provide supports where individual capacity is weak, these kinds of data strike us as essential.

NOTE

1. Notable exceptions to the second tendency include the work of Dohrenwend (1970) and of Myers et al. (1971) on social class, life events, and psychiatric disorder. In addition, the recent work of Catalano and Dooley (1977), which examines individual life stress and disorder as a function of macro-economic climate, represents a major effort to establish the relationship between personal life events and broader societal conditions.

REFERENCES

BRADBURN, N. M. *The structure of psychological well-being*. Chicago: Aldine, 1969.

BROWN, G. W., & HARRIS, T. *Social origins of depression*. London: Tavistock, 1978.

CARVETH, W. B., & GOTTLIEB, B. H. The measurement of social support and its relation to stress. *Canadian Journal of Behavioral Science*, 1979, *11*, 179-187.

CATALANO, R., & DOOLEY, D. The economic predictors of depressed mood and stressful life events in a metropolitan community. *Journal of Health and Social Behavior*, 1977, *18*, 292-307.

CODDINGTON, R. D. The significance of life events as etiologic factors in diseases of children, II. A study of a normal population. *Journal of Psychosomatic Research*, 1972, *16*, 205-213.

DEAN, A., LIN, N., TANSIG, M., & ENSEL, W. M. *Relating types of social support to depression in the life course*. Paper presented at the Annual Meeting of the American Sociological Association, New York, August, 1980.

DOHRENWEND, B. P. Problems in defining and sampling the relevant population of stressful life events. In B. S. Dohrenwend & B. P. Dohrenwend (Eds.), *Stressful life events: Their nature and effects*. New York: John Wiley, 1974.

DOHRENWEND, B. P., & DOHRENWEND, B. S. The problem of validity in field studies of psychological disorder. *Journal of Abnormal Psychology*, 1965, *70*, 52-69.

DOHRENWEND, B. P., & EGRI, G. *Recent stressful life events and schizophrenia.* Paper presented at the Conference on Stress, Social Support and Schizophrenia. Burlington, Vermont, September 24-25, 1979.

DOHRENWEND, B. S. *Anticipation and control of stressful life events: An exploratory analysis.* Paper presented at the Eastern Psychological Association Convention, New York, 1976.

DOHRENWEND, B. S. Social class and stressful events. In E. H. Hare & J. K. Wing (Eds.), *Psychiatric epidemiology: Proceedings of the international symposium held at Aberdeen University 22-25 July, 1969.* New York: Oxford University Press, 1970, 321-325.

DOHRENWEND, B. S., & DOHRENWEND, B. P. (Eds.). *Stressful life events: Their nature and effects.* New York: John Wiley, 1974.

EATON, W. W. Life events, social supports and psychiatric symptoms: A re-analysis of the New Haven data. *Journal of Health and Social Behavior,* 1978, *19,* 230-234.

GERSTEN, J. C., LANGNER, T. S., EISENBERG, J. G., & SIMCHA-FAGAN, O. An evaluation of the etiologic role of stressful life-change in psychological disorders. *Journal of Health and Social Behavior,* 1977, *18,* 228-243.

GORE, S. Stress-buffering functions of social supports: An appraisal and clarification of research models. In B. S. Dohrenwend & B. P. Dohrenwend (Eds.), *Life stress and illness.* New York: Neale Watson, 1980.

HOLMES, T. H., & MASUDA, M. Life change and illness susceptibility. In B. S. Dohrenwend & B. P. Dohrenwend (Eds.), *Stressful life events: Their nature and effects.* New York: John Wiley, 1974.

HOLMES, T. H., & RAHE, R. H. The Social Readjustment Rating Scale. *Journal of Psychosomatic Research,* 1967, *11,* 213-218.

HURST, M. W., JENKINS, C. D., & ROSE, R. M. The assessment of life change stress: A comparative and methodological inquiry. *Psychosomatic Medicine,* 1978, *40,* 126-141.

JONES, L. M., & FISCHER, C. S. *Studying egocentric networks by mass survey.* Working Paper No. 284, Institute of Urban and Regional Development, University of California, Berkeley, January 1978.

KESSLER, R. C, A strategy for studying differential vulnerability to the psychological consequences of stress. *Journal of Health and Social Behavior,* 1979, *20,* 100-108.

LAZARUS, R. S., & COHEN, J. B. Environmental stress. In I. Altman & J. Wohlwill (Eds.), *Human behavior and the environment: Current theory and research.* New York: Plenum, 1977.

LAZARUS, R. S., & LAUNIER, R. Stress-related transactions between person and environment. In L. A. Pervin and M. Lewis (Eds.), *Internal and external determinants of behavior.* New York: Plenum, forthcoming.

LIEM, R., & LIEM, J. Social class and mental illness reconsidered: The role of economic stress and social support. *Journal of Health and Social Behavior,* 1978, *19,* 129-156.

LIN, N., DEAN, A., & ENSEL, W. M. *Constructing social support scales: A methodological note.* Paper presented at the Conference on Stress, Social Support, and Schizophrenia, Burlington, Vermont, September 24-25, 1979.

McFARLANE, A.H., NORMAN, G.R., STREINER, D.C., ROY, R., & SCOTT, D.J. A longitudinal study of the influence of the psychosocial environment on health status: A preliminary report. *Journal of Health and Social Behavior,* 1980, *21,* 124-133.

McGRATH, J.E. (Ed.). *Social and psychological factors in stress.* New York: Holt, Rinehart & Winston, 1970.

MECHANIC, D. Discussion of research programs on relations between stressful life events and episodes and physical illness. In B.S. Dohrenwend & B.P. Dohrenwend (Eds.), *Stressful life events: Their nature and effects.* New York: John Wiley, 1974.

MYERS, J.K., LINDENTHAL, J.J., & PEPPER, M.P. Life events and psychiatric impairment. *Journal of Nervous and Mental Disease,* 1971, *152,* 149-157.

PAYKEL, E.S., MYERS, J.K., DIENELT, M.N., KLERMAN, G.L., LINDENTHAL, J.J., & PEPPER, M.P. Life events and depression: A controlled study. *Archives of General Psychiatry,* 1969, *21,* 753-760.

PEARLIN, L., & LIEBERMAN, M. Social sources of emotional distress. In R. Simmons (Ed.), *Research in community and mental health.* Greenwich, CT: JAI Press, 1977.

RABKIN, J.G., & STRUENING, E.C. Life events, stress and illness. *Science,* 1976, *194,* 1013-1020.

ROSENSTOCK, I.M. Why people use health services. *Milbank Memorial Fund Quarterly,* 1966, *44,* 94-124.

SARASON, I.G., JOHNSON, J.H., & SIEGEL, J.M. Assessing the impact of life changes: Development of the life experiences survey. In I.G. Sarason and C.D. Spielberger (Eds.), *Stress and anxiety.* New York: John Wiley, 1979.

SELYE, H. *The stress of life.* New York: McGraw-Hill, 1956.

SURTEES, P.G., & INGHAM, J.G. Life stress and depressive outcome: Application of a dissipation model to life events. *Social Psychiatry,* 1980, *15,* 21-31.

VINOKUR, A., & SELZER, M.C. Desirable versus undesirable life events: Their relationship to stress and mental distress. *Journal of Personality and Social Psychology,* 1975, *32,* 329-337.

Chapter 3

SOCIAL SUPPORT IN THE ADJUSTMENT OF PREGNANT ADOLESCENTS
Assessment Issues

MANUEL BARRERA, Jr.

Prior to initiating my own research on social support I reviewed the literature that was then somewhat sparse, but clearly provocative. A series of stimulating papers had recently been published to champion the role of social support in buffering stress, satisfying basic human needs, preventing disorders of all types, contributing to the remediation of illness and psychological distress, and influencing the provision of professional helping services (Caplan, 1974, 1976; Cassel, 1976; Cobb, 1976; Dean & Lin, 1977; Rabkin & Struening, 1976; Tolsdorf, 1976). My review of these articles and others led me to several conclusions about how social support was characterized in the literature and about what research topics ought to be pursued in the future. First, social support appeared to be a variable that was capable of having a broad impact on the well-being of community residents and, therefore, one that deserved the further attention of

---

Author's Note: Some of the research described in this chapter was supported by a faculty grant-in-aid that was awarded to the author by Arizona State University. Special appreciation is extended to Ms. Carol Lamond-Walker of the Phoenix Union School District, Ms. Pat Baird of the Maricopa County Health Department, and their coworkers, whose active cooperation made this study possible.

community researchers. Second, social support was portrayed as a ubiquitous yet indistinctly defined concept. Studies that used indicators as diverse as the presence of littermates, the "wantedness" of pregnancy, and involvement in self-help groups were equally interpreted as evidence of social support's effectiveness in ameliorating stress (e.g., Cobb, 1976). Finally, various approaches had been adopted to assess support, but few of these measures had been systematically developed and repeatedly used with different populations.

The present chapter is organized around two topics that were stimulated by these initial observations. First, I describe the development of several approaches to the assessment of what I feel are key dimensions of social support. In this context, concepts underlying the study of support and previous efforts to measure them are discussed. Second, I illustrate the application of these preliminary measures in the study of adolescents who were undergoing a major life change: pregnancy. Overall, the goal here is not only to make a methodological contribution to social support research, but also to increase our understanding of social support's potential role in the adjustment to stressful life events.

APPROACHES TO ASSESSING
SOCIAL SUPPORT

Social support assessment in previous research has adopted a variety of approaches. This diversity illustrates the multifaceted nature of support in that some measurement approaches have focused on the *providers* of support, some others on individuals' *subjective appraisal* of support, and still others on the *activities* involved in the provision of support.

A frequently assessed facet of support is its social context, that is, the people who are either potential or actual sources of support. Assessing this facet has often involved applications of social network analysis (Mitchell, 1974), a technique that offers methods for quantifying the structure and function of a set of people who constitute a system of significant exchanges. In a recent review (Mitchell & Trickett, 1980), applications of network analysis in social support research and the role of social networks in mediating the provision of support were critically discussed. In lieu of network analysis, several studies have used indices such as marital status (Eaton, 1978), access to a confidant (Brown et al., 1975), participation in community organizations and cultural activities (Lin et al., 1979), and presence of both parents in the household (Sandler, 1980). Similar to some network analysis measures, these indices provide information concerning the extent to which individuals are linked to significant people and have opportunities to interact in ways that might foster the expression of social support.

A second general approach to assessing support consists of those methods that emphasize individuals' subjective appraisal of relevant support dimensions. Unlike the quantitative assessments provided by social network analysis, qualitative indices have attempted to capture concepts such as satisfaction with support (Hirsch, 1979, 1980; Procidano & Heller, 1979), happiness with key relationships (Nuckolls et al., 1972), and adequacy of social attachments (Henderson et al., 1978). Cobb (1976) has argued that social support is essentially "information" that an individual is loved, esteemed, and part of a network of communication and mutual obligation. From this perspective, it is the cognitive appraisal of support that is regarded as the central target of necessarily qualitative measures of support.

A third approach to assessing support is directed at specific behavioral activities that are involved in the expression of natural forms of assistance, that is, natural helping behaviors. Relative to qualitative indices and quantitative measures of the presence of significant social relationships, attempts to assess natural helping behaviors have been rare. Cowen (1980: 278) commented that social support research has largely consisted of investigations of social support systems' structures rather than "what they actually do, how, and with what results." Similarly, Liem and Liem (1978: 19) made the following observation:

> An interesting related finding is that the amount of help received is not always related to perceptions of being supported. . . . While this finding is open to several explanations, its chief significance lies in the need it suggests for the development of social support measures that include more behaviorally oriented indices as well as subjective estimates of social support.

Calls for more explicit, behavioral accounts of support can also be found in papers by Gore (1978), Lieberman and Mullan (1978), and Tucker and Colten (1978). In addition, Gottlieb's (1978) recent study represents an important first step in specifying the activities involved in the delivery of natural forms of helping. He developed a scheme for the classification of natural helping behaviors by conducting content analyses of interviews with single mothers that were designed to elicit accounts of specific supportive activities.

The Development of a Multimethod
Approach to Assessing Social Support

In order ultimately to investigate substantive issues concerning social support's role in the adjustment to major life changes, there was an obvious need systematically to develop sound social support measures. This was, in fact, one of the major conclusions of Dean and Lin's (1977) review, which reported that they could find no social support scales with sufficient evidence of reliability or validity.

Recognizing the multifaceted nature of support, it appeared that studies incorporating a multimethod approach to assessing support would have distinct advantages over those that adopted a single approach. The simultaneous use of several different measures of support would allow for an examination of their interrelationships. It would be possible, for example, to begin to explore the relationship between subjective judgments regarding the adequacy of support and structural components of social networks. A multimethod approach to assessing support would also allow for a more precise specification of which aspects of support are predictive of adjustment for specific populations.

Measuring Socially Supportive Behaviors. As previously noted, Gottlieb's (1978) study is the only one that has assessed the perceived behavioral activities involved in the receipt of informal help. The categories of "informal helping behaviors" that he generated help to answer the question, What do support systems do? (Cowen, 1980). Ultimately, measures based on similar categories could be used to conduct fine-grained analyses for determining if specific supportive behaviors are predictive of satisfactory adjustment of certain individuals under certain life conditions. Although admittedly futuristic, one could envision community interventions that involve instructing natural helpers to deliver categories of supportive behaviors that have been empirically identified as predictive of adjustment.

In our work on the development of a behavioral measure of social support, the Inventory of Socially Supportive Behaviors (ISSB; Barrera et al., forthcoming), we began with the decision to employ a definition of support similar to the broad conceptualizations of Caplan (1976) and Hirsch (1979). From this perspective, social support provisions were thought to include activities directed at assisting others in mastering emotional distress, sharing tasks, giving advice, teaching skills, and providing material aid. Ideas for specific items came from a variety of sources (e.g., Asser, 1978; Brim, 1974; Caplan, 1976; Hirsch, 1979, 1980), but especially from Gottlieb's (1978) content analysis of interviews with single mothers which yielded twenty-six categories of helping behaviors.

Forty items were subsequently written according to three guidelines. First, behavioral specificity was stressed in order to minimize the need for subjective inferences. Second, wording that would make an item only applicable to a specific population was avoided. Since the scale was planned for eventual use with a wide variety of community populations, it was important to avoid overly restricted items. Finally, explicit references to states of psychological adjustment were omitted. An anticipated application of the scale was in research on the relationship between social support and adjustment. If the support scale itself included references to adjustment, any relationship between the scale and an adjustment measure could be explained by their direct content overlap.

Once the wording for the forty items was finalized, instructions were written requesting respondents to rate the frequency with which each item occurred during the preceding four weeks. Ratings were made on a 5-point Likert-type scale that ranged from "not at all" to "about every day."

The initial study of the ISSB evaluated its test-retest and internal consistency reliabilities. Seventy-one university students completed the ISSB in two assessment sessions that were separated by a two-day test interval. This interval was relatively brief, but it had to be short enough to prevent subjects from actually experiencing a substantial number of events during the testing interval, yet long enough to prevent the memory of initial test responses from seriously influencing subjects' retest responses.

The internal consistency reliability of the ISSB was analyzed and yielded coefficient alphas of .926 and .940 for the first and second administrations of the scale respectively. The high internal consistency justified the computation of a total ISSB score for each subject by summing the frequency ratings across all forty items. Subjects' total ISSB scores for the test and retest were substantially correlated (r[69] = .882, p < .001). Test-retest correlation coefficients for individual items ranged from a low of .441 to a high of .912.

In light of the encouraging results of the reliability analyses, an additional study was conducted to determine the ISSB's correlation with a qualitative index of social support, that is, a measure of perceived supportiveness. For this study the Cohesion subscale of the Family Environment Scale (Moos et al., 1974) was selected as the index of perceived supportiveness. This 9-item true-false subscale was described as assessing "the extent to which family members are helpful and supportive of each other" (Moos et al., 1974: 4). Forty-three university students voluntarily participated in a single assessment session in which the Cohesion subscale (embedded in nine filler items) and the ISSB were administered. Instructions for the ISSB were modified to request subjects to report the frequency of supportive behaviors received from family members only. Results confirmed the expectation that subjects who reported the greatest frequency of supportive interactions with family members on the ISSB would also tend to perceive their families as cohesive. Although these two measures were significantly correlated (r[41] = .359, p < .01), it was also apparent that they each were assessing some unique aspects of support.

In summary, the preliminary evaluation of the ISSB showed it to have high internal consistency and test-retest reliability. Despite the relatively short test-retest interval, this latter form of reliability was critical, since it would have been difficult to regard the ISSB as measuring *actual* supportive behaviors if subjects could not rate the frequency of their occurrence with some consistency.

Measuring Support Satisfaction, Need, and Social Network Indices. As a measure of supportive behaviors, the ISSB was designed neither to provide information concerning the *people* who supplied resources nor individuals' subjective appraisals of the *adequacy of support*. Both of these additional features represent prominent assessment approaches that have been previously adopted by social support researchers. Because the ultimate goal was to implement a multimethod approach in assessing the many facets of social support, procedures were developed for assessing social support network indices and subjects' satisfaction with and need for support. The Arizona Social Support Interview Schedule (ASSIS) was subsequently designed to measure these facets of support (Barrera, forthcoming).

The ASSIS's procedures for identifying support network membership differed substantially from methods used in some previous network studies (e.g., Hirsch, 1979, 1980; Pattison, 1977). Instructions for identifying network members in these studies have typically requested subjects to list people who were "significant" or "important" to them (see Mitchell & Trickett, 1980, for a review). While these instructions might be sufficient for identifying "social importance" networks, they fall short of calling for subjects to name people who specifically serve supportive functions. Thus, one objective in developing the ASSIS was to provide a method for subjects to identify individuals who more clearly serve supportive functions.

To accomplish this objective, procedures similar to those described by Jones and Fischer (1978) and Ratcliffe et al. (n.d.) were developed. These researchers specified functions that individuals would serve to qualify them as network members. By asking subjects to name people who met the described functions, network membership lists were constructed.

In the ASSIS, six rationally derived support functions formed the basis for questions that were used to elicit names of network members:

(1) Material Aid: providing material aid in the form of money and other physical objects;
(2) Physical Assistance: sharing of tasks;
(3) Intimate Interaction: interacting in a nondirective manner such that feelings and personal concerns are expressed;
(4) Guidance: offering advice and guidance;
(5) Feedback: providing individuals with information about themselves;
(6) Social Participation: engaging in social interactions for fun, relaxation, and diversion from demanding conditions.

These categories appeared to capture the range of activities that a number of social support researchers had described in their discussions of social support. Papers by Caplan (1976) and Hirsch (1980) were particularly influential in defining these categories.

A second interest in designing a network measure was to allow for drawing distinctions between strictly supportive network members and those who were, in addition, sources of interpersonal conflict. My own clinical work with distressed families and interviews I had conducted with counselors in a program for pregnant teenagers strongly suggested that major sources of support could also constitute major sources of strain. Furthermore, Henderson et al. (1978) found a significant relationship between the prominence of unpleasant social interactions and psychiatric morbidity. In light of these observations, the ASSIS not only included questions describing support functions, but also called for the identification of people who were sources of interpersonal conflict.

The ASSIS's qualitative indices of support satisfaction and need were based on the same six support categories that were used to identify network members. For each of the six categories, subjects were asked to use 3-point scales for rating their satisfaction with the support they had received and how much they needed that support during the past month.

Subsequent to the incorporation of the network, satisfaction, and need items into a structured interview schedule, a study was conducted to assess the reliability of the ASSIS indices and to correlate these indices with the ISSB. Its design was similar to that of the study that evaluated the ISSB's reliability: 45 university students participated in two assessment sessions that were separated by at least two days. Trained interviewers[1] individually administered the ASSIS to each subject, and they never interviewed the same subject twice. The ISSB was only administered during the second interview, and only after the ASSIS had been completed.

In accordance with Jones and Fischer (1978), *total network size*[2] was defined as the number of people who were named as providing at least one support function. *Conflicted network size* consisted of the number of support network members who were also sources of interpersonal conflict. Results of the study showed that subjects reported a mean of just over ten network members in the first (10.4) and second (10.8) interviews, and slightly more than two conflicted network members (2.5 and 2.6) in these assessments. Test-retest correlations showed that total network size was a stable indicator ($r[43] = .88$, $p < .001$). Additional analysis showed that a mean of 73.8 percent of the network members named in *either* the test *or* the retest interviews were named in *both* assessments. Conflicted network size had a significant but somewhat lower test-retest correlation ($r[43] = .54$, $p < .001$).

The support satisfaction measure suffered from a markedly skewed distribution that favored high satisfaction scores. A moderate test-retest correlation ($r[43] = .69$, $p < .001$) and low internal consistency (coefficient alpha = .33) were obtained. The support need measure demonstrated good test-retest reliability (r[43] = .80, p < .001) and moderate internal consistency (coefficient alpha = .52).

As noted earlier, the ISSB was administered along with the ASSIS during the retest assessment only. The ISSB showed a modest, but significant correlation with total network size (r[43] = .32, p < .05). The ISSB was not significantly correlated with either the satisfaction or the need measure.

With the exception of the low reliability of the support satisfaction measure, the scales included in the ASSIS demonstrated adequate reliability. Although social network analysis has been used frequently in social support research, this study was one of the few attempts to evaluate just how reliably network members can be identified. It was encouraging to discover that the ASSIS procedures led to a reliable measurement of total network size in this initial study of university students. The ISSB relationship to total network size was of a magnitude that approximated the ISSB's correlation with the Cohesion subscale of the Family Environment Scale. Although the ISSB and ASSIS scales can both be regarded as assessing facets of social support, these results suggest that they measure unique features of support as well.

SOCIAL SUPPORT AND THE ADJUSTMENT OF PREGNANT ADOLESCENTS

The goal of the scale development research was to provide assessment approaches that would be suitable for use in community-based research aimed at better understanding social support's role in the adjustment to major life events. Because the scales had been developed solely with college students, it was critical to substantiate their value in research with participant populations that not only differed from a university sample, but also had special relevance to the hypothesized role of social support as a moderator of stressful life conditions.

The decision to study the role of social support in the adjustment of pregnant adolescents was based on several factors. Perhaps the most influential was the attention that teenage pregnancy received in the community. A key informant survey on the needs of youth that had been conducted by a local community mental health center identified teen pregnancy as a high-priority problem (Balk, 1976). To address these needs, various school-health and social agencies created programs to alleviate the problems these young people faced. Because I served as a board member of a youth program that had launched a counseling/education program to serve pregnant teenagers, I was particularly sensitized to the stress of this life event. Adolescent pregnancy, in short, was a significant area of concern for residents of the local community. This concern, however, was clearly not restricted to the local community, since it paralleled national attention. In the popular press, teenage pregnancy was described as an epidemic with pervasive personal and social costs. Research indicated that children born to adolescents were not only at higher risk of death and a host of physical disorders, but also that teenage mothers were themselves at risk of physical impairments, disrupted education, weak economic power, and high divorce rates (Card & Wise, 1978; Furstenberg, 1976; Furstenberg & Crawford, 1978; Menken, 1972; Shinke & Gilchrist, 1977).

Pregnancy and childbirth are represented on several scales of stressful life events (e.g., Holmes & Rahe, 1967; Sarason et al., 1978). Among adolescent women, pregnancy is preceived to be particularly disruptive. In a study by Coddington (1972), over 200 teachers, pediatricians, and mental health workers were asked to rate the amount of social readjustment required by a number of major life events that might be experienced by preschool, elementary, junior high, and senior high school students. For junior high school students these key informants rated an unwed pregnancy as the single most stressful event while for senior high school students; it was rated second in stressfulness.

Not only is adolescent pregnancy a stressful event, but it is also an event whose impact on individuals' well-being could reasonably be influenced by the presence or absence of social support. For example, a study of women's appraisal of events associated with pregnancy (Helper et al., 1968) found that being unmarried and lacking the support of the baby's father served to increase the mother's perceived stressfulness of pregnancy. In a frequently cited study of primiparous, married women, Nuckolls et al. (1972) investigated the role of "psychosocial assets" in moderating the relationship between stressful life events and birth complications. Although possessing assets had no effect for women who experienced low levels of stress, women who reported high stress and low assets had three times more birth complications than those who reported high levels of psychosocial assets. It is important to note, however, that Nuckolls et al.'s measure of psychosocial assets included items concerning intrapersonal characteristics (e.g., self-esteem) and reactions toward pregnancy, in addition to items that at face value appeared to assess social support. Consequently, it is unclear to what extent social support alone accounted for the observed effects.

Social support has shown some relationship to the health of children born to teenage parents and to the long-term consequences for the parents' educational and occupational achievement (Baldwin & Cain, 1980; Furstenberg & Crawford, 1978). These studies have emphasized the role of the family in providing material aid (e.g., money, housing) and instrumental assistance (e.g., child care) *following* the birth of the child. Research has not included in-depth assessments of social support in an effort better to understand factors related to the adjustment of adolescents *during* their pregnancies.

A study was subsequently designed to examine the relationship between social support and the well-being of pregnant adolescents, using the support scales that had been developed in the preliminary studies. Participation in this study was restricted to women who were less than 20 years old and who did not have children from previous pregnancies. In order to obtain an ethnically diverse sample of volunteer participants who met these criteria, cooperative arrangements were made with two urban agencies that offered special services to pregnant adolescents. One of the agencies was an "alternative" school for pregnant high school students who elected to leave their home campuses in order to continue their studies at the alternative school. The second agency was a county health department clinic that conducted specialized pre- and postnatal clinics for adolescent women. In actuality, the populations of the two agencies overlapped, since many of the adolescents attending the alternative school received health care at the clinic. The health department clinic also served junior high school women and adolescents who had discontinued their education.

The final sample of 86 participants consisted of 22 Blacks, 32 Caucasians, 28 Mexican Americans, and 4 women who did not identify themselves as members of any of these ethnic groups. They had a mean age of 17.2 years and had been pregnant a mean of 6.6 months at the time of their interviews. Slightly over half (52.3 percent) of the sample were attending school, and 67.4 percent were not married.

Assessment Procedures and Measures

Over the duration of the project, eight female research assistants[3] were involved in interviewing the participants. The assessment battery consisted of self-administered scales as well as measures administered as part of a structured interview. Each assessment was conducted individually and began with the collection of background information such as age, school status, education, marital status, ethnicity, and other pertinent data. The order of presenting the remaining scales was uniquely determined for each participant.

Negative Life Events. A measure of negative life events consisted of twenty-seven undesirable events taken from Coddington's (1972) scale for senior high school students, and an additional eight items concerning victimization from violence and drug use that were written specifically for this study. These items were verbally administered by interviewers.

Social Support Network Indices. As previously described, the ASSIS, a social support network measure, yielded a number of scores. Total network size, unconflicted network size, conflicted network size, support satisfaction, and support need scores were all obtained from the ASSIS. Like the life events scale, the ASSIS was verbally administered by interviewers. In the administration of the ASSIS, the order of presenting the support categories was randomized for each research participant.

Receipt of Natural Helping Behaviors. Participants self-administered the 40-item ISSB.

Maladjustment. A self-administered scale, the Brief Symptom Inventory (BSI; Derogatis, 1977), was used as a measure of symptomatology. In addition to a total symptom score, three of the BSI's subscales — depression, anxiety, and somatization — were used as criterion variables. These symptom dimensions were selected because of their overall prevalence in the general population, and because they could conceivably be effected by the stress of early pregnancy.

Reliability of Social Support Measures

Although it was not possible to calculate test-retest reliability coefficients for the support measures in this study, internal consistency of the scales was again examined. Compared to results obtained for the college student sample, the internal consistency of the support satisfaction (.50) and support need (.70) scales of the ASSIS were notably higher. The coefficient alpha for the ISSB was high (.92) and almost identical to that obtained with the college student sample.

Relationships Between Social Support and Life Events Measures

One of the assumptions underlying the use of several measures of social support was that they assess different aspects of the structure and provisions of supportive social relationships. Table 3.1 shows an intercorrelation matrix of the social support measures and the stressful life events scale. Inspection of this matrix reveals that the support variables are at best only mildly related to each other. The ISSB is significantly related to only total and conflicted network size. Although support satisfaction and need are negatively related to each other ($r[84] = -.55$), these two variables are not significantly correlated with the ISSB or any of the network measures. It was particularly noteworthy that the measure of stressful life events was *positively* correlated with the ISSB ($r[84] = .41$, $p < .001$), *positively* correlated with support need ($r[84] = .36$, $p < .001$), and *negatively* correlated with support satisfaction ($r[84] = -.38$, $p < .001$). These results not only suggest that the ISSB possibly reflects increased supportive activities that are in response to stressful events, but also that the presence of negative events diminishes individuals' satisfaction with the support that they receive.

The Relationship Between Social Support and Adjustment

To examine the direct relationship between social support variables and measures of adjustment (symptoms), zero-order correlations were calculated. As shown in Table 3.2, total network size and one of its components, unconflicted network size, were not significantly related to any of the symptom dimensions. In fact, none of these correlations is significant, and all are conspicuously low. The ISSB, support need, and conflicted network size scores were all *positively* correlated with total symptomatology and many of the BSI subscales. In contrast, support satisfaction bore a significant negative relationship to all of the symptom dimensions, with the exception of somatization (which was not highly related to any of the variables examined in this study). Table 3.2 also shows that negative life events were

TABLE 3.1　Intercorrelations of Social Support and Life Event Measures (n = 86)

	2	3	4	5	6	7
1. ISSB	.24*	.12	.28**	−.13	.13	.41***
2. Total network size		.93***	.21*	−.00	.02	.15
3. Unconflicted network size			−.16	.00	−.02	.25**
4. Conflicted network size				−.02	.09	.04
5. Support satisfaction					−.55***	−.38***
6. Support need						.36***
7. Negative life events						

* p < .05; ** p < .01; *** p < .001

TABLE 3.2　The Relationship of Social Support and Life Events Measures to Maladjustment Scales (n = 86)

	Total Symptoms	Depression	Anxiety	Somatization
1. ISSB	.20*	.12	.10	.10
2. Total network size	.02	.00	−.05	−.03
3. Unconflicted network size	−.09	−.08	−.16	−.02
4. Conflicted network size	.29**	.23*	.30**	−.05
5. Support satisfaction	−.49***	−.49***	−.34***	−.12
6. Support need	.56***	.48***	.51***	.28**
7. Negative life events	.40***	.39***	.20*	.15

* p < .05; ** p < .01; *** p < .001

significantly correlated with total symptomatology, depression, and anxiety scales.

While these zero-order correlations were of some interest, the role of social support as a buffer of stressful life events was next examined. Similar to previous research that has examined the stress-buffering qualities of social support (Sandler, 1980; Wilcox, 1979), the effects of stressful life events, individual support variables, and the interaction of these two variables (represented by the product of life events and social support) were regressed on each of the symptom measures. The presence of a significant interaction term was interpreted as evidence of the stress-moderating effects of social support.

Analyses for which the overall Multiple R was significant are presented in Table 3.3. Support variables, negative life events, and

TABLE 3.3 Regression of Negative Life Events and Support on
Maladjustment Measures (n = 86)

Criterion	Predictors	Multiple R	R² Change	df	F
Total symptoms	NLE	.405	.164	1,84	16.48**
	ISSB	.406	.001	1,83	.11
	NLE × ISSB	.421	.012	1,82	1.25
	All predictors	.421		3,82	5.90*
Depression	NLE	.390	.152	1,84	15.08**
	ISSB	.392	.002	1,83	.18
	NLE × ISSB	.427	.028	1,82	2.81
	All predictors	.427		3,82	6.09*
Total symptoms	NLE	.405	.164	1,84	16.48**
	TNS	.407	.002	1,83	.15
	NLE × TNS	.431	.020	1,82	2.00
	All predictors	.431		3,82	6.22*
Depression	NLE	.390	.152	1,84	15.08**
	TNS	.394	.003	1,83	.33
	NLE × TNS	.441	.039	1,82	4.00*
	All predictors	.441		3,82	6.62*
Total symptoms	NLE	.405	.164	1,84	16.48**
	UNS	.429	.020	1,83	2.07
	NLE × UNS	.454	.021	1,82	2.19
	All predictors	.454		3,82	7.08*
Depression	NLE	.390	.152	1,84	15.08**
	UNS	.414	.019	1,83	1.93
	NLE × UNS	.460	.040	1,82	4.21*
	All predictors	.460		3,82	7.35**
Total symptoms	NLE	.405	.164	1,84	16.48**
	SAT	.546	.134	1,83	15.78**
	NLE × SAT	.548	.003	1,82	0.39
	All predictors	.548		3,82	11.76**
Depression	NLE	.390	.152	1,84	15.08**
	SAT	.540	.139	1,83	16.30**
	NLE × SAT	.549	.010	1,82	1.21
	All predictors	.549		3,82	11.81**

NOTES: NLE = Negative Life Events;
    ISSB = Inventory of Socially Supportive Behavior;
    TNS = Total Network Size;
    UNS = Unconflicted Network Size;
    SAT = Support Satisfaction.

* p < .05; ** p < .01

their interaction proved to be poor predictors of anxiety and somatization for this sample. In the regressions on the depression subscale scores, significant stress × social support interactions were shown for two support variables: total network size ($F[1, 82] = 4.00$, $p < .05$) and unconflicted network size ($F[1, 82] = 4.21$, $p < .05$).[4] To probe these interaction effects, the sample was divided at the median on each of the support network variables. Zero-order correlations between negative life events and depression scores were calculated for each of these subsamples. The correlation between stressful events and depression was smaller for those adolescents with large total ($r[44] = .25$) and large unconflicted ($r[49] = .26$) networks than for those with small total ($r[38] = .60$) and small unconflicted ($r[33] = .67$) networks.

Satisfaction with social support and stress did not show significant interaction effects. However, after accounting for the effects of stressful life events, satisfaction with social support still accounted for 13 percent of the variance in both the total symptom and depression subscale scores. The multiple Rs involving the support satisfaction measure were higher than those that included other support variables.

As previously noted, the ISSB was *positively* correlated with both the total symptom score and stressful life events. After accounting for the effects of negative life events, neither the effect of ISSB nor the interaction term was statistically significant.

While it does appear that social support plays an important role in the adjustment of pregnant adolescents, important distinctions should be made concerning the specific effects of the various social support measures used in this study. The ISSB proved to be a reliable index of the frequency with which individuals receive behavioral forms of social support. However, the salutary consequences of receiving this support are not demonstrated in this study. Instead, the ISSB appears to be a "barometer" of the amount of stress that these young women experienced, such that those who report the most undesirable events also appear to get the most help. Although it is still plausible that some forms of helping might actually have had a negative impact on the well-being of these women (e.g., overprotectiveness, interference, invasion of privacy), any relationship between the frequency of helping and symptoms disappears when the effects of stress are partialed out.

Network size shows the stress-buffering effect of social support similar to that reported by Wilcox (1979). The study also reveals the importance of drawing a distinction between those network members who are strictly the providers of positive forms of social support and those who, in addition, are sources of unpleasant social interactions. The size of the conflicted network, although small in an absolute sense, is positively correlated with several symptom dimensions, whereas the size of the unconflicted network tends to be negatively related to symptomatology. Furthermore, unconflicted network size contributes to buffering effects, whereas conflicted network size does not. Heller (1979) and Liem and Liem (1978) have expressed a need for research that examines the individual qualities of support providers and their effects on the support provided. Understanding more about the supporters who are also sources of conflict and the characteristics of the support that they provide should be on an agenda for future research.

The qualitative indices of support, i.e., satisfaction and need for support, prove to be the strongest predictors of symptomatology. One interpretation of this finding is that knowledge of people's subjective appraisals of the adequacy of support is more critical to the prediction of their well-being than simply collecting information about the number of supporters or the quantity of supportive behaviors to which they have access. But because support satisfaction and need are subjectively determined support measures, they are vulnerable to the criticism that they are simply a reflection of an individual's adjustment status. This was especially true in analyses involving the subscale of depression. Because one of the characteristics of depressed individuals is their negative evaluation of themselves and their world, it is conceivable that decreased satisfaction with supportive relationships could be just as much a *result* of depression as a cause of it. Henderson et al. (1978) have already noted this possibility. Future research will need to adopt research strategies to disentangle the causal direction of this relationship and to understand better the factors that contribute to satisfaction with support.

CONCLUSION

What is the role of social support in adolescents' adjustment to pregnancy? Based on the results of this study we can reply with what a colleague of mine has described as the Psychologist's Response: "It all depends." In this case, what "depends" is the manner in which social support is conceptualized and measured. If we consider pregnant adolescents' satisfaction with the support they receive, then social support appears to be a good predictor of psychological symptomatology, especially depression. There was also the suggestion that the number of supportive network members was related to their positive adjustment by buffering the impact of those stressful events that were experienced in addition to pregnancy. Finally, those adolescents who experienced the most stress also received the greatest frequency of supportive actions, but the beneficial effect of this help was not demonstrated in these data. Although social support appears to be an important factor in the adjustment of pregnant adolescents, it is equally apparent that not all measures of social support are related to adjustment in similar ways.

The study has several implications for efforts to develop and implement interventions directed at aiding pregnant adolescents and other groups facing critical life transitions. Strategies to assist community residents in expanding the number of their significant relationships that provide support appear to have potential value. Even those relationships that are supportive, however, might be ineffective in facilitating adjustment if they are also sources of interpersonal conflict. Interventions designed to eliminate conflict in otherwise supportive relationships would seemingly strengthen the role of social networks in aiding the adjustment of people undergoing major life changes.

The results of this study and others suggest that the receipt of satisfying support is related to positive adjustment, but the factors that contribute to the development of satisfying support are for the most part obscure. As previously noted, the direction of causality in the relationship between satisfying support and symptomatology is not clear in the present study. But the working assumption that satisfying, socially supportive relationships directly influence psychological adjustment would suggest that "satisfaction" should be a primary target of interventions. How do we go about changing community residents' sense of satisfaction with the support they receive? This question is beyond the scope of the present research, but it is one that naturally follows from this and other studies that have assessed qualitative dimensions of support (Hirsch, 1980; Procidano & Heller, 1979; Wilcox, 1979).

There is often a tendency to talk about social support as though it were a unitary concept. An awareness of the multifaceted nature of social support indicates that restraint should be exercised in making generalizations from studies that have adopted a single measure of social support. Gaining a better understanding of how social support might aid in the adjustment of community residents is a complex task. The development of comprehensive and differentiated methods of assessing support might provide a framework for improving our understanding of these processes, which appear to have such important implications for mental health in our communities.

Appendix 3.A
Inventory of Socially Supportive Behaviors (ISSB)

INSTRUCTIONS

We are interested in learning about some of the ways that you feel people have helped you or tried to make life more pleasant for you over the *past four weeks*. Below you will find a list of activities that other people might have done for you, to you, or with you in recent weeks. Please read each item carefully and indicate how often these activities happened to you during the *past four weeks*.

Use the following scale to make your ratings:

- A. Not at all
- B. Once or twice
- C. About once a week
- D. Several times a week
- E. About every day

Make all of your ratings on the answer sheet that has been provided. If, for example, the item:

45. Gave you a ride to the doctor.

happened once or twice during the past four weeks, you would make your rating like this:

      A   B   C   D   E
45. ☐   ■   ☐   ☐   ☐

Please read each item carefully and select the rating that you think is the most accurate.

During the past four weeks, how often did other people do these activities for you, to you, or with you:

1. Looked after a family member when you were away.
2. Was right there with you (physically) in a stressful situation.
3. Provided you with a place where you could get away for awhile.
4. Watched after your possessions when you were away (pets, plants, home, apartment, etc.).
5. Told you what she/he did in a situation that was similar to yours.
6. Did some activity with you to help you get your mind off of things.
7. Talked with you about some interests of yours.
8. Let you know that you did something well.
9. Went with you to someone who could take action.
10. Told you that you are OK just the way you are.
11. Told you that she/he would keep the things that you talk about private — just between the two of you.
12. Assisted you in setting a goal for yourself.
13. Made it clear what was expected of you.
14. Expressed esteem or respect for a competency or personal quality of yours.
15. Gave you some information on how to do something.
16. Suggested some action that you should take.
17. Gave you over $25.
18. Comforted you by showing you some physical affection.
19. Gave you some information to help you understand a situation you were in.
20. Provided you with some transportation.
21. Checked back with you to see if you followed the advice you were given.
22. Gave you under $25.
23. Helped you understand why you didn't do something well.
24. Listened to you talk about your private feelings.
25. Loaned or gave you something (a physical object other than money) that you needed.
26. Agreed that what you wanted to do was right.
27. Said things that made your situation clearer and easier to understand.
28. Told you how he/she felt in a situation that was similar to yours.

29. Let you know that he/she will always be around if you need assistance.
30. Expressed interest and concern in your well-being.
31. Told you that she/he feels very close to you.
32. Told you who you should see for assistance.
33. Told you what to expect in a situation that was about to happen.
34. Loaned you over $25.
35. Taught you how to do something.
36. Gave you feedback on how you were doing without saying it was good or bad.
37. Joked and kidded to try to cheer you up.
38. Provided you with a place to stay.
39. Pitched in to help you do something that needed to get done.
40. Loaned you under $25.

Appendix 3.B
Arizona Social Support Interview Schedule (ASSIS)

In the next few minutes I would like to get an idea of the people who are important to you in a number of different ways. I will be reading descriptions of ways that people are often important to us. After I read each description I will be asking you to give me the first names, initials, or nicknames of the people who fit the description. These people might be friends, family members, teachers, ministers, doctors, or other people you might know.

I will only want you to give me the names of people you actually know and that you have actually talked to during the last month. It's possible, then, that you won't get a chance to name some important people if for one reason or another you haven't had any contact with them in the last month.

If you have any questions about the descriptions after I read each one, please ask me to try and make it clearer.

A. PRIVATE FEELINGS

1. If you wanted to talk to someone about things that are very personal and private, who would you talk to? Give me the first names, initials, or

---

Author's Note: This version was used in the studies that are reported in the present chapter. The ASSIS is currently undergoing revision and additional evaluation.

nicknames of the people that you would talk to about things that are very personal and private.

PROBE: Is there anyone else that you can think of?

2. *During the last month,* which of these people did you actually talk to about things that were personal and private?

PROBE: Ask specifically about people who were listed in response to #1 but not listed in response to #2.

3. During the last month, would you have liked:
   1 = a lot more opportunities to talk to people about your personal and private feelings
   2 = a few more opportunities
   3 = or was this about right?

4. During the past month, how much do you think you needed people to talk about things that were very personal and private?
   1 = not at all
   2 = a little bit
   3 = quite a bit

B. MATERIAL AID

1. Who are the people you know that would lend or give you $25 or more if you needed it, or would lend or give you something (a physical object) that was valuable? You can name some of the same people that you named before if they fit this description, too, or you can name some other people.

PROBE: Is there anyone else that you can think of?

2. *During the past month,* which of these people actually loaned or gave you some money over $25 or gave or loaned you some valuable object that you needed?

PROBE: Ask about people named in response to #1 that were not named in response to #2.

3. During the past month, would you have liked people to have loaned you or to have given you:
   1 = a lot more
   2 = a little more
   3 = or was it about right?

4. During the past month, how much do you think you needed people who could give or lend you things that you needed?
   1 = not at all
   2 = a little bit
   3 = quite a bit

C. ADVICE

1. Who would you go to if a situation came up when you needed some advice? Remember, you can name some of the same people that you mentioned before, or you can name some new people.

PROBE: Anyone else?

2. *During the past month,* which of these people actually gave you some important advice?

PROBE: Inquire about people who were listed for #1 but not for #2.

3. During the past month, would you have liked:
    1 = a lot more advice
    2 = a little more advice
    3 = or was it about right?

4. During the past month, how much do you think you needed to get advice?
    1 = not at all
    2 = a little bit
    3 = quite a bit

D. POSITIVE FEEDBACK

1. Who are the people that you could expect to let you know when they like your ideas or the things that you do? These might be people you mentioned before or new people.

PROBE: Anyone else?

2. *During the past month,* which of these people actually let you know that they liked your ideas or liked the things that you did?

PROBE: Ask about individuals who were listed for #1 but not for #2.

3. During the past month, would you have liked people to tell you that they liked your ideas or things that you did:
    1 = a lot more often
    2 = a little more
    3 = or was it about right?

4. During the past month, how much do you think you needed to have people let you know when they liked your ideas or things that you did?
    1 = not at all
    2 = a little bit
    3 = quite a bit

E. PHYSICAL ASSISTANCE

1. Who are the people that you could call on to give up some of their time and energy to help you take care of something that you needed to do — things like driving you someplace you needed to go, helping you do some work around the house, going to the store for you, and things like that? Remember, you might have listed these people before or they could be new names.

PROBE: Anyone else you can think of?

2. *During the past month,* which of these people actually pitched in to help you do things that you needed some help with?

PROBE: Ask about people who were named in response to #1 but who were not named in response to #2.

3. During the past month, would you have liked:
   1 = a lot more help with things that you needed to do
   2 = a little more help
   3 = or was this about right?

4. During the past month, how much do you feel you needed people who would pitch in to help you do things?
   1 = not at all
   2 = a little bit
   3 = quite a bit

F. SOCIAL PARTICIPATION

1. Who are the people that you get together with to have fun or to relax? These could be new names or ones you listed before.

PROBE: Anyone else?

2. *During the past month,* which of these people did you actually get together with to have fun or to relax?

PROBE: Ask about people who were named in #1 but not in #2.

3. During the past month, would you have liked:
   1 = a lot more opportunities to get together with people for fun and relaxation
   2 = a few more
   3 = or was it about right?

4. How much do you think that you needed to get together with other people for fun and relaxation during the past month?
   1 = not at all
   2 = a little bit
   3 = quite a bit

G. NEGATIVE INTERACTIONS

1. Who are the people that you can expect to have some unpleasant disagreements with or people that you can expect to make you angry and upset? These could be new names or names you listed before.

PROBE: Anyone else?

2. *During the past month,* which of these people have you actually had some unpleasant disagreements with or have actually made you angry and upset?

PROBE: Ask about people listed for #1, but not for #2.

H. PERSONAL CHARACTERISTICS OF NETWORK MEMBERS

Now I would like to get some information about the people you have just listed. For each person on the list, could you tell me:

1. What is this person's relationship to you? For family members, specify the exact relationship (mother, father, brother, sister, grandmother, etc.). For professional people, also specify the exact profession (teacher, minister, doctor, counselor, etc.).

2. How old is this person?

3. What is this person's sex?

4. What is this person's ethnicity?
    1 = Black
    2 = Caucasian
    3 = Chicano, Latino, Mexican American
    4 = Native American
    5 = Asian American
    6 = Other (specify):

5. *For pregnant sample only:* Are any of the people you have listed the father of your baby? Indicate which person, if listed.

NOTES

1. Jody Falk, Linnard Lane, Guy Chadwick, and Daniela Jensen served as interviewers. Kurt Organista coordinated data collection and scheduling.

2. The ASSIS yielded two indices of total network size. Total *available* network size refers to the number of people who were perceived as being potentially available

for at least one form of support. Total *utilized* network size refers to the number of people who were reported to have actually provided at least one form of support during the preceding month. Because these two indices were highly correlated (r[43] = .92, p < .001), only total utilized network size is used in the present report.

3. Research assistants in this study were Sally DesCamp, Robyn Kay, Stephanie McFarland, Debbie Martinez, Jean Masciangelo, Carole Maynard, Linda Williams, and Jody Falk, who also served as study coordinator.

4. I fully recognize that because total and unconflicted network size are highly correlated (see Table 3.1), separate multiple regression analyses involving these two variables are redundant. I regard the uncorrelated indices of unconflicted and conflicted network size to be the key network indicators for these analyses. Analyses that include total network size have been reported because total network size has been the most frequently used network indicator in previous studies.

REFERENCES

ASSER, E. S. Social class and help-seeking behavior. *American Journal of Community Psychology,* 1978, *6,* 465-475.

BALDWIN, W., & CAIN, V. S. The children of teenage parents. *Family Planning Perspectives,* 1980, *12,* 34-43.

BALK, D. *The catchment area and its target populations: A needs assessment synthesis.* Unpublished manuscript, Phoenix South Community Mental Health Center, 1976.

BARRERA, M., Jr. A method for the assessment of social support networks in community survey research. *Connections,* forthcoming.

BARRERA, M., Jr., SANDLER, I. N., & RAMSAY, T. B. Preliminary development of a scale of social support: Studies on college students. *American Journal of Community Psychology,* forthcoming.

BRIM, J. A. Social network correlates of avowed happiness. *Journal of Nervous and Mental Disease,* 1974, *158,* 432-439.

BROWN, G. W., BHROLCHAIN, M. N., & HARRIS, T. Social class and psychiatric disturbance among women in an urban population. *Sociology,* 1975, *9,* 225-254.

CAPLAN, G. *Support systems and community mental health: Lectures on concept development.* New York: Behavioral Publications, 1974.

CAPLAN, G. The family as support system. In G. Caplan & M. Killilea (Eds.), *Support systems and mutual help: Multidisciplinary explorations.* New York: Grune & Stratton, 1976.

CARD, J. J., & WISE, L. L. Teenage mothers and teenage fathers: The impact of early childbearing on the parents' personal and professional lives. *Family Planning Perspectives,* 1978, *10,* 199-235.

CASSEL, J. The contribution of the social environment to host resistance. *American Journal of Epidemiology,* 1976, *104,* 107-123.

COBB, S. Social support as a moderator of life stress. *Psychosomatic Medicine,* 1976, *38,* 300-314.

CODDINGTON, R. D. The significance of life events as etiologic factors in the diseases of children: I-A survey of professional workers. *Journal of Psychosomatic Research,* 1972, *16,* 7-18.

COWEN, E. L. The wooing of primary prevention. *American Journal of Community Psychology,* 1980, *8,* 258-284.

DEAN, A., & LIN, N. The stress-buffering role of social support. *Journal of Nervous and Mental Disease,* 1977, *165,* 403-417.

DEROGATIS, L. R. *SCL-90: Administration, scoring, and procedures manual-I for the R version.* Baltimore: Author, 1977.

EATON, W.W. Life events, social supports, and psychiatric symptoms: A re-analysis of the New Haven data. *Journal of Health and Social Behavior,* 1978, *19,* 230-234.

FURSTENBERG, F. F. The social consequences of teenage parenthood. *Family Planning Perspectives,* 1976, *8,* 148-164.

FURSTENBERG, F. F., & CRAWFORD, A. G. Family support: Helping teenage mothers to cope. *Family Planning Perspectives,* 1978, *10,* 322-333.

GORE, S. The effect of social support in moderating the health consequences of unemployment. *Journal of Health and Social Behavior,* 1978, *19,* 157-165.

GOTTLIEB, B. H. The development and application of a classification scheme of informal helping behaviours. *Canadian Journal of Behavioural Science,* 1978, *10,* 105-115.

HELLER, K. The effects of social support: Prevention and treatment implications. In A. P. Goldstein & F. H. Kanfer (Eds.), *Maximizing treatment gains: Transfer enhancement in psychotherapy.* New York: Academic Press, 1979.

HELPER, M. M., COHEN, R. L., BEITENMAN, E. T., & EATON, L. F. Life events and acceptance of pregnancy. *Journal of Psychosomatic Research,* 1968, *12,* 183-188.

HENDERSON, S., BYRNE, D. G., DUNCAN-JONES, P., ADCOCK, S., SCOTT, R., & STEELE, G. P. Social bonds in the epidemiology of neurosis: A preliminary communication. *British Journal of Psychiatry,* 1978, *132,* 463-466.

HIRSCH, B.J. Psychological dimensions of social networks: A multimethod analysis. *American Journal of Community Psychology,* 1979, *7,* 263-277.

HIRSCH, B.J. Natural support systems and coping with major life changes. *American Journal of Community Psychology,* 1980, *8,* 159-172.

HOLMES, T.H., & RAHE, R.H. The social readjustment rating scale. *Psychosomatic Medicine,* 1967, *11,* 213-218.

JONES, L.M., & FISCHER, C.S. *Studying egocentric networks by mass survey.* Working Paper No. 284, Institute of Urban and Regional Development, University of California, Berkeley, January 1978.

LIEBERMAN, M.A., & MULLAN, J.T. Does help help? The adaptive consequences of obtaining help from professionals and social networks. *American Journal of Community Psychology,* 1978, *6,* 499-517.

LIEM, G.R., & LIEM, J. H. *Social support and stress: Some general issues and their application to the problems of unemployment.* Unpublished manuscript, Boston College and University of Massachusetts — Boston, 1978.

LIN, N., SIMEONE, R.S., ENSEL, W.M., & KUO, W. Social support, stressful life events, and illness: A model and an empirical test. *Journal of Health and Social Behavior,* 1979, *20,* 108-119.

MENKEN, J. The health and social consequences of teenage childbearing. *Family Planning Perspectives,* 1972, *4,* 45-53.

MITCHELL, J.C. Social networks. *Annual Review of Anthropology,* 1974, *3,* 279-300.

MITCHELL, R.E., & TRICKETT, E.J. An analysis of the effects and determinants of social networks. *Community Mental Health Journal,* 1980, *16,* 27-44.

MOOS, R.H., INSEL, P.M., & HUMPHREY, B. *Family, work, and group environment scales: Combined preliminary manual.* Palo Alto, CA: Consulting Psychologists Press, 1974.

NUCKOLLS, K.B., CASSEL, J., & KAPLAN, B.H. Psychosocial assets, life crises and the prognosis of pregnancy. *American Journal of Epidemiology,* 1972, *95,* 431-441.

PATTISON, E.M. A theoretical-empirical base for social system therapy. In E.F. Feulks, R.M. Wintrob, J. Westermeyer, & A.R. Favazza (Eds.), *Current perspectives in cultural psychiatry.* New York: Spectrum, 1977.

PROCIDANO, M.E., & HELLER, K. *Toward the assessment of perceived social support.* Paper presented at the meeting of the American Psychological Association, New York, 1979.

RABKIN, J.G., & STRUENING, E.L. Life events, stress, and illness. *Science,* 1976, *194,* 1013-1020.

RATCLIFFE, W.D., ZELHART, P.F., & AZIM, H.F.A. *Social networks and psychopathology.* Unpublished manuscript, University of Alberta.

SANDLER, I.N. Social support resources, stress and maladjustment of poor children. *American Journal of Community Psychology,* 1980, *8,* 41-52.

SARASON, I.G., JOHNSON, J.H., & SIEGEL, J.M. Assessing the impact of life changes: Development of the life experiences survey. *Journal of Consulting and Clinical Psychology,* 1978, *46,* 932-946.

SCHINKE, S.P., & GILCHRIST, L.D. Adolescent pregnancy: An interpersonal skill training approach to prevention. *Social Work in Health Care,* 1977, *3,* 159-167.

TOLSDORF, C. Social networks, support, and coping: An exploratory study. *Family Process,* 1976, *15,* 407-417.

TUCKER, M.B., & COLTEN, M.B. *The stress buffering effect of social support in heroin addicted women.* Paper presented at the Symposium on Mothering, Child Abuse and the Addicted Woman, National Drug Abuse Conference, Seattle, 1978.

WILCOX, B.L. *Social support, life stress and psychological adjustment.* Paper presented at the meeting of the Western Psychological Association, San Diego, 1979.

Chapter 4

SOCIAL SUPPORT IN ADJUSTING TO MARITAL DISRUPTION
A Network Analysis

BRIAN L. WILCOX

Supportive social relationships have long been recognized, at least at an intuitive level, as playing many important roles in the lives of people. Sociologists and anthropologists have pointed to the primary group as the major environmental influence on the behavior and attitudes of the individual. While the importance of "significant others" in the development and maintenance of norms, values, beliefs, and attitudes has been recognized by social scientists for a considerable period of time, psychologists, epidemiologists, and sociologists have recently begun to turn their attention to another hypothesized consequence of these types of supportive relationships.

In a series of influential papers, John Cassel (1974, 1976) proposed a functional relationship between psychosocial factors and stress-related disorders. According to Cassel (1974: 478), social supports (a major psychosocial factor) serve as "protective factors buffering or cushioning the individual from the physiologic or psychologic consequences of exposure to the stressor situation." In support of this "buffering hypothesis," he cites a number of laboratory animal studies and human epidemiological investigations that found that organisms experiencing stressful events were protected from the negative adaptational outcomes of such events if they were part of a supportive milieu. The empirical evidence provided by most of these studies, however, is indirect at best.

More recently, three lines of research have provided additional support for the buffering hypothesis. One line of research has examined the relationships between well-being, social support, and specific social stressors. LaRocco et al. (1980) found social support to significantly moderate the influence of job stress on several indices of physical health. Gore (1978) found that men who received high levels of emotional support from friends and family following the closing of the plant in which they were employed showed lower levels of physiological strain than did those workers with low levels of support. Social support, in and of itself, did not influence the level of strain in a matched control group of stably employed men.

A second line of research has examined the effect of social support on the relationship between well-being and measures assessing the joint contributions of a variety of social stressors. A series of studies have reported statistically significant relationships between measures of stressful life events, such as those appearing on the Schedule of Recent Events (Holmes & Rahe, 1967), and a variety of health-related "outcome" measures.[1] The magnitude of the obtained correlations, however, has not been particularly impressive; they generally range between .30 and .40. More recently, stressful life events researchers have begun investigating the mediating role played by a variety of biological, psychological, behavioral, and situational variables in the relationship between life stress and well-being. Much of this research has focused on the stress-buffering role of social support. Wilcox (forthcoming) found that the relationship between stressful life events and psychological distress is conditional on the individual's level of social support. Cases with high levels of support show only a slight regression of psychological distress on life events; low support cases, on the other hand, show substantial linear regression. As social support decreases, the relationship between life events and psychological distress becomes stronger.

The concept of social support has been operationalized in a somewhat bewildering assortment of ways in those studies constituting these two lines of research. The common thread in these operationalizations of the construct is a focus on the quality of one or more dyadic relationships. Thus, investigators have equated the concept of social support with marital status (married = higher support), having a "confidant," and/or having a number of "close friends."

A third, more recent, line of research on stress, social support, and adjustment differs from the previous two primarily in the manner in which social support is assessed. Tolsdorf (1976) and Hirsch (1979,

1980) have applied the analytic tool of network analysis in an attempt to develop valid and reliable quantitative measures of support. Network analysis was originally developed by social anthropologists (Barnes, 1954; Bott, 1955; Mitchell, 1969) to operationalize the notion of social structure. Social networks have been defined by Barnes (1954: 43) as "a set of points, some of which are joined by lines. The points of the image are people . . . and the lines indicate which people interact with each other." Social scientists such as Mitchell (1969) and Fischer et al. (1977) have argued that the morphological and interactional characteristics of personal social networks influence the behavior of the individuals who are part of those networks. For example, it is possible that different network structural characteristics (such as density, range, or multiplexity) may influence the nature of the social support available to a person and, hence, the person's well-being. Hirsch's research (which he reviews in this volume) suggests that this is the case.

The present study was conducted with the intent of examining the relationship of network structure to the psychosocial adjustment of women to marital separation and divorce. Marital disruption has been shown to be a significant disruptive force in the lives of those who experience it. Bloom et al. (1978) have reviewed a vast number of studies linking marital disruption with a variety of physical and emotional disorders. Epidemiologists have consistently found marital status to be associated with both treated and true prevalence rates of psychopathology, with separated and divorced individuals having higher rates of psychopathology than their married counterparts (Bachrach, 1976; Crago, 1972). Much of this research also suggests that this relationship appears to be stronger for men than for women (Bloom et al., 1978). Several epidemiological investigations have uncovered strong associations between marital status and morbidity as well. Verbrugge (1979) found that divorced and separated persons had the poorest health status of all marital categories. They also had the highest rates of acute conditions, chronic conditions, complete and partial work disability, short-term disability, and utilization of health services. Similar results can be found in a number of other studies (Berkman, 1969; LaHorgue, 1960; Renne, 1971). These marital status morbidity differentials do not appear to be spurious; when race and income are statistically controlled, the differences persist (National Center for Health Statistics, 1976). Mortality differentials have also been consistently reported, showing essentially the same pattern as the morbidity differentials (Gove, 1973; Verbrugge, 1979). The probability of acquiring a mortal illness or injury as an adult appears to be much greater for the formerly married than for single or married individuals. Additional studies have found the formerly married to be at excessive risk for suicide, homicide, and traffic accidents (see Bloom et al., 1978).

It appears, then, that the formerly married (more specifically, separated and divorced individuals) are at high risk for a wide variety of psychological, physical, and behavioral problems. A number of hypotheses have been offered in an attempt to account for these findings. In recent years a sizable literature has developed in which marital disruption is viewed as a specific stressor and placed within the context of the stress and coping literature. Marital disruption, it appears, often requires a number of ecological transitions on the part of the formerly married individual. Changes in economic status following marital disruption appear to be a potent source of stress, particularly for women (Brandwein et al., 1974; Espenshade, 1979). Hetherington et al. (1977, 1978) have also noted that persons experiencing separation or divorce are likely to experience intense negative emotional reactions and changes in self-concept. Characteristic emotions experienced by divorcing individuals include anger, depression, rejection, and incompetence, among others. Household maintenance also seems to be a particular source of stress for many separated and divorced individuals, especially men (Hetherington et al., 1978). Another major source of stress for the maritally disrupted is in the arena of parent-child relations. Hetherington et al. (1977, 1978) found that the negative emotional reactions of divorced parents are often exacerbated by the negative reactions of their children to the marital disruption. The multiple sources of stress bearing upon the single parent often result in ineffective parenting strategies and aversive parent-child interactions. These behavior patterns were not observed in a comparison group of intact families.

In addition to detailing the risks and stresses associated with marital disruption, past research has also detailed the demographic, social, and psychological characteristics of those who have failed to adapt, relatively speaking, to the demands of marital disruption. Surprisingly little attention, however, has been directed to the study of the characteristics of those persons who have successfully adjusted to the stressors associated with marital disruption. This is unfortunate, in that much can be learned about adaptational failure and the stress and coping process itself by attending to the "environmental resistors" — those persons who successfully and gracefully adapt to significant life stressors. Indeed, in spite of the significant risks associated with marital disruption, most persons who experience it do not develop significant long-term pathologies.

Those few studies that have attempted to determine the factors that differentiate between persons who adapt to marital disruption successfully as opposed to unsuccessfully are quite limited, in that they have dealt largely with the role of demographic factors, to the relative exclusion of social and psychological factors. Social support is one factor that appears to be a potentially important moderator of the marital disruption-distress relationship. Many writers have speculated that individuals who are enmeshed in supportive social networks will find the transition from marriage to singlehood a smoother one. As was mentioned at the beginning of this chapter, a growing body of research suggests that social support seems to buffer persons from the negative consequences of a wide variety of social stressors.

While speculation regarding the role of social support in the process of coping with marital disruption has been extensive, empirical research directly relevant to the question has been limited, with the bulk of this literature descriptive in nature. Weiss (1975, 1979) notes that a great deal of support is received by divorced individuals from friends and family members. Such persons are seen as key sources of emotional support and instrumental aid. Bernard (1964) echoes this point, noting that in her studies of single-parent families, divorced women who were part of a nurturant network of friends and family members seemed to cope more effectively with single parenthood. Those women who were unable to acquire needed assistance from an informal network of friends and relatives complained about feelings of isolation, depression, and a general dissatisfaction with the course of their lives.

Two recent surveys also suggest that social support plays a significant role in the postdivorce adjustment process. Colletta (1979) found that the amount of support received and satisfaction with that support was significantly related to the child-rearing practices of a sample of 72 single-parent mothers. Divorced mothers who reported unsatisfactory levels of social support appeared to interact with their children in a harsher and more restrictive manner than did those divorced mothers receiving more satisfying levels of support. Chiriboga et al. (1979) found that the divorced turned to a variety of sources for needed support following marital disruption. Friends, relatives, and counselors were most frequently turned to for help. Utilization of social supports was found to be linked to the degree of perceived stress evoked by the divorce: the greater the perceived stress, the higher the level of support utilization.

A third study examined the role of social support in postdivorce adjustment (Raschke, 1977). Postdivorce stress was found to be significantly correlated with level of support and social participation. Subjects reporting low levels of social participation and support reported high levels of stress on the average. The relationship between stress and support remained significant even when sex and age were controlled for statistically.

SOCIAL NETWORKS AND ADJUSTMENT: AN EMPIRICAL INVESTIGATION

These reports suggest that social support may be an important moderator of the marital disruption-adjustment relationship. The present study was designed to contribute further data on this issue by approaching it from a slightly different, although complementary, perspective. As previously mentioned, some researchers have approached the topic of social support by focusing on the structural and interactional characteristics of the network of supportive others. Network analysts have argued that an individual's behavior is influenced in important ways by the structure of his or her social network (Fischer et al., 1977; Hirsch, 1979, 1980; Tolsdorf, 1976). Some researchers have suggested that the size (or "range") of an individual's network, that is, the number of supporters one has available to call on, is positively related to adjustment to social stress (Wilcox, forthcoming). Others have noted that the proportion of interrelationships between members of an individual's network ("network density") can influence adaptation to stress. In a study of women undergoing certain stressful transitions, Hirsch (1980) found that low-density networks (those in which interrelations between network members are sparse) aided their adaptive strivings more than high-density networks. Other researchers have also investigated the relationship between network density and coping (see Mitchell & Trickett, 1980, for a review). The present study sought to further this line of research by examining the size (range) and density of the networks among two contrasting groups of women: those who had experienced considerable difficulties coping with divorce and those who seem to have adapted easily to the demands of marital disruption.

The vast majority of research in the social support field has tended to examine only the positive aspects of support networks. Research in the divorce field, however, indicates that one of the more stressful aspects of the divorce process is the change that occurs in the social network following marital disruption. Bohannan (1970: 60) reports that major changes in one's network of friends and supporters "is an almost universal experience of divorcees in America." Bohannan refers to this process as the "community divorce" and notes that while most divorced persons cope with this aspect of divorce successfully, some have considerable difficulty dealing with the loss of friends. It would appear, then, that changes in the makeup of the social network can contribute to the stress associated with marital disruption. This leads to our hypothesis that women whose networks of supporters underwent significant change following separation and divorce would experience greater levels of stress and adjustment difficulties than women whose support networks remained relatively stable. In a similar vein, we hypothesized that women whose preseparation networks overlapped minimally with their former spouses' preseparation networks would experience fewer adjustment difficulties than would those women whose preseparation networks overlapped extensively with their former spouses' preseparation networks. The logic underlying this hypothesis is that people often find it uncomfortable, if not difficult, to maintain relationships with both members of the separated couple. Pilot interviews further suggested that the wife rather than the husband typically lost contact with old friends.

METHODOLOGY

Subjects

Data for this study were derived from interviews conducted with 50 recently divorced women who were identified as either successfully (n = 25) or unsuccessfully (n = 25) adjusting to their new marital status during the course of a larger study on separation and divorce. Subjects were assigned to groups on the basis of their scores on the Profile of Mood States (McNair et al., 1971), the 22-Item Symptom Checklist (Langner, 1962), and on ratings of adjustment made by interviewers. All of the women were still single at the time of the interview. A summary of selected descriptive characteristics of the two groups is presented in Table 4.1. Brief interviews were also conducted with the subjects' former spouses in order to gather data necessary for one aspect of the study.

TABLE 4.1   Summary (means) of Descriptive Characteristics of
            Subsamples, by Group

	S.A.	U.A.
Age	31.6	32.6
Number of children	1.08	.88
Duration of separation and divorce (months)	18.6	20.9
Education (years)	12.4	11.6
Income	$11,600	$11,600

NOTE: S.A. = successfully adjusting group; U.A. = unsuccessfully adjusting group.

Procedure

Each woman took part in a two-hour interview, which was conducted in her home. Subjects were questioned about the circumstances surrounding the marital separation, the nature of the
separation, current concerns about adjustment, social participation,
and support, and demographic information.

Particular attention was paid to the task of assessing social support networks. Previous studies by this investigator, as well as others,
pointed out numerous problems with some of the typical approaches
to network assessment. The usual manner of eliciting names of network members is to ask the subject to name her "best friends," "close
friends," or people she feels "closest to." The method used to elicit
names of network members must be considered carefully, because
different methods will elicit different names and, hence, represent
different operationalizations of the concept of "network." For example, asking respondents to name their "best friends" presents a
number of measurement problems. The term "best friend" is a vague
construct that is subject to widely varying interpretations. Another
problem with this method is that a single probe often results in a poor
degree of recall and, thus, an underestimation of the network.

In an attempt to maximize recall and minimize the measurement
problems just mentioned, we elicited the names of network members
by asking a series of questions intended to identify network members
who provided the respondent with emotional and tangible support. A
series of pretest interviews resulted in a final list of twelve questions,
which were used to elicit members of what we call the "support"

network. These questions, listed in Appendix 4.A, were intended to tap several life domains of concern to the divorced woman (Hetherington et al., 1978; Weiss, 1975). For example, one question asked respondents to name persons they turn to for help with child care.[2]

Each subject was asked to report information about her support network (1) six months prior to the separation (retrospectively), and (2) at the time of the interview. These data allowed us to examine the relationship between changes in network structure over time and adjustment. Additionally, brief interviews were conducted with the former spouses of each of the subjects. These men were asked to report information about their support networks six months prior to the separation. These data allowed us to test our hunches concerning the influence of husband-wife network overlap (boundary density) on later adjustment to marital disruption.

Network Variables

Range. This variable is defined as the number of network members named by the respondent. Range was measured for both the preseparation and the postdivorce networks. Changes in network range were assessed by comparing the two measures.

Density. This variable is defined as the proportion of actual relationships among network members (excluding the respondent) to the total number of relationships possible. A density coefficient is arrived at by using the following formula:

$$\text{Density} = \frac{\text{Na} \times 100}{\frac{1}{2} \text{N} \times (\text{N-1})}$$

where Na is the number of actual interrelationships, N is network range, and $\frac{1}{2}$ N × N-1 is the number of theoretically possible interrelationships. The density coefficient can be interpreted as the proportion of possible interrelationships actualized, or the probability that any randomly selected network member has a relationship with any other randomly selected network member. The higher is the density coefficient (which can vary between 0 and 1 like any probability), the greater is the degree of interconnections between network members. Density was assessed for both the preseparation and the postdivorce networks. Changes in network density were assessed by comparing the two density measures.

Boundary Density. This variable is defined as the proportion of possible interconnections existing between two different networks. As such, it assesses the density of interconnections crossing the boundary between two networks. Two boundary density coefficients were calculated for each subject. First, the respondents' preseparation and postdivorce networks were treated as separate networks. An interconnection between the two networks was said to exist if the same member appeared in both networks. Thus, the more stable was the composition of the network over time, the higher was the preseparation-postdivorce (P-P) boundary density. Second, boundary density coefficients were calculated for the interconnections between the respondents' preseparation networks and their spouses' preseparation networks (H-W boundary density). An interconnection was said to exist if either a person who was named to the respondent's network was also named to her spouse's network, or a person named to the respondent's network was intimately connected to a member of her spouse's network through marriage or blood.

RESULTS

Before presenting the results of the data analyses, a caveat is in order. These results should be interpreted cautiously because the group n's are quite modest and the two groups are nonequivalent (nonrandomly assigned); thus, any differences between them may be due to preexisting differences other than those used to create the groups.

There are a number of interesting findings concerning the networks of the two groups. The first analysis tested the null hypothesis regarding the range and density of the networks six months prior to separation. Hotelling's T^2 statistic was calculated to test this hypothesis. The obtained T^2 was nonsignificant; the networks of the two groups six months prior to separation did not differ in either range or density.[3] The mean network range for the successfully adjusting (S.A.) group is 16.6, while for the unsuccessfully adjusting (U.A.) group it is 15.8. Density figures are slightly more discrepant, although still not statistically significant: 16.7 for the S.A. group and 20.2 for the U.A. group.

The second analysis contrasted network range and density for the two groups at the time of interview. Hotelling's T^2 is significant in this case ($p<.01$). The mean network range for the S.A. group is 14.9, while for the U.A. group it is 11.1. This difference does not quite reach statistical significance. Density figures, however, are significantly

TABLE 4.2   Mean Network Range by Group, Pre- and Postdivorce

| | Range | | |
	S.A.	U.A.	Difference (S.A.-U.A.)
Preseparation	16.6	15.8	.6
Postdivorce	14.9	11.1	3.8
Difference Pre-post	1.7	4.7	

different (statistically speaking)[4]: 16.4 for the S.A. group and 29.3 for the U.A. group. Means for the first two analyses are presented in Tables 4.2 and 4.3.

The third analysis examined the boundary densities between the preseparation networks of the respondents and the preseparation networks of their spouses. Boundary density is significantly greater in the U.A. group than it is in the S.A. group. The two groups also differ significantly in terms of the boundary density between the respondents' preseparation and postdivorce networks. Mean boundary density values for these two analyses are presented in Table 4.4.

DISCUSSION

The data regarding network range and density (provided in Tables 4.2 and 4.3) suggest that the two groups differ neither in the range nor the density of their preseparation networks. Women in the U.A. group have slightly smaller and more dense networks at this point than women in the S.A. group, but these differences are not significant. At the time of the interview, however, there was a sizable (though statistically nonsignificant) difference in network range. Women who showed more positive postdivorce adjustment have somewhat larger networks than women who adjusted less positively. The S.A. group also has significantly *less dense* postdivorce networks than the U.A. group.

What can be said about these findings? Why might lower-density networks be associated with more positive adjustments? One potential explanation centers on the fact that lower-density networks generally are associated with more flexible norms and access to a greater variety of roles. Hirsch (1979) has noted that low-density networks may be more adaptive in situations (such as separation) that result in a great deal of life change because (1) access to a greater diversity of

TABLE 4.3   Mean Network Density by Group, Pre- and Postdivorce

	Density		Difference (S.A.-U.A.)
	S.A.	U.A.	
Preseparation	16.7%	20.2%	−3.5%
Postdivorce	16.4%	29.%	−12.6%
Difference Pre-post	.3%	−8.8%	

TABLE 4.4   Boundary Densities Between Preseparation Network and (1) Spouse's Network, and (2) Postdivorce Network, by Group

	Boundary Density	
	S.A.	U.A.
With spouse	17.4%	36.3%
Pre-/postdivorce	76.0%	59.1%

roles-partners can enhance one's coping repertoire; (2) dyadic relationships are more amenable to change than group relationships; and (3) as a person's needs and interests change, less dense network structures increase the probability of finding someone whose needs and interests are congruent with one's own.

A second explanation is suggested by closely examining the makeup of the postdivorce networks of these two groups. A larger proportion of the supporters named by the less positively adjusted women were kin than was the case for the S.A. women. This finding can help explain the differences in both network density and psychosocial adjustment for the two groups. Networks composed largely of family members are, for obvious reasons, more likely to be relatively close-knit (highly interconnected). In a large-scale community study, Wellman (1979) found that support networks composed primarily of kin were more dense than were nonkin-dominated networks. Interestingly, the preseparation networks of the two groups do not differ appreciably concerning their kin-nonkin makeup. The U.A. women apparently relied more on their kin after the separation than they had prior to its occurrence. As one respondent noted, "Who else was I going to ask for help or talk to about the way I was feeling? My old friends seemed to vanish into thin air when Bill and I separated." According to another U.A. respondent, "In some ways the divorce brought me closer to my family. I was never very close to my brothers and sisters, but they were about the only people I knew who were around to help when things got bad." This change does not occur for the S.A. women; the composition of their networks with respect to the percentage of kin versus nonkin appears to remain relatively stable over time.

Research on the separation and divorce process provides a basis for speculation as to why kin-dominated (high-density) networks might be associated with less positive adjustment. Goode (1956) and Weiss (1975) note that family members, while often providing reassurance and support, frequently find it difficult to accept the fact that the marriage is over. Once the end of the relationship is accepted, kin often react with greater anger than would nonkin intimates. As Weiss (1975: 132) has noted, "parents, especially, assume the right to comment on the separation, to criticize it, to disapprove or approve of it, perhaps going on until the separated individual is driven to exasperation." During our interviews, many women noted that relationships with family members were at once the most supportive and the most stress-producing. Even though they frequently offered high degrees of emotional sustenance, family members were more likely to be judgmental than were nonkin. According to one U.A. woman, "As helpful as my parents tried to be, they couldn't avoid letting me know what a disappointment I was to them. When I told them that it was my idea to leave Walter, they blew up. 'How can you do this to your child?' they kept asking."

An additional finding sheds further light on the reason for the difference in the networks of the two groups. As was mentioned earlier, the boundary density (i.e., degree of overlap) between the respondents' preseparation networks and their spouses' preseparation networks (H-W boundary density) was greater for the U.A. women than for the S.A. women (see Table 4.4). According to the U.A. women, many of their friends prior to separation were the spouses of their husbands' business associates and friends. For many of these women, the marital relationship provided the basis and context for many of their friendships. Friendships dependent on the link between husband and wife almost always cooled or completely died following separation. As one respondent put it, "If I could tell women who are getting married one thing, it would be to keep some friends of your own. Most of my friends were women who were married to friends of my husband. When Phil left he took my friends with him. That hurt almost as much as the divorce." High H-W network boundary density might be hypothesized to be an important risk factor for divorcing women. Further research should be directed at this question.

The loss of these friendships is reflected in Table 4.2 by a mean decrease of 4.7 network members for the U.A. group. Network membership turnover, however, is actually greater than this. As is indicated in Table 4.4, the preseparation network-postdivorce network (P-P) boundary density is much greater for the S.A. women than for the U.A. women. P-P boundary density reflects the stability of actual network membership (as opposed to range and density) over time, with higher P-P boundary density coefficients indicating greater network membership stability. The P-P coefficient for the U.A. group is 59 percent. This group, then, experienced a 41 percent turnover in network membership following marital disruption. The corresponding figure for the S.A. group is 76 percent. Thus, it appears that the networks of the U.A. women changed quite markedly in response to the disruption of marriage, while the S.A. women's networks appear to have remained remarkably stable. The U.A. women told us that they relied more on kin for support as a result of the disruption of their predivorce networks. Said one such respondent, "All of a sudden all of my old friends seemed to be gone. All of them had excuses for why we could never get together. Making new friends at my age isn't all that easy. . . . So I seem to spend a lot more time visiting my family now." Low P-P network boundary density might be hypothesized as another significant risk factor for divorcing women. Again, further research is needed to answer this question.

The present study testifies to the complexity inherent in research concerning the role of social support in the stress and coping process. One generally neglected aspect of support networks is that they are dynamic in nature. Social networks, as noted by Srinivas and Béteille (1964), are in a near-constant state of flux. In her classic study of family and social network, Bott (1971) pointed out that five of her twenty study families underwent major restructuring of their social networks during the course of the study. Networks expand and contract, become more or less dense, and change in a number of other ways. Most researchers have viewed support systems in a static fashion, attempting to relate network characteristics derived from measurements taken at one point in time to some health outcome. The present findings, however, suggest that changes in networks over time may provide more detailed clues concerning the role of social support in the stress process than will "still photographs" of networks. The dynamic nature of people's social lives should be reflected in the tools we use to assess their lives. The appropriate research designs will likely be quite complex and tax the methodological and creative abilities of the investigator. Yet only by recognizing the dynamic nature of social support within our research designs will we make progress toward the development of an ecologically valid model of the stress and coping process (Holahan & Spearly, 1980).

The present study also confirms the importance of blending quantitative data derived from the social network interview schedule with qualitative information gathered during the open-ended portion of the interview. The two styles of research, quantitative and qualitative, are certainly complementary, not mutually exclusive. As Campbell (forthcoming: 30), among others (see Cook & Reichardt, 1979), points out, "Quantification both builds upon and is cross-validated by the scientist's pervasive qualitative knowledge." In the present study, the interpretation of the quantitative network data was greatly enhanced by the available qualitative data. Network data are particularly susceptible to inappropriate interpretation in the absence of such information. Quantitative network data must be grounded in qualitative data.

This study began with the hope of uncovering social network variables that might differentiate between divorced women who were known to be adapting successfully and those adapting less successfully to marital disruption. The results of this investigation, while certainly limited by the design employed, suggest a number of fruitful avenues for future study. The identification of significant risk factors associated with coping with marital disruption has important theoretical and practical ramifications. The study of the social support network appears to be one fruitful area for investigation.

Appendix 4.A

Questions Used to Elicit
Names of Network Members

1. Who have your turned to in the past for help with child care? Who might look after your children if you had to go out of town for a day?
2. Who do you talk with about problems you have with your children?
3. Do you have a fiancee or one best friend you are dating or seeing regularly? If so, who is this person?
4. In an emergency, who might you be able to borrow up to $100 from?
5. Are there any people who help with small chores around your house, like cleaning, cooking, painting, or small repairs?
6. When you are bothered by a personal problem, who might you get together with to talk about the problem?
7. Are you a part of a group of people who all know one another and get together as a group? Who is in that group?
8. Are there any people whose advice you particularly value when making an important decision? Who are these people?
9. Who do you talk with about problems at work?
10. Who might you be able to borrow a car from or get a ride from if your car was broken down?
11. Who might you call up if you wanted to just get together with someone for some recreation, like going to a movie or a bar?
12. Are there any people who are very dear to you or very important in your life these days who you have not mentioned so far? Who are these people?

NOTES

1. "Outcome" is placed in quotation marks because the vast majority of these studies have used retrospective designs that preclude causal inferences. Hence, the adjustment measures do not necessarily reflect "effects" produced by stressful life events. They may in fact be conceived of as causal antecedents of stressful life change in many instances. See Rabkin and Struening (1976) for a discussion of this issue.

2. The final network questionnaire is quite similar to the one developed by Jones and Fischer (1978).

3. Density estimates were calculated using a method that excludes links between the respondent and network members. These ties exist by definition, and their inclusion results in a confounding of network size and density (see Wilcox, 1980).

4. Alpha level was set at .01 for all significance tests. Thus, for all findings reported to be statistically significant, $p < .01$.

REFERENCES

BACHRACH, L.L. *Marital status and mental disorder: An analytical review.* DHEW Publication No. (ADM) 75-217, National Institute of Mental Health, Rockville, Maryland, 1976.

BARNES, J. A. Class and committees in a Norwegian island parish. *Human Relations,* 1954, *7,* 39-58.

BERKMAN, P. L. Spouseless motherhood, psychological stress, and physical morbidity. *Journal of Health and Social Behavior,* 1969, *10,* 323-334.

BERNARD, S. *Fatherless families: Their economic and social adjustment.* In Papers in Social Welfare #7. Waltham, MA: Florence Heller Graduate School for Advanced Studies in Social Welfare, Brandeis University, 1964.

BLOOM, B. L., ASHER, S. J., & WHITE, S. W. Marital disruption as a stressor: A review and analysis. *Psychological Bulletin,* 1978, *85,* 867-894.

BOHANNAN, P. The six stages of divorce. In P. Bohannan (Ed.), *Divorce and after.* Garden City, NY: Doubleday, 1970.

BOTT, E. Urban families: Conjugal roles and social networks. *Human Relations,* 1955, *8,* 345-383.

BOTT, E. *Family and social network* (2nd ed.). New York: Free Press, 1971.

BRANDWEIN, R. A., BROWN, C. A., & FOX, E. M. Women and children last: The social situation of divorced mothers and their families. *Journal of Marriage and the Family,* 1974, *36,* 498-514.

CAMPBELL, D. T. Qualitative knowing in action research. *Journal of Social Issues,* forthcoming.

CASSEL, J. Psychosocial processes and "stress": Theoretical formulations. *International Journal of Health Services,* 1974, *6,* 471-482.

CASSEL, J. The contribution of the social environment to host resistance. *American Journal of Epidemiology,* 1976, *104,* 107-123.

CHIRIBOGA, D. A., COHO, A., STEIN, J. A., & ROBERTS, J. Divorce, stress and social supports: A study in help-seeking behavior. *Journal of Divorce,* 1979, *3,* 121-135.

COLLETTA, N. D. Support systems after divorce: Incidence and impact. *Journal of Marriage and the Family,* 1979, *41,* 837-846.

COOK, T. D., & REICHARDT, C. S. (Eds.). *Qualitative and quantitative methods in evaluation research.* Beverly Hills, CA: Sage Publications, 1979.

CRAGO, M. A. Psychopathology in married couples. *Psychological Bulletin,* 1972, *77,* 114-128.

ESPENSHADE, T. J. The economic consequences of divorce. *Journal of Marriage and the Family,* 1979, *42,* 615-626.

FISCHER, C.S., JACKSON, R.M., STUEVE, C.A., GERSON, K., JONES, L.M., & BALDASSARE, M. *Networks and places: Social relations in the urban setting.* New York: Free Press, 1977.

GOODE, W.J. *After divorce.* New York: Free Press, 1956.

GORE, S. The effect of social support in moderating the health consequences of unemployment. *Journal of Health and Social Behavior,* 1978, *17,* 157-165.

GOVE, W.R. Sex, marital status, and mortality. *American Journal of Sociology,* 1973, *79,* 45-67.

HETHERINGTON, E.M., COX, M., & COX, R. The aftermath of divorce. In J.H. Stevens, Jr., & M. Matthews (Eds.), *Mother-child, father-child relations.* Washington, DC: National Association for the Education of Young Children, 1977.

HETHERINGTON, E.M., COX, M., & COX, R. Stress and coping in divorce: A focus on women. In J. Gullahorn (Ed.), *Psychology and transition.* New York: B.H. Winston, 1978.

HIRSCH, B.J. Psychological dimensions of social networks: A multimethod analysis. *American Journal of Community Psychology,* 1979, *7,* 263-277.

HIRSCH, B.J. Natural support systems and coping with major life changes. *American Journal of Community Psychology,* 1980, *8,* 159-172.

HOLAHAN, C.J., & SPEARLY, J.L. Coping and ecology: An integrative model for community psychology. *American Journal of Community Psychology,* 1980, *8,* 671-685.

HOLMES, T.H., & RAHE, R.H. The social readjustment rating scale. *Journal of Psychosomatic Research,* 1967, *11,* 213-218.

JONES, L.M., & FISCHER, C.S. *Studying egocentric networks by mass survey.* Working Paper No. 284, Institute of Urban and Regional Development, University of California, Berkeley, January 1978.

LaHORGUE, A. Morbidity and marital status. *Journal of Chronic Diseases,* 1960, *12,* 476-498.

LANGNER, T.S. A twenty-two item screening score of psychiatric symptoms indicating impairment. *Journal of Health and Social Behavior,* 1962, *3,* 269-276.

LaROCCO, J.M., HOUSE, J.S., & FRENCH, J.R.P., Jr. Social support, occupational stress, and health. *Journal of Health and Social Behavior,* 1980, *21,* 202-218.

McNAIR, D.M., LORR, M., & DROPPLEMAN, L.F. *Profile of Mood States* (POMS). San Diego, CA: Educational and Industrial Testing Service, 1971.

MITCHELL, J.C. The concept and use of social networks. In J.C. Mitchell (Ed.), *Social networks in urban situations.* Manchester, England: University of Manchester Press, 1969.

MITCHELL, R.E., & TRICKETT, E.J. Social network research and psychosocial adaptation: Implications for community mental health practice. In P. Insel (Ed.), *Environmental variables and the prevention of mental illness.* Lexington, MA: D.C. Heath, 1980.

National Center for Health Statistic. *Differentials in health characteristics by marital status: United States, 1971-1972* (Vital Health and Statistics Series 10, No. 104). Washington, DC: Government Printing Office, 1976.

RABKIN, J.G., & STRUENING, E.L. Life events, stress, and illness. *Science,* 1976, *194,* 1013-1020.

RASCHKE, H.J. The role of social participation in postseparation and postdivorce adjustment. *Journal of Divorce,* 1977, *1,* 129-140.

RENNE, K.S. Health and marital experience in an urban population. *Journal of Marriage and the Family,* 1971, *34,* 338-350.

SRINIVAS, M.M., & BÉTEILLE, A. Networks in Indian social structure. *Man,* 1964, *64,* 164-168.

TOLSDORF, C.C. Social networks, support and coping: An exploratory study. *Family Process,* 1976, *15,* 407-417.

VERBRUGGE, L.M. Marital status and health. *Journal of Marriage and the Family,* 1979, *41,* 267-285.

WEISS, R.S. *Marital separation.* New York: Basic Books, 1975.

WEISS, R.S. *Going it alone.* New York: Basic Books, 1979.

WELLMAN, B. The community question: The intimate networks of East Yorkers. *American Journal of Sociology,* 1979, *84,* 1201-1231.

WILCOX, B.L. *Assessing support networks: An empirical comparison of methods.* Unpublished manuscript, 1980.

WILCOX, B.L. Social support, life stress, and psychological adjustment: A test of the buffering hypothesis. *American Journal of Community Psychology,* forthcoming.

Chapter 5

SOCIAL SUPPORT AND SERIOUS ILLNESS

M. ROBIN DiMATTEO and RON HAYS

> Social support . . . has beneficial effects on a wide variety of health variables throughout the life course from conception to just before death, and on the bereaved who are left behind after a death. . . . One cannot escape the conclusion that the world would be a healthier place if training in supportive behaviors were built into the routines of our homes and schools, and support worker roles were institutionalized [Cobb, 1979: 113].

Recent developments in the field of Health Psychology have directed attention to the influence of social factors in physical illness. As suggested in the preceding quotation, social support figures prominently among those social factors purported to influence health states. While this proposition may be intuitively appealing, how much do we really know about the relationship between social support and physical well-being? Since the question is quite broad, this chapter covers only a limited aspect of it. Hence, our aim is to assess the effectiveness of social support in promoting recovery and coping with serious physical illness and injury.

Authors' Note: Preparation of this chapter was supported by the University of California, Riverside, Intramural Research Grant, and an Affirmative Action Faculty Development Award, both to the first author. Thanks are due to Benjamin Gottlieb and Alan Stacy for their comments on drafts of this chapter.

We define various sources and kinds of social support, detail how they have been operationalized and applied in the study of serious illness, and examine a range of health outcome variables to which they have been related. We consider factors that mediate the effects of social support, and situations in which it is potentially harmful. The existing literature on social support and serious illness is critiqued and recommendations for further research are made.

We have adopted a *somatopsychic* rather than a psychosomatic orientation, choosing to examine whether social support is capable of ameliorating or reducing social-psychological and physical problems resulting from the onset of an illness or injury. We do not consider issues of mental health nor do we examine the psychosomatic issue of whether social support can act as a buffer against psychological stress to prevent illness. Inclusion of these topics would have taken our literature review and analysis far afield of its original intent and would have demanded a careful investigation of the literature on stress, coping, and illness. Excellent examinations of those areas are already available (Antonovsky, 1979; Cohen, 1979; LaRocco et al., 1980).

Our review of the literature was less straightforward than we had anticipated, for three major reasons. First, the concept of social support has not yet been uniformly recognized by social scientists, nor has it acquired a consensual definition. Second, as Dean and Lin (1977) noted, nowhere in the social-psychological or measurement literature is there a measure of social support with known or acceptable properties of reliability and validity. Finally, although the importance of social support has often been asserted and intervention strategies have been advocated to improve existing social support (Cahners, 1978; Cahners & Bernstein, 1979; Cobb, 1959; Cutler & Beigel, 1978; Davidson, 1979; Foster & Mendel, 1979; Hamburg & Adams, 1967; Henderson, 1977; Johnson et al., 1979; Lipowski, 1969; Mangurten et al., 1979; Perrault et al., 1979), such assertions are handicapped by the paucity of empirical research. Limitations of the existing research on social support have been cogently summarized by Kaplan et al. (1977: 47):

> There is little strong empirical evidence to confirm the role it may play in health and illness. This is not surprising; attempts at conceptualization and measurement have been inadequate, discipline-bound (or study-bound), and usually formulated for post-hoc interpretation of unexpected, but striking findings.

THE MEANING OF SOCIAL SUPPORT

Determining the importance of social support requires a complete understanding of the concept. Does social support involve purely emotional support, such as understanding or communication from other people, or does it also include tangible services such as financial help, physical care, and household assistance? What aspects of serious illness are affected — the actual physical outcome of treatment, the well-being of the patient, or the social rehabilitation of the patient? Further, while the connection between social support and well-being in serious illness might seem obvious, it is also important to identify any harm it might bring about.

Social support is actually not a single concept; instead, it is interpreted in several ways and includes a range of phenomena. In fact, Carveth and Gottlieb (1979: 181) concluded that "there is little agreement about the definition of social support nor is there consensus about the utility of distinguishing among sources of support." Sidney Cobb, for example, has specified three kinds of social support, all of which focus on the interpersonal aspects of a person's life (Cobb, 1976, 1979; Cobb & Erbe, 1978). Emotional support is "information that one is cared for and loved," esteem support is "information that one is valued and esteemed," and network support is "information that one belongs to a network of mutual obligation" (Cobb, 1976; 300-301). Social support has also been defined in a less strictly interpersonal way, as "any input, directly provided by an individual (or group), which moves the receiver of that input towards goals which the receiver desires" (Caplan et al., 1976: 211). A similar definition was adopted by Tolsdorf (1976: 410), who stated that social support is "any action or behavior that functions to assist the focal person in meeting his personal goals or in dealing with the demands of any particular situation." Kahn has defined it as "interpersonal transactions that include one or more of the following: the expression of positive affect of one person toward another; the endorsement of another person's behaviors, perceptions, or expressed views; and/or the giving of symbolic or material aid to another" (see Dimond, 1979: 102). All of these definitions, while instructive, are not entirely complete.

A more comprehensive definition has been provided by Robert Caplan (1979). He has specified two dimensions — objective-subjective and tangible-psychological — that form four variations of social support. *Objective tangible support* is "behavior directed toward providing the person with tangible resources that are hypothesized to benefit his or her mental or physical well-being (1979: 85). *Objective psychological support* is "behavior directed toward providing the person with cognitions (values, attitudes, beliefs, and perceptions) and toward inducing affective states that are hypothesized to promote well-being" (1979: 85). Objective support (tangible and psychological) is measured by an outside observer. *Subjective tangible support* and *subjective psychological support* are analogous to their "objective" counterparts, but they are determined by the target person's perception that supportive conditions exist.

Caplan's distinction between objective and subjective social support is critical. Social support can be measured from the frame of reference of the target person — the subjective or phenomenological approach — or from the perspective of an outside observer — the objective approach. Objective assessment is not prone to the self-reporting biases inherent in the phenomenological approach, and it provides a standard of comparison across individuals. But the phenomenological approach is also valuable (Donald et al., 1978; Kiritz & Moos, 1974; Lipowski, 1969). Donald et al. (1978: 5) note that "in favor of the more subjective approach is the argument that individuals have different needs and tastes; therefore, the nature and number of interpersonal contacts with friends, relatives, and others necessary to achieve social health may vary greatly. These differences may not be adequately reflected in measures of objective social health constructs." Similarly, Kiritz and Moos (1974: 109) have suggested that "the most efficient predictor of a person's physiological behavior in a given environment may consist of how he perceives that environment." The phenomenological approach has also been supported with the argument that "what an individual experiences is directly known only to him, and we may learn about it by obtaining his introspective reports" (Lipowski, 1969: 1198). It is important, then, that both objective and subjective (or external and internal) perspectives receive consideration in measurements of social support, because "there is a relatively low correlation between objective measures of a condition and subjective measures of the way that condition is perceived by a populace" (Milbrath, 1979: 34).

The concepts of recovery and coping are also interpreted in various ways in studies of social support. By way of illustration, think about this comparison. We would not consider it particularly surprising or profound if we were to discover that pleasant family visits to the hospital make ill people happy. We would, however, be rather surprised (and enthused) to find that a family therapy meeting in which members of the family are taught to communicate their feelings more effectively to one another has a salutary effect on the physical well-being of the patient, such that he or she experiences more frequent and lengthier remissions from the disease and greater mobility. The two situations are quite distinct and their differences demonstrate that social support can be broadly defined, as can the coping and recovery processes it may influence. A careful and systematic examination of the many aspects of social support and their effects on each of the numerous possible outcomes is needed in order to determine which kinds of social support affect which kinds of outcomes.

THE EMPIRICAL RESEARCH

Table 5.1 presents all the major empirical studies of social support and illness that we were able to locate in the literature in psychology, sociology, public health, and medicine. We believe that the list of studies, if not entirely complete, is representative of the available literature. The studies were sometimes difficult to find because few were catalogued under "social support." In two computerized literature searches we specified key words that covered the range of social support sources and forms, including terms such as family, friends, community, support groups, and self-help groups. The references appearing in the table are empirical studies that involve some operationalization and quantification (however simple) of social support and of its outcomes. Theoretical papers and statements based solely on anecdotes, case studies, or "clinical experience" are not included. For each study, the table contains the illness condition(s) of the patients studied, the provider, recipient, and form of the social support, and the outcome(s) measured in the study.

Taken as a whole, the research suggests that social support may, in fact, be associated with recovery, and coping with serious physical illness and injury. For example, Berle et al. (1952) found that scores on their prognosis scale, which included items measuring emotional support provided to patients by their parents and spouses, correlated with clinical appraisal of symptom change in a sample of 209 patients with asthma, migraine headaches, or essential hypertension. The same prognosis scale correlated with the dosage of prednisone needed to control intrinsic asthma in another study (De Araujo et al., 1973). In addition, anxiety was reported to decrease in relatives of patients with life-threatening illnesses or injuries after they received supportive, empathic counseling (Bunn & Clarke, 1979). Interestingly, human

(text continued on p. 131)

TABLE 5.1 Provider, Recipient, Assessed Outcome, and Type of Social Support Used in Empirical Studies of Recovery from Serious Illness and Risk States

Study	Illness	Provider	Recipient	Type of Support	Outcome
SERIOUS ILLNESS					
Berle, Pinsky, Wolf & Wolff (1952) (NE)	essential hypertension, migraine, asthma[a]	Parents, spouse (F)	Patients (P)	Emotional (SP)	Clinical Appraisal of symptom change (P)
Bloom (1979) (NE)	Mastectomy	"A variety of social supports" (?)[b]	Patients (P)	(?)	Coping, mood disturbance, self-esteem locus of control (E)
Bloom, Ross, & Burnell (1978) (E)	Mastectomy	Interdisciplinary team (H, P)	Patients (P)	Individual and group supportive counseling, transmittal of information (OP)	Health locus of control, affect response (E)

TABLE 5.1 (continued)

Study	Illness	Provider	Recipient	Type of Support	Outcome
Bracken, Bracken, & Landry (1977) (?E)	Myocardial infarction	Lecturers vs. videotape (H)	Patients (P)	Information (OP)	Knowledge about MI, rejection of sick role, attitude toward therapy (S), psychological adaptation, feelings of anxiety, depression, and hostility, denial and guilt (E, S)
Bunn & Clarke (1979) (E)	Life-threatening injury or illness	Hospital staff (H)	Relatives of patient (F)	Emphatic, supportive crisis counseling (OP)	Anxiety (E)
Carey (1974) (NE)	Terminal illness	Kin, clergy, friends, physician, nurses, hospital chaplain (F, H)	Patients (P)	Concern, closeness to another, disclosure about death (SP, ST)	Emotional adjustment (E)
Davidson, Bowden, & Tholen (1979) (NE)	Burns	Family, friends, peers (F, P)	Patients (P)	"Support" (?)	Life-satisfaction, self-esteem, social & recreational activity (E, S)

(continued)

123

TABLE 5.1 (continued)

Study	Illness	Provider	Recipient	Type of Support	Outcome
De Araujo, Van Arsdel, Holmes, & Dudley (1973) (NE)	Chronic intrinsic asthma	Parents, spouse (F)	Patients (P)	Psychosocial assets (SP)	Dosage of adreno-corticosteroids needed to control illness (P)
Dimond (1979) (NE)	Hemodialysis	Family, spouse and confidant (F)	Patients (P)	Cohesion and Expressiveness of family environment, encouragement, sensitivity, avail-ability, and involve-ment of spouse, pre-sence of confidant (OP, SP)	Morale, change in social functioning (E, S)
Dzau & Boehme (1978) (?E)	Stroke	Medical term (H)	Family members of the patient (F)	Educational lec-tures, therapeutic listening (OP)	Anxiety, under-standing of stroke and the treatment regimen, comfort in visits with relatives (E)

TABLE 5.1

Study	Illness	Provider	Recipient	Type of Support	Outcome
Finlayson (1976) (NE)	Myocardial infarction	Kin, children, nonkin (F)	Family (F) of the patient	Driving to hospital, babysitting, providing reassurance (ST, SP)	Wife's perception of whether disease is over, employment of husband (S)
Garrity (1973) – (NE)[c]	Myocardial infarction	Family (F)	Patients (P)	Concern about patient's health (SP)	Vocational adjustment (S)
Hyman (1971) – (NE)	Chronic physical illness; cardiovascular, gastrointestinal	Family, others (F)	Patients (P)	Preferential treatment (SP)	Disability in job, household, recreational, social (S)
Jamison, Wellisch, & Pasnau (1978) (NE)	Mastectomy	Physicians, spouses, surgeons, nursing staff, children (H, F)	Patients (P)	Understanding, emotional support (SP)	Postmastectomy adjustment (E)
Järvinen (1955) (NE)	Myocardial infarction	Hospital staff (H)	Patients (P)	Behavior of physicians during ward rounds (OP)	Survival (P)

(continued)

125

TABLE 5.1 (continued)

Study	Illness	Provider	Recipient	Type of Support	Outcome
Klein, Dean, & Bogdonoff (1967) (NE)	Chronic medical & psychosomatic illness	Spouse-patient (F)	Patient-spouse (P, F)	Role tension (SP)	Nervousness, fatigue, tiredness, depression, jitters, work activity (P, S, E)
Klein, Kliner, Zipes, Troyer, & Wallace (1968) (NE)	Myocardial infarction	Coronary care team (H)	Patients (P)	Removal of support and predictability of environment (OP, OT)	Emotional reaction, cardiovascular complication (E, P)
Krant & Johnston (1978) (NE)	Advanced cancer	Family, physician (F, H)	Patients, family (P, F)	Communication (SP)	Comfort in visiting patient, feeling helpless and sensing patient helpless (E)
Lesser & Watt (1978) (NE)	Stroke, dysphasia	Volunteer organization (H)	Patients (P)	Encouragement, reassurance, social confidence enhancement, home visits (OP)	Language improvement, social confidence (P, E)

TABLE 5.1 (continued)

Study	Illness	Provider	Recipient	Type of Support	Outcome
Lewis (1966) – (NE)	Congestive heart failure	Family (F)	Patients (P)	Attitude toward patient (SP)	Return to work (S)
Litman (1966) (NE)	Orthopedic disabilities	Family (F)	Patients (P)	Family integration, encouragement, acceptance (OP)	Response to rehabilitation (P, S, E)
Lynch, Thomas, Mills, Malinow, & Katcher (1974) (NE)	Coronary disease and myocardial infarction	Nurse, Physician, family, friends (F, H)	Patients (P)	Human contact (OP, OT)	Cardiac arrhythmia (P)
Porritt (1979) (NE)	Hospitalized for road injuries	Family, friends, physicians, boss, clergy (F, H)	Patients (P)	Natural Support: empathic understanding, respect, genuineness, availability (SP) Intervention: practical, emotional and social support (OT, OP, ST, SP)	Emotional distress, work adjustment, life enjoyment, health deterioration (E, S, P)
Robertson & Suinn (1968) (NE)	Stroke	Family (F)	Patients (P)	Empathy (OP)	Rehabilitation progress (P, S)

(continued)

127

TABLE 5.1 (continued)

Study	Illness	Provider	Recipient	Type of Support	Outcome
Weisman & Worden (1975) (NE)	Cancer	Family, friends (F)	Patients (P)	Degree of intimacy with others (OP)	Length of survival beyond "expected" (P)
Whitley, Branscomb, & Moreno (1979) (E)	Childhood cancer	Cancer rehabilitation counselor (H)	Patients, family (P, F)	Assistance with problems (OP, OT)	Problems solved after assistance (E)
Williams, Darbyshire, & Brown (1978) (NE)	Hearing impairment in children	Medical profession (H)	Family (F)	Information, counseling (S, P)	Ease of transition from normal to handicapped (E)
AT RISK					
Black, Hersher, & Steinschneider (1978) (NE)	Cyanotic episodes	Medical profession (H)	Parents (P)	Apnea monitor, tangible aid (OT)	Reduction of anxiety (E)

128

TABLE 5.1 (continued)

Study	Illness	Provider	Recipient	Type of Support	Outcome
Caplan, Robinson, French, Caldwell, & Shinn (1976) (NE)	High blood pressure	Medical staff (H)	Patients (P)	Patient education and emotional support (OP)	Adherence, motivation to adhere, self-esteem, psychological strain of the regimen (E)
Carveth & Gottlieb (1979) (NE)	New motherhood	Family, friends, physician (F, H)	Mothers (P)	Amount of contact, problem-centered feedback, importance of relationship (SP)	Stress (E)
Earp (1979) (E)	Hypertension	Public health nurses and pharmacists, relative or friend, (H, F)	Patients (P)	Home visits, monitored blood pressure (OP, OT)	Blood pressure (P)
McGuire & Gottlieb (1979) (E)	New parenthood	Physician, peer groups (H, P)	Parents (P)	Groups encouraging sharing of experiences (OP)	Health status; number of people and frequency discussing child-rearing; social comparison, problem-solving (P, E, S)

(continued)

TABLE 5.1 (continued)

Study	Illness	Provider	Recipient	Type of Support	Outcome
Paykel, Emms, Fletcher, & Rassaby (1980) (NE)	Pregnancy	Husband, confidant (F)	Wife (P)	Marital adjustment, communication, tangible help from husband, adequacy of confidant (OT, OP)	Puerperal depression (E)
Wellons, Caplan, Van Harrison, & French (1979) (E)	Hypertension	RN, significant other (F, H)	Patient (P)	Help with getting to facility or fulfilling behavioral pre-scriptions (OT, OP)	Blood pressure (P)

NOTE: Letters in parentheses represent the following: **Study:** NE = nonexperimental, E = experimental. **Provider:** F = friends and family, P = peer groups, H = helping professionals. **Recipient:** P = patient, F = family and significant others. **Type of support:** SP = subjective psychological, OP = objective psychological, ST = subjective tangible, OT = objective tangible. **Outcome:** P = physical, S = social role, E = socioemotional.

a. This study was classified as "serious illness" rather than "at risk," although it examines patients from both categories.

b. When it was not possible to classify a study based on the information given in the citation, question marks appear in the table. This occurred either because insufficient information was given by the authors or the study design itself did not permit such classification.

c. A negative sign in the far left column under the authors' names indicates that negative effects of social support were found on some outcome measures.

130

contact by itself has been linked to patients' heart rates and rhythms, and the frequency of ectopic beats (Lynch et al., 1974; Lynch, 1977). Furthermore, while Porritt (1979) found little correspondence between the availability of social support sources and outcome in a crisis (a composite of emotional distress, work adjustment, life enjoyment, and health deterioration), the quality of social support (empathic understanding, respect, and constructive genuineness) was related to outcome. Social support has also been an important predictor of coping with mastectomy (Bloom, 1979; Jamison et al., 1978) and self-efficacy following breast surgery (Bloom et al., 1978).

Response to rehabilitation also may be linked with social support. Robertson and Suinn (1968) found that empathy (defined as the ability of the family to predict the patient's attitudes) between stroke patients and their families correlated with recovery rate. Family reinforcement was associated with patient response to rehabilitation in a sample of 100 orthopedically disabled patients (Litman, 1966). Lesser and Watt (1978) noted an increase in social confidence in stroke victims following involvement in a speech-after-stroke club. Social support has also been found to correlate with subjectively assessed rehabilitation outcomes (Davidson et al., 1979), "morale" (Dimond, 1979), and more favorable outcomes following husbands' myocardial infarctions (Finlayson, 1976).

Social support may play an important role in terminal illness as well. In one study, cancer patients who lived significantly longer than was the norm for patients with their condition tended to maintain cooperative and mutually responsive relationships with others (Weisman & Worden, 1975). Carey (1974) found higher-quality interpersonal relationships (greater concern shown by nearest of kin and one's local clergyman) related to greater emotional adjustment (the extent to which the patient copes with limited life expectancy) in a sample of 84 terminal patients.

Social support has not always been considered beneficial, however. In a sample of men recovering from congestive heart failure and myocardial infarction, Garrity (1973) found that the more worried the family was about a man's health, the fewer hours he worked after the attack. Likewise, Lewis (1966) reported that patients from overprotective families were less likely to return to work. Moreover, perceived preferential treatment from the family was related to disability (e.g., job, household, recreation) among a sample of patients with various illness conditions (Hyman, 1971).

Motivation to adhere to medical regimens (Caplan et al., 1976), perceived consequences of not adhering (Caplan et al., 1976), increased patient compliance (Earp, 1979), less puerperal depression (Paykel et al., 1980), and obtaining control over blood pressure (Wellons et al., 1979) have each been associated with measures of social support. Social support in serious illness or injury was also examined in several other studies listed in Table 5.1 (Black et al., 1978; Bracken et al., 1977; Dzau & Boehme, 1978; Järvinen, 1955; Klein et al., 1968; Krant & Johnston, 1978; McGuire & Gottlieb, 1979; Whitely et al., 1979; Williams et al., 1978).

THE OUTCOME VARIABLES

Coping with and recovering from serious illness and injury involve multifaceted outcomes. They range from the patient's feelings of happiness and hopefulness to cohesiveness and comfort with family members, and may even extend to the patient's capacity to overcome physical limitations and deterioration. Based on the findings in the literature, and on our own conceptualizations, we compiled, a list of eighteen general outcomes representing a range of beneficial results. Eleven psychologists (six faculty members and five graduate students) were asked to indicate which of the eighteen outcomes were conceptually related to one another by arranging them in three to five theoretical factors (they were free to determine the number of factors within this range). There was high agreement among the judges, with the following three factors clearly emerging..

Physical recovery involved five outcomes related to physical well-being, including increased longevity, greater physical mobility, reduction in the need for medication (particularly for pain), symptom amelioration, and quicker recovery. *Social role recovery* involved three outcomes related to the individual's resumption of role-related activities, including greater productivity (defined in terms of contribution to work and home life), reduction in the use of health services (indicating a relinquishing of the sick role), and greater compliance or cooperation with a health regimen (reflecting desire to recover and become healthy once again). Finally, *socioemotional recovery* involved nine psychological outcome variables and an interpersonal item: greater life satisfaction and happiness, greater harmony in interpersonal relationships, increased ability to cope emotionally with illness, restored self-esteem, reduced anxiety, reduced fear, reduced stress, and increased "morale" and hope for survival.

In Table 5.1, the column labeled "outcome" lists the outcome measures used in the empirical research on social support. Next to each is one or more letters, indicating our coding of the type of outcome measured (P = physical, S = social role, E = socioemotional). This coding is provided for easier reference to entries in the table.

THE PROVIDERS, RECIPIENTS,
AND FORMS OF
SOCIAL SUPPORT

Social support can be provided by a number of different sources, and the character of the support is also quite variable. In Table 5.1, the provider of the social support is listed and labeled as F (friends and family), P (peer groups consisting of other ill persons, self-help groups, and group therapy) and/or H (helping professionals, including physicians, nurses, rehabilitation counselors, social workers, and other group leaders). The recipient of social support (P = patient, F = family and significant others) is coded in the column labeled "recipient."

Type of support provided was difficult to code, primarily because it rarely occurs in just one form. "The quantity of human contact," for example, could range from intimate conversation and physical contact to the communication of specific information. When it was possible to determine from the report a reasonable operational definition of the social support used, Caplan's (1979) two-dimensional scheme was employed: support was coded as T (tangible) or P (psychological), and as O (objective: assessed by outside observers) or S (subjective: purely a function of the perceptions of the recipient). Examples of the four kinds of support follow. Objective tangible support involves help such as financial assistance, the running of errands, child care, and clean up. Objective psychological support involves the communication of information about the illness and about care, and the expression of specific behaviors such as touching, listening, disclosing, and smiling, which are expected to produce a more positive affective state in the patient. Subjective tangible support is involved when the recipient believes that he or she is receiving tangible assistance like financial help, help in running errands, child care, or cleanup. Subjective psychological support, while perhaps the most nebulous, is the most common. It involves the recipient's perception of comfort, esteem, intimacy, and hope received through social interaction.

The coding of all variables in the table is based solely on the opinions of the two authors; this coding procedure has helped us to organize and understand the general trends in the literature. It is useful for examining consistencies in the research, and in determining what is already known, what is missing, and what needs further empirical examination. Different coding schemes are, of course, possible.

Note that the empirical studies have been divided into two kinds: those dealing with serious illness and injury (such as cancer and myocardial infarction, 27 studies) and those focusing on potentially serious, though presently "at-risk" populations (included are hypertension, cyanotic episodes, and pregnancy/new parenthood, 7 studies).

TRENDS IN THE SOCIAL SUPPORT LITERATURE

Assessment of the current status of research on social support and serious illness or injury is possible by examining the trends in Table 5.1. The table reveals that in most of the studies the family provided the social support, and in somewhat fewer studies it was provided by a health professional or counselor. A small number of studies looked at the influence of self-help groups or peer groups on recovery and coping. Most of the studies examined social support provided to the patient. Few studied the effects of providing social support to family members, despite the fact that stresses experienced by the family are enormous at times of serious illness. In addition, most of the research assessed the effects of psychological rather than tangible support. Though there appears to be an equal number of studies that assessed objective and subjective measures of social support, only a small number of studies measured both types. (As noted earlier, it is advantageous to include both objective and subjective measures in order to obtain a more complete understanding of social support.) Various outcomes have been measured in the different studies, but only in a small number of these have more than one kind of outcome been assessed. Examination of all three outcome dimensions (physical, social role, socioemotional) within each study is needed in order to develop the most comprehensive perspective on the effects of each form of social support.

Only a minority of the studies in the table are "experimental" or actually tested an intervention. Whether each study is experimental (E: included an intervention and a control or comparison group), or nonexperimental (NE: usually "correlational") is coded in the first column of the table. Two studies that were experimental, but weak in methodology (lacking an adequate, comparable control group but including a "control group" nonetheless or lacking random assignment to conditions), are coded with a question mark (?E).

LIMITATIONS OF THE EXISTING RESEARCH

While there is considerable evidence from other areas of research that variables such as social class, education, and ethnicity do indeed influence perceptions of medical care (DiMatteo & Hays, 1980; Mechanic, 1966; Ware et al., 1978), pain perceptions and reactions to illness (Zborowski, 1952; Zola, 1966), and family structure and cohesiveness (Udry, 1974), the effect of these sociodemographic factors on the relationship between social support and illness outcome has largely been ignored. It is important to examine whether sociodemographic variables interact with various forms of social support. For example, individuals from certain ethnic groups and social classes are more comfortable with physical contact and touching than are those from other groups (Montagu, 1978), and the relative influence of health professionals, family, and the lay referral network (Gottlieb, 1976) often varies as a function of the patient's ethnic identification and social class (Kirscht, 1976).

Another overlooked area in empirical research on social support is the patient's personality and usual coping style. Personality factors are likely to mediate the effects of social support interventions. For example, Harker (1972: 166) has suggested that some patients become "depressed and uncommunicative, and others, taking their cue from him, leave him alone, reduce conversation, or become visibly anxious or even irritated. An interpersonal stalemate is reached." Caplan (1979) cites his own current research, as well as a study by De-Nour and Czaczkes (1976), as evidence that patients who need social support the most are often the least likely to get it. Unfortunately, some individuals tend to undermine or impair their own support, but we know very little about the circumstances in which they do this, or for what reason. The current neglect of this important issue prompted Mitchell and Trickett's (1980: 34) statement: "It is somewhat surprising that one feature of current research on social networks is the lack of discussion of the role that individuals play in influencing the quality of their networks." In short, the study of social support as it relates to coping with and recovery from serious illness should take into consideration not only information about the support itself, but also differences among recipients. With regard to this point, Henderson and Byrne (1977: 166) have stated that "there is probably much variation between individuals in the requirement for support. So there are both situational and personality factors to be allowed for." A concerted effort on the part of researchers to examine coping styles such as repression-sensitization (Byrne, 1961), internal-external locus of control (Rotter et al., 1972), and defensive styles (Meyerowitz, 1980) is necessary if programs are to be designed to be flexible and responsive to patients' individual needs, and if progress is to be made in understanding the function of social support for patients with different coping styles.

The seriousness of a patient's illness is one of the most important variables affecting his or her responses to various forms of social support, as well as his or her ability to adjust to various outcomes. "Seriousness" of an illness or injury is determined by many factors, including the amount of pain, physical limitation, and disfigurement that results; the difficulty of following the treatment regimen; the chronicity of the condition; the likelihood of recovery; and the threat to survival. During the course of illness, all of these factors affect the patient's reactions to other people and the reactions of others to the patient. While the various research studies on social support, as presented in Table 5.1, have examined a wide range of conditions from hypertension to metastatic cancer, there has been no systematic examination of the effects of social support variables (such as type and source) on conditions varying in chronicity, threat to survival, pain, type and location of symptoms, physiological impairment, and psychological import. Just as the phenomenology of various illness conditions differs, so there are changes in the character of naturally occurring social support over the course of serious illness.

Another limitation of the empirical research is the paucity of experimental studies. In few studies has the degree or kind of social support provided been systematically varied as an independent variable, and its effects on an outcome measure determined. More often, the approach has been "correlational," examining the effects on health of naturally occurring support in the person's life. Causal inferences cannot be drawn in these studies, because while it might be true that social support influences the physical and emotional state of the patient, it is equally likely that the physical and emotional state of the patient influences the social support he or she receives. A third variable, such as the patient's optimism, is likely to influence both support and outcome. Experimental intervention studies are not always feasible, however, and while useful, they certainly cannot establish causality. Other methods should be applied (e.g., path analysis was employed by LaRocco et al., 1980 in an effort to increase our explanatory power).

THE PROCESS OF SOCIAL SUPPORT

A thorough knowledge and understanding of prior empirical research is essential for determining the importance of various forms of social support. In addition, careful theoretical analysis is needed in order to elucidate the process of social support in serious illness. While there is no shortage of writing on general theoretical issues, a detailed social psychological analysis is presently needed. In this section we formulate and elaborate on some of the effects of social support in serious illness or injury.

The usefulness of tangible social support is probably apparent. Financial help, the running of errands, and child care, while generally welcome at any time, tend to be more highly valued when one is ill and incapacitated. Objective tangible supports as well as subjective ones (such as the patient's perceptions of available financial security and sense of control over the environment) may help to reduce the ill person's pain, fatigue, and worry. Tangible social support can also make it physically easier to comply with therapeutic regimens.

The importance of psychological social support (objective and subjective) requires more careful analysis. Precisely because they are intangible, psychological supports may operate subtly. Psychological social support is primarily an interpersonal phenomenon, and during a time of crisis and disequilibrium, a patient is likely to be especially receptive to social influence of this kind. This is a classic assertion of Gerald Caplan's (1964) crisis theory. "This greater accessibility [during crisis] offers health professionals and others who deal with patients an unusual opportunity to have a strong constructive impact" (Moos & Tsu, 1977: 7-8). There may be several reasons for this effect.

The human environment provides a means for the individual to engage in "social comparison" (Festinger, 1954). By looking at the reactions of others, individuals can judge the appropriateness of their own reactions. They may learn from others how to define their own emotional arousal, and to assess the threatening quality of a situation based on the emotional expressions of others around them (Schachter, 1959). This suggests that the emotional states of individuals who interact with the patient (family, friends, health professionals) have a profound influence on the emotional state of the patient. Therefore, social support in the form of calmness, caring, and reassurance may operate to reduce anxiety and modify debilitating emotional arousal in the patient.

People usually look to others, particularly members of their primary reference group, for validation of their value and worth, for assessments of their personal characteristics, and for feedback about their behavior (Caplan, 1974; Mead, 1934). This is particularly true when a person is physically ill or disfigured (Moos & Tsu, 1977). The reactions of others to the patient (social validation) can have an important effect on his or her self-image and feelings of self-esteem. Levy (1976) notes that one of the hallmarks of self-help group functioning is the reduction or elimination, through social comparison and consensual validation, of members' sense of isolation or uniqueness regarding their problems and experiences. Self-help groups also provide members "an opportunity to build an new identity, and hence, a new base from which they can face the world and their predicaments" (Levy, 1976: 320).

At times of crisis such as illness, just as at other times, a close social environment provides the individual with an opportunity to discuss feelings, develop intimacy by disclosing private information, and express emotion. A good deal of evidence suggests that self-disclosure (including the expression of feelings) to a few close persons is an important component of healthy personality adjustment (Chelune, 1979; Cozby, 1973; Jourard, 1971).

Close individuals such as family, friends, and health professionals who have come to know the patient intimately are likely to be much better able than those who only know him or her superficially to understand his or her emotional communications and expressions of needs. They are also likely to communicate better with the patient. This is primarily because repeated exposure and experience contribute to the support person's ability to understand the nonverbal cues of the patient (Rosenthal et al., 1979) — particularly facial expressions, body movements and postures, and voice tone — and to recognize which of his or her own nonverbal behaviors will be most effective with the patient. For example, the use of touch can be very effective in comforting a patient who is distressed (Friedman, 1979; Montagu, 1978), but touch will be most effective if the supporter has and appropriately uses prior knowledge of the patient's willingness to be touched and preference for type and frequency of touching. The patient's nonverbal style is likely to project the style he or she prefers in others (e.g., relaxed, unhurried behavior versus agitated, energetic behavior). Matching the patient's nonverbal style may be essential for empathic communication to occur. Knowledge of the patient's typical nonverbal expressions (facial, voice, body) can thus represent the essence of "knowing" the patient and render verbal communications with the patient more effective as well.

Those close to the patient are likely to have the most "leverage" in influencing and changing the patient's attitudes and behaviors. This is important in the matter of compliance, particularly with medical regimens that require a difficult change in lifestyle for the patient. Studies of attitude change (reviewed in Zimbardo et al., 1977) suggest that the greater the credibility of the source of persuasive communication, the more likely it is that attitude change will occur. Since credibility of the source involves liking, respect, and a belief that his or her motives are altruistic and not selfish, it is probable that the source will be effective in influencing the patient's attitudes and behaviors toward the goal of cooperation with the medical treatment regimen.

NEGATIVE OR HARMFUL ASPECTS
OF SOCIAL SUPPORT

Up to this point, we have concentrated on the positive effects of social support on patients' well-being and capacity to cope with and recover from physical illness or injury. Earlier, though, we cited empirical evidence of instances that suggest social support may also be detrimental to a patient (Garrity, 1973; Hyman, 1971; Lewis, 1966). Here we consider ways in which social support could result in negative consequences.

Negative effects on "family equilibrium" might result from illness. Even a well-functioning family is strained by serious illness or injury to one of its members if that individual receives too much attention and support and family functioning is disrupted. Demands by the ill individual may become quite unreasonable as a result of his or her feeling entitled to a lot of support and consideration from others

(Jourard, 1963). In fact, many families do not withstand serious physical illness or impairment of a member, and divorce or separation
results. Illness represents a new entity — something not initially
bargained for by those in the relationship. Spouses of seriously ill or
injured individuals may experience a variety of chronic illness conditions and symptoms in addition to frustration and interpersonal conflict (Klein et al., 1967). Because of the detrimental effects on the
family, they need social support too, preferably from the patient
(Caplan, 1979).

The extent to which family members support the patient may
depend in part on the degree of support they themselves receive. It is
therefore important that the patient, despite the problems of illness,
make an effort to provide some emotional return to those supporting
her or him, if only through understanding, gratitude, and encouragement. Counseling and rehabilitation programs for the seriously ill or
injured should focus on issues of equity and reciprocity, and help
family members restore equilibrium in their relationships, taking the
illness or injury into account. Work with the family or network as a
whole may be necessary to prevent disengagement of its members
and destruction of emotional bonds. Effective techniques for involving all members of the individual's social orbit at once are demonstrated in the fields of family therapy (Goldenberg & Goldenberg,
1980) and network therapy (Speck & Attneave, 1973).

The provision of support for health professionals may also be
important. Research on the phenomenon of "burnout" (Maslach,
1976) has pointed to the need for support groups and other emotional
outlets for health professionals who care for seriously ill patients.
Other outlets have also been suggested, such as sharing feelings
openly with family members of the patient, or with professionals
trained to deal with the problem of burnout as a mental health issue.
Caplan (1979) feels that the delivery of social support by providers
must become an integral part of institutional operation if it is to be
used consistently, and rewards must be built into the system if the
provision of social support by providers is to be maintained.

Social support might be detrimental because it may interfere with
compliance. If the treatment is acceptable to them, family members
and other close persons may help the patient remember his treatment
regimen and encourage him to follow it. But if the treatment
prescribed for the patient goes against the values, beliefs, and usual
patterns of conduct of the family, they may subvert the treatment

regimen or cause it to be ignored. Therefore, a holistic view of the patient is necessary, one that focuses on the entire social ecology, taking into account both positive and negative influences from the patient's social network. Involvement of the family and workmates in the planning and implementation of the treatment regimen might also be initiated.

Social support may also undermine the patient's self-esteem, to the extent that it reflects his/her status as an "impaired person" vis-à-vis the supportive others. Two aspects of this problem are particularly noteworthy. First, there is evidence that patients are often distressed by the "burden" (emotional, physical, financial) that they place on their loved ones as a result of their illness. Tangible and even psychological support are seen by some patients as infringements on their loved ones' time and energy (Harker, 1972; Schwartz, 1977). Second, receiving support from others requires the patient to recognize his or her status as an impaired person. In order to conceal their "stigmatized" identity from others (Goffman, 1963; Gussow & Tracy, 1968), some patients may exhibit social detachment and not disclose information about themselves and their feelings. The patient may perceive the costs of self-disclosure to his or her social support network to be greater than the benefits. At the expense of demanding too much attention from the support group, a patient may refuse all attention, protecting others from the impairment and retaining self-esteem (Harker, 1972). Unfortunately, this social detachment may have the effect of alienating the person from his or her social support system, separating family members emotionally from one another, straining interactions, and eroding trust.

RECOMMENDATIONS FOR
FUTURE RESEARCH

The importance of sound social science research methodology, while obvious, cannot be emphasized enough. Adequate sample size, random sampling, and the inclusion of control groups (in experimental studies) are critical to the achievement of valid conclusions about the role of social support in the face of serious illness or injury. Similarly, researchers must lend more precision to their definition of "social support." We suggest that this definition incorporate the four types of social support proposed by Caplan (1979) described earlier, and specify aspects of the social network (those individuals who provide social support) such as provided in previous work in this area (e.g., Cobb, 1979). In addition, future investigations should be more comprehensive than those conducted thus far. Most of the research has failed to assess more than one kind of support, provider, or recipient, and it has focused on only a single illness and one or two outcomes at a time. Multiple sources, kinds of support, types of illnesses, and recovery and coping outcomes need to be explored. Furthermore, the influence of various forms of social support may also depend on factors like the characteristics of the patient to whom it is addressed. Hence, sociodemographic and personality variables should be assessed and examined for their interaction with social support variables.

Since some studies (Garrity, 1973; Hyman, 1971; Lewis, 1966) have indicated possible negative effects of social support on well-being, investigators need to consider both positive and negative consequences in subsequent research. Before recommending the institution of social support programs for patients, costs and benefits of any proposed interventions should be carefully weighed (Bloom et al., 1978; Gottlieb, 1979; Mitchell & Trickett, 1980).

INSTITUTING SOCIAL SUPPORT: A CONCLUDING NOTE

Social support is beginning to emerge as a central psychosocial issue in health research. The time, effort, and resources needed to assess its effects adequately are extensive. Even with the most adequate methodology and statistical analysis, the research data will be subject to different interpretations and the issues may remain complex and somewhat ambiguous. Though its potential in any humanistic approach to patient care should be acknowledged, the value of social support must not be blindly accepted. We must consider whether there presently exists enough evidence in the research literature to justify a wholehearted effort to improve patients' current level of social support. Based on this review, we suggest that, although intervention may be important, not enough is yet understood about how social support operates to warrant liberal implementation of social support programs. Instead, a more conservative approach is recommended. Campbell (1969) has argued for instituting reforms in the context of experiments, evaluating promising programs through the use of both randomization and appropriate control groups. We feel that researchers should further explore the effects of social support by employing this "reforms as experiments" procedure. A careful balance of theory, empirical research, and frequent, open-minded evaluation is necessary if we are to progress in the scientific study of social support.

REFERENCES

ANTONOVSKY, A. *Health, stress, and coping.* San Francisco: Jossey-Bass, 1979.

BERLE, B. B., PINSKY, R. H., WOLF, S., & WOLFF, H. G. A clinical guide to prognosis in stress diseases. *Journal of the American Medical Association,* 1952, *149,* 1624-1628.

BLACK, L., HERSHER, L., & STEINSCHNEIDER, A. Impact of the apnea monitor on family life. *Pediatrics,* 1978, *62*(5), 681-685.

BLOOM, J. R. Social support, coping and adjustment to mastectomy. *American Association for Cancer Research: Proceedings,* 1979, *20,* 360. (Abstract)

BLOOM, J. R., ROSS, R. D., & BURNELL, G. The effect of social support on patient adjustment after breast surgery. *Patient Counseling and Health Education,* 1978, *1*(2), 50-59.

BRACKEN, M. B., BRACKEN, M., & LANDRY, A. B. Patient education by videotape after myocardial infarction: An empirical evaluation. *Archives of Physical Medicine and Rehabilitation,* 1977, *58*(5), 213-219.

BUNN, T. A., & CLARKE, A. M. Crisis intervention: An experimental study of the effects of a brief period of counselling on the anxiety of relatives of seriously injured or ill hospital patients. *British Journal of Medical Psychology,* 1979, *52,* 191-195.

BYRNE, D. The repression-sensitization scale: Rationale, reliability, and validity. *Journal of Personality,* 1961, *29,* 334-349.

CAHNERS, S. S. Group meetings for families of burned children. *Health and Social Work,* 1978, *3*(3), 165-172.

CAHNERS, S. S., & BERNSTEIN, N. R. Rehabilitating families with burned children. *Scandinavian Journal of Plastic and Reconstructive Surgery,* 1979, *13,* 173-175.

CAMPBELL, D. T. Reforms as experiments. *American Psychologist,* 1969, *24*(4), 409-429.

CAPLAN, G. *Principles of preventive psychiatry.* New York: Basic Books, 1964.

CAPLAN, G. *Support systems and community mental health.* New York: Behavioral Publications, 1974.

CAPLAN, R. Patient, provider, and organization: Hypothesized determinants of adherence. In S.J.Cohen (Ed.), *New directions in patient compliance.* Lexington, MA: D.C.Heath,1979.

CAPLAN, R.D., ROBINSON, E.A.R., FRENCH, J.R.P.,Jr., CALDWELL, J.R., & SHINN, M. *Adhering to medical regiments: Pilot experiments in patient education and social support.* Ann Arbor: University of Michigan, 1976.

CAREY, R.G. Emotional adjustment in terminal patients: A quantitative approach. *Journal of Counseling Psychology,* 1974, *21*(5), 433-439.

CARVETH, W.B., & GOTTLIEB, B.H. The measurement of social support and its relation to stress. *Canadian Journal of Behavioural Science,* 1979, *11*(3), 179-188.

CHELUNE, G.J. *Self-disclosure: Origins, patterns, and implications of openness in interpersonal relationships.* San Francisco: Jossey-Bass, 1979.

COBB, B. Emotional problems of adult cancer patients. *Journal of the American Geriatrics Society,* 1959, *7,* 274-285.

COBB, S. Social support as a moderator of life stress. *Psychosomatic Medicine,* 1976, *38*(5), 300-314.

COBB, S. Social support and health through the life course. In M.W.Riley (Ed.), *Aging from birth to death.* Boulder, CO: Westview Press, 1979.

COBB, S., & ERBE, C. Social support for the cancer patient. *Forum on Medicine,* 1978, *1*(8), 24-29.

COHEN, F. Personality, stress, and the development of physical illness. In G.C.Stone, F.Cohen, & N.E.Adler (Eds.), *Health psychology.* San Francisco: Jossey-Bass, 1979.

COZBY, P.C. Self-disclosure: A literature review. *Psychological Bulletin,* 1973, *79*(2), 73-91.

CUTLER, D.L., & BEIGEL, A. A church-based program of community activities for chronic patients. *Hospital and Community Psychiatry,* 1978, *29*(8), 497-501.

DAVIDSON, D.M. The family and cardiac rehabilitation. *Journal of Family Practice,* 1979, *8*(2), 253-261.

DAVIDSON, T.N., BOWDEN, L., & THOLEN, D. Social support as a moderator of burn rehabilitation. *Archives of Physical Medicine and Rehabilitation,* 1979, *60,* 556. (Abstract)

DEAN, A., & LIN, N. The stress-buffering role of social support: Problems and prospects for systematic investigation. *Journal of Nervous and Mental Disease,* 1977, *165*(6), 403-417.

DeARAUJO, G., VAN ARSDEL, P.P., HOLMES, T.H., & DUDLEY, D.L. Life change, coping ability and chronic intrinsic asthma. *Journal of Psychosomatic Research,* 1973, *17,* 359-363.

De-NOUR, A.K., & CZACZKES, J.W. The influence of patient's personality on adjustment to chronic dialysis. *Journal of Nervous and Mental Disease,* 1976, *162*(5), 323-333.

DiMATTEO, M.R., & HAYS, R. The significance of patients' perceptions of physician conduct: A study of patient satisfaction in a family practice center. *Journal of Community Health,* 1980, *6*(1), 18-34.

DIMOND, M. Social support and adaptation to chronic illness: The case of maintenance hemodialysis. *Research in Nursing and Health,* 1979, *2,* 101-108.

DONALD, C. A., WARE, J. E., BROOK, R. H., & DAVIES-AVERY, A. *Conceptualization and measurement of health for adults in the health insurance study: Volume IV, Social health.* Publication No. R-1987, The Rand Corporation, Santa Monica, California, 1978.

DZAU, R. E., & BOEHME, A. R. Stroke rehabilitation: A family-team education program. *Archives of Physical Medicine and Rehabilitation,* 1978, *59,* 236-239.

EARP, J. A. L. The effects of social support and health professional home visits on patient adherence to hypertension regiments. *Preventive Medicine,* 1979, *8*(2), 155. (Abstract)

FESTINGER, L. A. A theory of social comparison processes. *Human Relations,* 1954, *7,* 117-140.

FINLAYSON, A. Social networks as coping resources: Lay help and consultation patterns used by women in husbands' post-infarction career. *Social Science and Medicine,* 1976, *10,* 97-103.

FOSTER, Z., & MENDEL, S. Mutual-help group for patients: Taking steps toward change. *Health and Social Work,* 1979, *4*(3), 82-98.

FRIEDMAN, H. S. Nonverbal communication between patients and medical practitioners. *Journal of Social Issues,* 1979, *35,* 82-99.

GARRITY, T. F. Vocational adjustment after first myocardial infarction; Comparative assessment of several variables suggested in the literature. *Social Science and Medicine,* 1973, *7,* 705-717.

GOFFMAN, E. *Stigma: Notes on the management of a spoiled identity.* Englewood Cliffs, NJ: Prentice-Hall, 1963.

GOLDENBERG, I., & GOLDENBERG, H. *Family therapy: An overview.* Monterey, CA: Brooks/Cole, 1980.

GOTTLIEB, B. H. Lay influences on the utilization and provision of health services: A review. *Canadian Psychological Review,* 1976, *17,* 126-136.

GOTTLIEB, B. H. The primary group as supportive milieu: Applications to community psychology. *American Journal of Community Psychology,* 1979, *7*(5), 469-480.

GUSSOW, Z., & TRACY, G. S. Status, ideology, and adaptation to stigmatized illness: A study of leprosy. *Human Organization,* 1968, *27*(4), 316-325.

HAMBURG, D. A., & ADAMS, J. E. A perspective on coping behavior: Seeking and utilizing information in major transitions. *Archives of General Psychiatry,* 1967, *17,* 277-284.

HARKER, B. L. Cancer and communication problems: A personal experience. *Psychiatry in Medicine,* 1972, *3*(2), 163-171.

HENDERSON, S. The social network, support and neurosis: The function of attachment in adult life. *British Journal of Psychiatry,* 1977, *131,* 185-191.

HENDERSON, S., & BYRNE, D. Towards a method for assessing social support systems. *Mental Health and Society,* 1977, *4,* 164-170.

HYMAN, M. D. Disability and patients' perceptions of preferential treatment: Some preliminary findings. *Journal of Chronic Diseases,* 1971, *24,* 329-342.

JAMISON, K. R., WELLISCH, D. K., & PASNAU, R. O Psychosocial aspects of mastectomy: I. The woman's perspective. *American Journal of Psychiatry,* 1978, *135*(4), 432-436.

JÄRVINEN, K. A. J. Can ward rounds be a danger to patients with myocardial infarction? *British Medical Journal*, 1955, *1*, 318-320.

JOHNSON, F. L., RUDOLPH, L. A., & HARTMANN, J. R. Helping the family cope with childhood cancer. *Psychosomatics*, 1979, *20*(4), 241, 245-247, 251.

JOURARD, S. M. *Personal adjustment: An approach through the study of healthy personality* (2nd ed.). London: Macmillan, 1963.

JOURARD, S. M *The transparent self.* New York: D. Van Nostrand, 1971.

KAPLAN, B. H., CASSEL, J. C., & GORE, S. Social support and health. *Medical Care*, 1977, *15*(5), 47-58.

KIRITZ, S., & MOOS, R. H. Physiological effects of social environments. *Psychosomatic Medicine*, 1974, *36*(2), 96-114.

KIRSCHT, J. P. The health belief model and illness behavior. In M. H. Becker (Ed.), *The health belief model and personal health behavior.* Thorofare, NJ: Charles B. Slack, Inc., 1976.

KLEIN, R. F., DEAN, A., & BOGDONOFF, M. D. The impact of illness upon the spouse. *Journal of Chronic Diseases*, 1967, *20*, 241-248.

KLEIN, R. F., KLINER, V. A., ZIPES, D. P., TROYER, W. G., & WALLACE, A. G. Transfer from a coronary care unit: Some adverse responses. *Archives of Internal Medicine*, 1968, *122*, 104-108.

KRANT, M. J., & JOHNSTON, L. Family members' perceptions of communications in late stage cancer. *International Journal of Psychiatry in Medicine*, 1978, *8*(2), 203-216.

LaROCCO, J. M., HOUSE, J. S., & FRENCH, J. R. P., Jr. Social support, occupational stress, and health. *Journal of Health and Human Behavior*, 1980, *21*, 202-218.

LESSER, R., & WATT, M. Untrained community help in the rehabilitation of stroke sufferers with language disorder. *British Medical Journal*, 1978, *2*, 1045-1048.

LEVY, L. H. Self-help groups: Types and psychological processes. *Journal of Applied Behavioral Science*, 1976, *12*(3), 310-322.

LEWIS, C. E. Factors influencing the return to work of men with congestive heart failure. *Journal of Chronic Diseases*, 1966, *19*, 1193-1209.

LIPOWSKI, Z. J. Psychosocial aspects of disease. *Annals of Internal Medicine*, 1969, *71*, 1197-1206.

LITMAN, T. J. The family and physical rehabilitation. *Journal of Chronic Diseases*, 1966, *19*, 211-217.

LYNCH, J. J. *The broken heart: The medical consequences of loneliness.* New York: Basic Books, 1977.

LYNCH, J. J., THOMAS, S. A., MILLS, M. E., MALINOW, K., & KATCHER, A. H. The effects of human contact on cardiac arrhythmia in coronary care patients. *Journal of Nervous and Mental Disease*, 1974, *158*(2), 88-99.

MANGURTEN, H. H., SLADE, C., & FITZSIMONS, D. Parent-parent support in the care of high-risk newborns. *J.O.G.N. Nursing*, 1979, *8*(5), 275-277.

MASLACH, C. Burned out. *Human Behavior*, 1976, *5*(9), 16-22.

McGUIRE, J. C., & GOTTLIEB, B. H. Social support groups among new parents: An experimental study in primary prevention. *Journal of Clinical Child Psychology*, 1979, *8*, 111-116.

MEAD, G. H. *Mind, self, and society*. Chicago: University of Chicago Press, 1934.

MECHANIC, D. Response factors in illness: The study of illness behavior. *Social Psychiatry*, 1966, *1*, 11-20.

MEYEROWITZ, B. E. Psychosocial correlates of breast cancer and its treatment. *Psychological Bulletin*, 1980, *87*(1), 108-131.

MILBRATH, L. W. Policy relevant quality of life research. *Annals of the American Academy of Political and Social Science*, 1979, *444*, 32-45.

MITCHELL, R. E., & TRICKETT, E. J. Social networks as mediators of social support: An analysis of the effects and determinants of social networks. *Community Mental Health Journal*, 1980, *16*(1), 27-44.

MONTAGU, A. *Touching*. New York: Harper & Row, 1978.

MOOS, R. H., & TSU, V. D. The crisis of physical illness: An overview. In R. H. Moos (Ed.), *Coping with physical illness*. New York: Plenum, 1977.

PAYKEL, E. S., EMMS, E. M., FLETCHER, J., & RASSABY, E. S. Life events and social support in puerperal depression. *British Journal of Psychiatry*, 1980, *136*, 339-346.

PERRAULT, C., COLLINGE, J., & OUTERBRIDGE, E. W. Family support in the neonatal intensive care unit. *Dimensions in Health Services*, 1979, *56*(5), 16-18.

PORRITT, D. Social support in crisis: Quantity or quality. *Social Science and Medicine*, 1979, *13A*, 715-721.

ROBERTSON, E. K., & SUINN, R. M. The determination of rate of progress of stroke patients through empathy measures of patient and family. *Journal of Psychosomatic Research*, 1968, *12*, 189-191.

ROSENTHAL, R., HALL, J. A., DiMATTEO, M. R., ROGERS, P. L., & ARCHER, D. *Sensitivity to nonverbal communication: The PONS test*. Baltimore: Johns Hopkins University Press, 1979.

ROTTER, J. B., CHANCE, J. E., & PHARES, E. J. *Applications of a social learning theory of personality*. New York: Holt, Rinehart & Winston, 1972.

SCHACHTER, S. *The psychology of affiliation*. Stanford, CA: Stanford University Press, 1959.

SCHWARTZ, M. D. An information and discussion program for women after a mastectomy. *Archives of Surgery*, 1977, *112*(3), 276-281.

SPECK, R. V., & ATTNEAVE, C. L. *Family networks*. New York: Pantheon, 1973.

TOLSDORF, C. C. Social networks, support, and coping: An exploratory study. *Family Process*, 1976, *15*, 407-417.

UDRY, J. R. *The social context of marriage* (3rd ed.). Philadelphia: J. B. Lippincott, 1974.

WARE, J. E., DAVIES-AVERY, A., & STEWART, A. The measurement and meaning of patient satisfaction. *Health and Medical Care Services Review*, 1978, *1*, 3-15.

WEISMAN, A. D., & WORDEN, J. W. Psychosocial analysis of cancer deaths. *Omega*, 1975, *6*(1), 61-75.

WELLONS, R. V., CAPLAN, R. D., VAN HARRISON, R., & FRENCH, J. R. P., Jr. Effects of social support on adherence to therapeutic regimens. *Preventive Medicine*, 1979, *8*(2), 248. (Abstract)

WHITLEY, S. B., BRANSCOMB, B. V., & MORENO, H. Identification and management of psychosocial and environmental problems of children with cancer. *American Journal of Occupational Therapy,* 1979, *33*(11), 711-716.

WILLIAMS, D. M. L., DARBYSHIRE, J. O., & BROWN, B. Families of young, hearing-impaired children: The impact of diagnosis. *Journal of Otolaryngology,* 1978, *7*(6), 500-506.

ZBOROWSKI, M. Cultural components in responses to pain. *Journal of Social Issues,* 1952, *8,* 16-30.

ZIMBARDO, P. G., EBBESEN, E., & MASLACH, C. *Influencing attitudes and changing behavior* (2nd ed.). Reading, MA: Addison-Wesley, 1977.

ZOLA, I. K. Culture and symptoms — an analysis of patients' presenting complaints. *American Sociological Review,* 1966, *31,* 615-630.

Chapter 6

SOCIAL NETWORKS AND THE COPING PROCESS
Creating Personal Communities

BARTON J. HIRSCH

Interest in the health-enhancing potential of social networks has mushroomed among social scientists and mental health professionals. It is presently unknown whether this interest is destined to be merely a fad, or instead to make a serious contribution to our understanding and ability to promote mental health. To prevent the former possibility it is necessary to raise some critical questions regarding the presuppositions and implications of current research. I shall argue that the several research strategies that have been developed differ fundamentally in their capacity to elaborate viable paradigms for this emerging field. In doing so, I argue the value of research that includes the identification of each network member and the use of dyadic and systems analytical categories for network analysis. Several studies that illustrate this approach are discussed. I then sketch the initial formulation of a model that seeks to relate social networks to coping and mental health. The model conceptualizes social networks as

Author's Note: For helpful comments on drafts of this chapter, the author is grateful to John C. Glidewell, Benjamin H. Gottlieb, Roger E. Mitchell, Rudolf H. Moos, and Barry Wellman. The author is also pleased to acknowledge the support of an individual NIMH National Research Service Postdoctoral Fellowship (1 F32 MH07787-02); additional funding was provided via NIAAA Grant AA02863 and Veterans Administration Medical Research Funds.

personal communities and emphasizes their capability for embedding
a repertoire of satisfactory social identities. I conclude by considering
implications of this model for the design and evaluation of social-
community interventions.

TRADITIONAL SOCIAL NETWORK
RESEARCH STRATEGIES

The most traditional approach to assessing how social ties may
affect mental health is essentially demographic and family-oriented.
Typically, it consists of ascertaining the marital, or living alone versus
with others, status of the respondent. For example, Eaton (1978)
found the effect of life events on symptoms to be stronger for those
unmarried and living alone than for those either married or living with
others. In a similar vein, Sandler (1980) shows that for elementary
school children, living with two parents and elder siblings reduces the
effect of stress on maladaptation. The implications of such studies are
metatheoretical: Social ties seem important and we ought to study
them. It is difficult to draw any substantive implications from such
work, nor are specific implications for practice readily discernible.

Studies that assess the quantity or quality of social support available from family and friends, but do not include an identification of
each specific network member, represent an alternative methodology.
Typically using written questionnaires, these studies may assess the
number of one's friends, the amount of crisis help thought available,
the quality of cognitive guidance or tangible assistance provided, and
so on. Supports are assessed from categories of network members,
such as "friends," with questions typically directed, for example, at
whether "I have a friend who would loan me $50."

Perhaps the most notable study of this type was an epidemiological investigation reported by Berkman and Syme (1979). Their 9-year
longitudinal study tracked the health outcome (mortality) of approximately 7000 adults of varied ages. The principal independent variable
was a social network index consisting of responses to questions
regarding the number of close friends and relatives respondents felt
close to, and how often both sets of people were seen each month.
This network index was significantly related to mortality rates even
after controlling for age, initial physical health status, socioeconomic
status, health practices (smoking, alcohol consumption, obesity,
physical activity), and utilization of health services. These are cer-

tainly impressive findings! Nonetheless, their implications seem again primarily metatheoretical: something seems to be going on, but exactly what, we do not know. It seems quite possible, however, for studies using this general research strategy to generate data that would be of substantive theoretical import. This would be the case, for example, if the Berkman and Syme findings were to be considered in conjunction with research indicating that support X was related to mental health more than support Y. Even in this case, however, the failure to identify and assess relationships with specific network members fundamentally limits the import of such findings for our understanding of social support. As I suggest below, this is so because studies of specific relationships are necessary to address critical issues regarding the influence of dyadic and systemic variables on support (see Gottlieb, 1980; Wellman, 1980).

Social support is provided by other people and arises within the context of interpersonal relationships. Different types of relationships may provide different types of support (Weiss, 1974). Thus, while we certainly need to distinguish among types of supports, we will be severely restricted in the conclusions we may draw from such data if we do not also classify and understand the relationships from which these supports emerge. Categorizing relationships as being with family or friends, while not unimportant, is by itself only an initial, rudimentary characterization. We need as well to be able to differentiate relationships according to their content, process, and development. This objective can be accomplished only by identifying and studying a variety of specific network relationships. We shall see later in the chapter how such classifications may enable us better to understand the nature, availability, and value of supports provided for diverse coping tasks.

If we do not identify specific network members, we also will be unable to obtain precise data regarding relationships *among* network members. Failure to obtain these data precludes study of how social networks may function as support *systems*. There is a considerable body of theory and research suggesting that a systems perspective is critical to understanding the social psychology of mental health (Glidewell, 1972). Indeed, later in this chapter I present research suggesting that network interrelationships reflect important dimensions of our lives and can significantly affect coping processes and outcomes. Here again, then, failure to identify each specific network member severely curtails our ability to address important issues and thus develop a more sophisticated understanding of social support.

In the remainder of the chapter I wish to explore an alternative research strategy. This approach aims to provide a more comprehensive analysis of ties with specific network members, and includes the use of both dyadic and systems levels of analysis. Specifically, I shall discuss three studies that were conducted using *social network analysis,* a methodology initially developed by anthropologists and sociologists (see reviews by Barnes, 1972; Mitchell, 1969, 1974; Wellman, 1980; Whitten and Wolfe, 1973). After presenting these studies I explore the conceptualization of social networks that they suggest.

SOCIAL NETWORK ANALYSIS

Tolsdorf: Psychiatric and Medical Inpatients

Christopher Tolsdorf was the first psychologist to employ social network analysis for studying the coping process. Tolsdorf's (1976) research focused on the networks and coping patterns of ten male hospitalized psychiatric patients (all first-admission schizophrenics) and ten male medical inpatients matched on demographic variables.

Tolsdorf first considered the strength of ties between patients and their network members. One variable that he assessed was the number of "content areas" encompassed by each relationship out of a possible total of ten (e.g., engage in recreational or economic activities together). Relationships that included more than one content area were termed "multiplex," and those that included only one were termed "uniplex." Previous research had suggested that multiplex ties were stronger, and, indeed, medical patients were found to have a higher proportion of multiplex ties in their networks, and schizophrenics a higher proportion of uniplex ties. Additional analyses were consistent in indicating that medical patients had stronger, more varied ties to network members than did schizophrenics. For example, for medical inpatients, the amount of support they extended and received was symmetrical, while the schizophrenics tended to receive more support than they gave. In contrast to the medical patients' networks, those of the schizophrenics tended to be kin-dominated, with kin frequently reported to be hostile. As might be expected in kin-dominated networks, Tolsdorf's data suggest that there were more interrelationships among members of the schizophrenics' networks. Thus, while the schizophrenics were generally restricted to often hostile families or kin, the medical patients could draw on a broader variety of multiplex ties.

Drawing on qualitative interview data, Tolsdorf went on to delineate between-group differences regarding their orientation to and utilization of network supports during stress. The schizophrenics were seen to hold a negative network orientation, a set that "it is inadvisable, impossible, useless, or potentially dangerous to draw on network resources" (Tolsdorf, 1976: 413). The medical group, by and large, held a more positive orientation, believing it "safe, advisable, and in some cases necessary to confide in the social network and draw on it for advice, support, and feedback in a crisis situation" (1976: 413). Additionally, the medical patients tended to have less superficial and more self-disclosing interactions, and to solicit and follow advice more frequently than was the case for the schizophrenics. Thus, not only did the schizophrenics have fewer network resources to begin with, but they made less use of what resources they had.

Tolsdorf then examines how both sets of patients coped with stressful life events, taking account of both their individual cognitive and behavioral responses ("individual mobilization") and their utilization of their social networks. Considering these personal and network variables simultaneously,

> it becomes possible to identify two contrasting constellations for the two groups of subjects. Specifically, the psychiatric subjects experienced some significant life stress with which they attempted to cope using individual mobilization. When this strategy failed, they chose not to mobilize their networks, relying instead on their own resources, which had already been shown to be inadequate. This resulted in more failure, higher anxiety, a drop in performance and self-esteem, followed eventually by a psychotic episode. The medical patients showed a variety of constellations, but in no case was the psychiatric constellation replicated. Some medical subjects did not report any significant life stress, but when stress was reported the medical subjects coped with it initially using individual mobilization. If this failed they would employ network mobilization, and in all cases this coping strategy resulted in either a constructive resolution of the stress or at least a compromise control of the stress situation to keep it within manageable and reasonable limits [1976: 416].

Tolsdorf's study suggests how social network analysis may inform our understanding of the coping process. Of particular value is his delineation of some of the complex factors affecting network mobilization, and his portrayal of a coping ecology in which individuals can make use of both personal and network resources in responding to the impact of life events. The schizophrenics lacked both sets of resources. The high level of family conflict and hostility guaranteed that what little positive support they did receive was paid for dearly. Previous family research suggests that the negative effect of family members may have been potentiated by their discouraging the development of nonfamily friendships (e.g., Laing & Esterson, 1964; Lidz et al., 1965). The failure of the schizophrenics to develop strong nonfamily ties, and thus break their excessive dependence on their families, may be attributed as well to their own negative network orientation and, no doubt, to their lack of adequate social skills.

While Tolsdorf's research suggests network variables that may be related to coping and mental health, his emphasis on the schizophrenics limits our ability to specify and understand how networks may be used adaptively. To develop such knowledge it is necessary to consider in greater detail the ways in which networks may facilitate successful coping.

Kapferer: A Conflictual Work Situation

In its use of social exchange concepts to analyze dyadic and, especially, group or systems relationships, Bruce Kapferer's (1969) ethnographic study of a conflict in an African zinc mine provides a provocative illustration of unique ways in which social network analysis can further our understanding of the coping process. While not explicitly concerned with "mental health," there is little doubt that the conflict had a major impact on the lives of the central individuals.

The two protagonists in this conflict, Abraham and Donald, work with thirteen others in a unit designed to purify zinc before it is marketed. The dispute begins with Abraham's objection to Donald's fast-working pace. Donald's brief period of angry opposition to Abraham follows, and eventually Donald acquiesces to Abraham's demands.

Kapferer is concerned with why Abraham was able to mobilize more support for his position than Donald. Appeals to norms and values regarding rate-busting (Abraham's accusation against Donald) and witchcraft (Donald's accusation against Abraham) are deemed insufficient to account for the differential mobilization of support. Instead, Kapferer argues that in their choice of whom to support, fellow workers act to minimize negative consequences to the total set of their own relationships in the work setting. This involves considering not only the effects of their choice on their relationship to the protagonists (if there is such a relationship), but also the effects of their choice on their relationships with allies of the protagonists.

Let us consider first the effects of direct ties between protagonists and coworkers. While there were only fifteen workers in the unit, not all the workers had relationships with each other. Each potential relationship was characterized as to whether it regularly involved the following five interactional content areas: conversation, joking behavior, job assistance, personal service, and cash assistance. Relationships that involved only one of those areas were termed "uniplex," while those that involved any two or more of those areas were termed "multiplex." While neither Abraham nor Donald had many direct ties to the others in the room (nine and eight ties respectively), several of Abraham's relationships were multiplex, as compared to only one of Donald's. Multiplex ties in general proved to be more reliable and potent sources of support, for coworkers had more to lose by failing to provide support to a multiplex rather than a uniplex friend.

Many of the workers, however, including several in positions of considerable influence, had relationships with neither Abraham nor Donald. That they too supported Abraham can be seen as a function of their multiplex ties to individuals who in turn were directly tied to Abraham. While for the sake of brevity I must omit the rich ethnographic details of Kapferer's analysis, his conclusion is that these coworkers had more to lose by failing to support Abraham's allies than by failing to support Donald's allies. Thus, via a social exchange analysis of multiplexity and complex interrelationships among the workers, Kapferer explains why Abraham was able to mobilize more support than was Donald.

The outcome of this conflict came as a considerable surprise to Donald, who thought that his ties and status in the unit were much stronger than they proved to be. The crisis apparently shattered his illusions and led him to make a major change in his life which entailed additional hardship: He transferred to a different unit, where he now worked twice as long as previously for less daily pay. Abraham, on the other hand, enhanced his position, for not only had the work rate slowed down (his original objective), but his own ties and status in the unit had been strengthened. Thus, while this study was not explicitly concerned with mental health, it seems reasonable to infer that the conflict affected the psychosocial well-being of the protagonists.

Kapferer's account of how network ties contributed to these outcomes suggests the importance of comprehensively assessing network relationships. Without such an assessment, it would have been impossible to explain why support had been provided in such a manner. Moreover, his analysis adds to Tolsdorf's account of factors affecting network mobilization by considering the positions and perspectives of the network members who were being mobilized. Their own stance was determined not by the intrinsic merits of the case, but in large part by their ties to individuals other than the protagonists. This finding underscores our need to consider network ties at group as well as at dyadic levels.

Hirsch: Young Widows and Returning Women Students

Elsewhere (Hirsch, 1980), I have reported the results of a study concerning how social networks might foster adaptive coping among two groups of women: 20 recently widowed younger women and 14 mature women (aged 30 or over) recently returned to college full-time. Recent younger widows are a group at particularly high risk for both mortality and the development of severe depression (Parkes, 1972). Returning women students assume highly ambiguous roles as they reenter a competitive, often career-directed social institution after having already begun raising a family. Both groups were in the midst of major life changes, with a level of symptomatology at approximately the midpoint between the means for clinical and normal populations. Mental health was assessed via standard measures of symptomatology (Hopkins Symptom Checklist), mood (Profile of Mood States), and self-esteem (evaluation scale of the Semantic Differential).

Both dyadic and systemic network variables were assessed. On the dyadic level, this involved measuring two different variables: the provision of five alternative types of supports to respondents (cognitive guidance, socializing, social reinforcement, tangible assistance, and emotional support), and the categorization of friendships as multi- versus unidimensional. A relationship for any individual is termed *multidimensional* if and only if it involves engaging in at least two different kinds of activities important to that individual (e.g., shared recreation, verbal confidences). A unidimensional relationship, by contrast, reflects involvement in no more than one kind of activity with the other that is considered important (Hirsch, 1979). Multidimensional relationships differ from multiplex relationships insofar as multiplexity measures only whether relationships involve two or more activities, while multidimensionality allows for individual differences in the importance of activities to subjects.

On a systems level, the principal variable assessed was network density. Density is defined as the proportion of actual to potential relationships that exist *among* the members of an individual's network. As the focal individual, by definition, has a relationship with all members of his or her network, these relationships are not included in calculating density (see Hirsch, 1979, for the formula).

Findings indicated that multidimensional friendships were significantly related to higher self-esteem, and more satisfying socializing and tangible assistance. Density was negatively related to mental health.

Further analyses were conducted to determine the precise set of relationships accounting for the negative effect of density. Separate analyses of the density of the combined nuclear family-relative subnetwork, and then of the density of the friendship subnetwork, indicated that the density of neither of these subnetworks was significantly associated with either of the mental health or support variables.

A very strong effect, however, is revealed for the nuclear family-friendship (NF-F) boundary density. This NF-F boundary density is defined as the proportion of actual to potential relationships existing between nuclear family members, on the one hand (in this study, principally children), and friends, on the other (see Hirsch, 1981, for the formula). Figure 6.1 illustrates this graphically. As can be seen in Table 6.1, a denser NF-F boundary is significantly related to greater symptomatology, poorer mood, and lower self-esteem. A denser NF-F boundary is negatively related to all five supports, these statistical relationships being significant in three instances. Finally, a denser NF-F boundary is significantly associated with friendships that are uni- rather than multidimensional.

To interpret these network findings we must first analyze the coping tasks confronting these women. For both groups of women, developing intensified involvements outside the family sphere emerged as an overarching requirement for social adaptation (Hirsch,

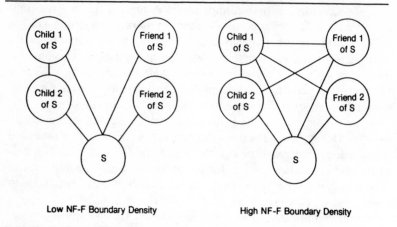

Low NF-F Boundary Density   High NF-F Boundary Density

Figure 6.1 Diagrammatic Illustration of Nuclear Family (NF)-Friendship (F) Boundary Density

1980). Typically the widows already had strong ties to their children, and thus needed to look outside the family to fill the social void left by their husbands' deaths. The students now considered school and an eventual career, in addition to their family, as important parts of their lives.

Social networks differed considerably in their ability to serve as a support system for intensified nonfamily involvements. In high-density networks, the greater involvement of friends with children may have led friendships to have become focused unidimensionally on child- or family-related events and topics. Access to and support for nonfamily involvements were not as readily available.

Low-density, multidimensional networks were better suited to support nonfamily life. A low NF-F boundary density enhanced separation of family and nonfamily roles and activities, thereby providing a structural resource for intensified nonfamily involvements. Multidimensional friendships often involved valued interactions outside the family sphere. Women in these networks may merely have had to change the extent of already existing commitments or identifications with particular nonfamily activities and relationships, rather than to develop entirely new ones (see Coser, 1975; Sieber, 1974). Intensified nonfamily pursuits may, accordingly, be appraised

TABLE 6.1   Correlates of Density

| Variable | Density of Overall Network | | Density of Nuclear Family Friendship Boundary | |
	r	n	r	n
Symptoms	.18	34	.36**	29
Mood	.25	34	.39**	29
Self-esteem	−.28	34	−.44***	29
Socializing	−.48***	34	−.61***	29
Social Reinforcement	−.37**	33	−.34*	28
Emotional Support	−.46***	33	−.18	28
Tangible Assistance	−.23	32	−.40**	28
Cognitive Guidance	−.30*	32	−.09	27
Multidimensional friendships	−.47***	32	−.49***	28

* p n .05; ** p n .03; *** p n .01
SOURCE: Hirsch, 1980.

as less threatening and be pursued more confidently, as these women have a greater backlog of actual experiences indicating that these alternatives are feasible and satisfying. Thus, these networks provided greater access to rewarding alternative social identities and activities, facilitating a smoother reorganization of their lives at less psychic cost.

In this manner, low-density, multidimensional social networks could serve as the cornerstone for a successful coping strategy. This strategy was designed to cultivate relationships outside the family sphere in order to develop a repertoire of satisfying social roles. The strategy involved fundamental choices regarding the kind of social network to be created. Should important, personally valued activities be compartmentalized among network relationships, or should several such activities be incorporated in multidimensional relationships? Multidimensional friendships emerged as an important source of support for a reorganized identity structure. Should family and nonfamily life be totally integrated? A low NF-F boundary density, reflecting a high degree of family/nonfamily segregation, provided an important structural resource for achieving coping objectives. In his study of divorced women, Wilcox (Chapter 4) has also found low-density networks to be associated with better mental health.

I do not, however, wish to suggest that this is the only kind of social network that can promote successful coping. For example, one widow in particular demonstrated how successful coping could be combined with membership in a high-density network. She used a variety of network and nonnetwork resources to intensify nonfamily involvements and to develop a repertoire of satisfying social roles. Her friendships, for example, had been developed through her church, which provided a focal point for valued interactions in which her family affairs did not predominate. In addition, on a personal level, she appeared quite skillful in directing conversations toward nonfamily areas (Hirsch, 1981).

Thus, there is not just one kind of social network that can facilitate successful coping. Indeed, if we wish to identify different successful coping strategies, this discussion illustrates one method of doing so: studying individuals who are coping successfully but are in contrasting social networks. This method allows us to identify prototypes of successful coping strategies based on varied configurations of personal and environmental resources (Hirsch, 1981). Later in this chapter I elaborate on the potential benefits of such research for theory and practice. First, however, we must consider the implications of these studies for our understanding of how networks may relate to coping and mental health.

SOCIAL NETWORKS AS PERSONAL COMMUNITIES

We have seen that social networks — composed of family members and relatives, friends, work associates and professional colleagues, fellow PTA members, and so on — involve far more than the provision of narrow categories of "help." Instead, networks reflect the nature and value of our participation in the major life spheres. We must understand this broader linkage to explain how networks relate to coping and mental health. As a step in this direction, I propose a conceptualization of the social network as a personal community that embeds and supports critical social identities. Let me explain what I mean by this and explore how personal communities may relate to psychosocial well-being.

Achieving meaningful participation in one's culture and society is an important task confronting us throughout our lives. The nature of our participation can be suitably captured or characterized by our social identities. Each of the various life spheres — family, friends, vocational, moral/ethical, leisure, sexual, and so on — has its own set of possible identities, some of which overlap. These identities may include, for example, being a spouse, a lover, and a respected community leader, as well as being someone who is loved, cherished, and wise. Many identities evolve and change over the life-span. We may go from student to professional, protegé to mentor, Young Turk to Old Guard; and the meanings we attach to certain identities, such as masculine and feminine, youthful and mature, may differ over the life span as well. Social identities are thus related to roles and to role performances, as well as to other relevant aspects of the self-concept.

The viability of a social identity depends significantly on its recognition in the social network. To be wise or sexy, or to be a spouse, a social worker, or an expert tennis player, necessarily involves having certain kinds of interactions or relationships with others. Indeed, identities are often associated with a wide range of interpersonal activities. A union organizer, for example, interacts with the workers he or she is trying to organize, has dealings with other union or community figures, and discusses aspects of these activities with family members and friends. In this manner, social identities are recognized and supported by being embedded in relationships. Without sharing our activities with others, whether by word or deed, our identities would be tenuous and at times even illusory.

By expressing and embedding our social identities in a social network, we make our social network a personal community. These personal communities reflect our involvement in the major spheres of life, as well as the degree to and manner in which these spheres are integrated or segregated (see Craven and Wellman, 1973; Fischer et al., 1977; Henry, 1963). These personal communities also reflect our values and choices. In creating and maintaining a particular personal community, we are at least implicitly choosing, from among feasible alternatives, how we seek to achieve meaningful participation in our culture and society.

These considerations are especially salient during times of major life change. An attempt to build a new identity structure that better serves current or emerging developmental tasks may "require" a person to initiate events, as with the returning women students. When environmentally produced, as was the case with the widows, events can disrupt or shatter an existing satisfactory identity structure (see Brown and Harris, 1978). In either case, rebuilding a more satisfactory identity structure, and a personal community that supports it, is paramount. The criterion of satisfactoriness must be emphasized, for by definition everyone will have an identity structure and personal community of some sort.

What, then, determines the satisfactoriness of an identity structure and a personal community? As an initial step in answering this question, Levinson et al. (1978) have suggested that identities be considered satisfactory to the extent that they are personally valued and viable in the larger society. Both Levinson et al. (1978) and Erikson (1950) suggest that satisfactoriness must be considered within the appropriate developmental context as well. Furthermore, both these authors have argued for the importance of a repertoire of satisfactory social identities, as satisfactory identities need to be established in each of the major life spheres.

While this tentative formulation of satisfactoriness needs to be worked out in more detail, it has some important implications for our previous discussion. First, overinvestment in particular spheres to the neglect of others may have deleterious consequences, as seemed to be the case with several of the young widows, returning women students, and schizophrenics. Second, this formulation emphasizes the importance of a life-span approach to social networks. To achieve a repertoire of satisfactory social identities appropriate to each developmental stage, it seems necessary that a series of significant life changes take place periodically. For example, we typically move from being a student and a dating partner to entering an occupation and an intimate adult relationship. Thus, as new social identities need to be embedded and supported in network relationships, significant adjustments in one's personal community also appear periodically necessary. As we gain increased knowledge about development over the entire life span, we may discover that many such readjustments are necessary. These network changes may be elicited both by network events (e.g., children leaving home, death of spouse) and by nonnetwork events (e.g., reaching a final plateau in career advancement).

Social Networks and
Psychosocial Well-Being:
An Ecological Formulation

To analyze social networks, social identities, and life events in this manner is to study the ecology of human development (for descriptions of social ecology, see Bronfenbrenner, 1979; Kelly, 1979; Moos, 1976). It involves considering the reciprocal relations of individuals and their environments over time, how individuals make use of, cope with, adapt to, and modify environmental opportunities and environmental constraints (see Kelly, 1977; Mitchell and Trickett, 1980). Using the ecological concept of person-environment fit, let us delineate more systematically possible person-network outcomes of such efforts.

A healthy outcome consists of a social network that reflects and supports a repertoire of satisfactory social identities and, over time, provides opportunities for further development and enrichment. There is thus a good fit between the person and his or her social network relative to salient developmental tasks. This goodness of fit permits the individual to be integrated with and to participate actively in a viable segment of the larger culture and society.

Less healthy outcomes consist of either the lack of a sufficient repertoire of personally valued and developmentally appropriate identities, or their failure to find adequate expression and support in the social network. I will mention here only a few of the personal and environmental factors that can contribute to this outcome. On the environmental side of the equation, opportunities may be limited, as is certainly true for many segments of our society. Limited opportunities restrict the range of feasible alternatives from which satisfactory social identities and personal communities may be created (Fischer et al., 1977; Sarbin, 1970). For example, women may have difficulty establishing nonfamily involvements, given the low availability of jobs to displaced homemakers (Hirsch, 1981). The network may also have developed highly constricting norms and roles, impermeable to change (Hirsch, 1979); or, as Kapferer's (1969) analysis suggests, recognition for particular identities may be withheld because it threatens the (perceived) self-interest of network members. On the person side of the equation, individuals may lack the requisite personal or social competencies needed to capitalize on available opportunities (Heller, 1979); or they may have an illusory sense of their own identity, as was probably the case with Donald (in the Kapferer study), and only in a crisis come to realize the actual nature of their network relationships.

Network Paths to Identity
Recognition and Support

Given this overarching conceptualization, let us now consider more specifically how networks may provide recognition and support for social identities. This discussion is based primarily on additional data and clinical impressions gained from semistructured interviews with the young widows and returning women students. In that study, five potentially supportive interactions were assessed (see the list in Table 6.1). From analyzing these other data, I believe that we may delineate three alternative paths by which networks may recognize and support social identities. These paths are termed "explicit," "implicit," and "indirect." Each path is presented in turn.

EXPLICIT AND IMPLICIT PATHS

The most easily understood path by which networks may support identities is through explicit verbal acknowledgment or reinforcement. Identities here are clearly labeled and recognized, as in telling another that he or she is a "fine accountant," "terrific parent," or a "close friend."

Networks probably provide more frequent identity support via more subtle, implicit interactions. Two types of interactions within this category may be described. The first involves everyday, normal socializing with family and friends, as well as routine interactions with coworkers, fellow union or PTA members, and so on, that are directed to the usual concerns of individuals in those settings and positions. The second type of interaction involves "specific helping," such as the provision of cognitive guidance or tangible assistance relevant to some task. Meaningful everyday and specific helping interactions (i.e., without pretense) can provide support for one's identities insofar as such interaction *presumes* that one has a viable claim on the relevant role or identity. For example, others can talk to me in such a manner that it is clear that they consider me a good clinician or a close friend, and that they would not have interacted with me in such a manner had they not considered me to be such a person. These interactions may provide recognition and support for valued identities.

There appear to be a number of parameters governing the extent to which explicit or implicit interactions can provide identity support. We may hypothesize that a network interaction will provide support for a particular identity to the extent that the other is in a meaningful position to provide such acknowledgment; the other conveys this acknowledgment competently and sincerely (whether by word or deed); and the recipient is able to "hear" or recognize the (level of) acknowledgment without neurotic or other misunderstandings.

AN INDIRECT PATH

Network interactions that can provide either explicit or implicit identity support can, in addition, provide identity support indirectly via their impact on problem-solving efforts and efforts to maintain an adaptive emotional equilibrium under stress. For example, I may be having difficulty resolving a particularly thorny research or clinical problem. Some colleagues give me advice on how to proceed. From the manner of the interactions and the nature of their advice, I may receive implicit identity recognition: Those interactions would have taken place only if they considered me a competent professional. It may also be the case that they have given me very good advice which, when implemented, leads to a satisfactory resolution of the problem. This new therapeutic gain or research finding may, in turn, lead to an enhanced professional identity. Thus, the collegial interaction may lead to identity recognition and support via two different paths.

This indirect path is important because problems always arise in achieving and maintaining the work, family, leisure, and other objectives upon which social identities are largely based. It is necessary to resolve those problems in order to create and maintain a satisfactory identity structure and personal community. Network interactions that facilitate successful problem resolution therefore lead indirectly to identity recognition

Given the significance of problem-solving and maintaining an adaptive emotional equilibrium under stress in the coping process (see Coelho et al., 1974; Lazarus, 1980), I discuss below some ways in which network interactions can facilitate these aspects of coping. I limit myself to discussing some unexpected effects of everyday and specific helping interactions.

Everyday interactions, while often not explicitly focused on problem-solving, may nonetheless function to facilitate this activity. This is so because such interactions, particularly when experienced as especially enjoyable and rewarding, can serve to clarify and reinforce underlying values and life objectives. They can remind one of and bring to the fore the basic choices and issues involved in the situation. In Levinson et al.'s (1978) vocabulary, such experiences can highlight one's "dream" of the kind of life one desires. This may promote problem-solving by leading to a finer specification of the problem(s) at hand and by ruling out goals and tactics incompatible with these fundamental values. Such interactions can also emphasize the extent to which particular others can serve as resources for problem resolution. For example, I may now realize more fully how certain friends of mine share interests I am considering pursuing, and how enjoyable interactions with them in this area can be. This may lead to a reappraisal of the viability of a particular life change. I may also come to appreciate the concern they have about my welfare, and thus consider it appropriate to ask them for certain kinds of assistance.

While specific helping interactions may not be focused on providing emotional support, they may nonetheless function in such a manner. Several women described instances when a good suggestion or piece of advice, or the lending of a helping hand for household chores, perked up their spirits tremendously. These transactions provided reassurance that there was light at the end of the tunnel and that they did not have to go it alone.

FUTURE DIRECTIONS

I have sketched in this chapter the initial, broad contours of a model that seeks to relate social networks to coping and psychosocial well-being. The model conceives of social networks as personal communities and emphasizes their capability to embed a repertoire of satisfactory social identities over the life span. I presented this model in the hope that it might suggest previously unexplored possibilities of conceptualization and thereby aid in the design and interpretation of social network research. Others may wish merely to use this model as a basis for elaborating contrasting ones. In the words of the philosopher Abraham Kaplan (1964: 293), "The dangers are not in working with models but in working with too few, and those too much alike, and above all, in belittling any effort to work with anything else."

While this formulation of the model has been rather broad, its future specificity will depend in large measure on more carefully articulating criteria for a satisfactory repertoire of social identities at given stages of the life cycle. It will also be necessary to specify the scope (limiting) conditions under which such repertoires are hypothesized to have adaptive value. Social network research may well be able to contribute to achieving these objectives via the study of prototypical networks associated with successful adaptation. In this approach, successful adaptation would be defined initially according to nonnetwork criteria — e.g., scores on traditional measures of adjustment, as in the study of widows and returning women students. Since network relationships are behavioral measures of social identities, these prototypical networks would be expected to embed a repertoire of satisfactory social identities. By delineating the identity repertoires embedded in these networks, we might thus "bootstrap" (Cronbach and Meehl, 1955) our way from measures largely of symptomatology to positive criteria for and measures of satisfactory identity repertoires.

While I have focused my remarks in this chapter on research and conceptualization, there is clearly a great deal of interest in the implications of social network research for social-community interventions. This is an interest I have shared and sought to develop in my own work as a community and clinical psychologist. I will therefore conclude this chapter by briefly considering how this conceptualiztion of social networks may inform the design and evaluation of social-community interventions.

Given the integral relation between social identities and social networks, any intervention that increases opportunities or resources for creating satisfactory social identities can impact networks. These interventions include, for example, change efforts in existing settings or the creation of new settings that lead to more satisfactory roles or activities. Social policy changes, such as increased hiring of displaced homemakers, also represent important targets for efforts to increase available options for identity formation.

In the future, the impact interventions may have on the *repertoire* of social identities and the structural composition of the network needs to be more carefully considered and evaluated. Most interventions have hitherto been designed with only one sphere of life (e.g., work, neighborhood) as the explicit target. Significant changes in one sphere, however, may well affect other spheres, as well as the integration/segregation of the separate spheres. Even if our goals in a particular setting are reached, these "other" changes may not be as positive — or they may represent a substantial bonus!

Furthermore, as the dyadic and systemic structure of a network provides resources and constraints for the articulation of a satisfactory identity repertoire, we should also begin to include network changes as explicit targets of our intervention. At present, network workshops have emerged as the principal vehicle by which a network perspective has been communicated. These workshops focus on imparting skills in network analysis, and in linking multidimensional relationships, density, and so on, to participants' objectives regarding social identities, work/life segmentation, coping with stress, and the like (see Brennan, 1977; Gottlieb and Todd, 1979). Workshop participants have included the general public or more specialized groups, such as policy makers or staff in particular settings. From my own experiences in leading several such workshops, I believe there is much enthusiasm for acquiring these network competencies and much potential in this approach for aiding people in their efforts to create more satisfactory personal communities. Network interventions are still in an exploratory stage, though, as befits our current state of knowledge. These workshops need to be further developed and systematically evaluated. In particular, for maximum impact these workshops need to be integrated with other interventions designed to create increased resources for identity and network development. For example, in my own work I am exploring how this kind of network intervention may be incorporated with other social-community programs and policies in a long-term effort to reduce job burnout in a human service agency.

In our enthusiasm for exploring the potential of social network interventions, we should not overlook the critical importance of expanding our knowledge base. Both objectives may be furthered by conducting our interventions as action-research (see Rappaport, 1977). This action-research approach would be designed to transform knowledge about social networks into interventions to promote psychosocial well-being, and to evaluate such social action for the purpose of generating new knowledge about identity repertoires and personal communities. Such an approach seems best suited to enhance the development and vitality of the field.

REFERENCES

BARNES, J. A. Social networks. *Addison-Wesley Module in Anthropology,* 1972, *26,* 1-29.

BERKMAN, L., & SYME, S. Social Networks, host resistance and mortality: A nine-year followup study of Alameda County residents. *American Journal of Epidemiology,* 1979, *109,* 186-204.

BRENNAN, G. *Work/Life segmentation and human service professionals: A social network approach.* Unpublished doctoral dissertation, University of Massachusetts at Amherst, 1977.

BRONFENBRENNER, U. *The ecology of human development.* Cambridge, MA: Harvard University Press, 1979.

BROWN, G., & HARRIS, T. *Social origins of depression: A study of psychiatric disorder in women.* New York: Free Press, 1978.

COELHO, G., HAMBURG, D., & ADAMS, J. (Eds.). *Coping and adaptation.* New York: Basic Books, 1974.

COSER, R. L. The complexity of roles as a seedbed of individual autonomy. In L. A. Coser (Ed.), *The idea of social structure: Papers in honor of Robert K. Merton.* New York: Harcourt Brace Jovanovich, 1975.

CRAVEN, P., & WELLMAN, B. The network city. *Sociological Inquiry,* 1973, *43,* 57-88.

CRONBACH, L., & MEEHL, P. Construct validity in psychological tests. *Psychological Bulletin,* 1955, *52,* 281-302.

EATON, W. Life events, social supports and psychiatric symptoms: A re-analysis of the New Haven data. *Journal of Health and Social Behavior,* 1978, *19,* 230-234.

ERIKSON, E. *Childhood and society.* New York: Norton, 1950.

FISCHER, C., JACKSON, R., STUEVE, C., GERSON, K., & JONES, L., with BALDASSARE, M. *Networks and places: Social relations in the urban setting.* New York: Free Press, 1977.

GLIDEWELL, J. A social psychology of mental health. In S. Golann & C. Eisdorfer (Eds.), *Handbook of community mental health.* Englewood Cliffs, NJ: Prentice-Hall, 1972.

GOTTLIEB, B. H. *Social networks and social support in the design of preventive interventions.* Paper presented at the Symposium on Helping Networks and the Welfare State, University of Toronto, Toronto, May 1980.

GOTTLIEB, B. H., & TODD, D. Characterizing and promoting social support in natural settings. In R. Munoz, L. Snowden, & J. Kelly (Eds.), *Social and psychological research in community settings.* San Francisco: Jossey-Bass, 1979.

HELLER, K. The effects of social support: Prevention and treatment implications. In A. Goldstein & F. Kanfer (Eds.), *Maximizing treatment gains: Transfer enhancement in psychotherapy.* New York: Academic Press, 1979.

HENRY, J. *Culture against man.* New York: Random House, 1963.

HIRSCH, B. Psychological dimensions of social networks: A multimethod analysis. *American Journal of Community Psychology,* 1979, *7,* 263-277.

HIRSCH, B. Natural support systems and coping with major life changes. *American Journal of Community Psychology,* 1980, *8,* 159-172.

HIRSCH, B. Coping and adaptation in high-risk populations: Toward an integrative model. *Schizophrenia Bulletin,* 1981, *7,* 164-172.

KAPFERER, B. Norms and the manipulation of relationships in a work context. In J. C. Mitchell (Ed.), *Social networks in urban situations.* New York: Humanities Press, 1969.

KAPLAN, A. *The conduct of inquiry.* San Francisco: Chandler, 1964.

KELLY, J. *The ecology of social support systems: Footnotes to a theory.* Paper presented at the 85th Annual Meeting of the American Psychological Association, San Francisco, September 1977.

KELLY, J. (Ed.). *Adolescent boys in high school: A psychological study of coping and adaptation.* Hillsdale, NJ: Erlbaum, 1979.

LAING, R., & ESTERSON, A. *Sanity, madness and the family.* Baltimore: Penguin, 1964.

LAZARUS, R. The stress and coping paradigm. In C. Eisdorfer, D. Cohen, A. Kleinman, & P. Maxim (Eds.), *Theoretical bases for psychopathology.* New York: Spectrum, 1980.

LEVINSON, D., with C. DARROW, E. KLEIN, M. LEVINSON, & B. McKEE. *The seasons of a man's life.* New York: Random House, 1978.

LIDZ, T., FLECK, S., & CORNELISON, A. *Schizophrenia and the family.* New York: International Universities Press, 1965.

MITCHELL, J. C. (Ed.). *Social networks in urban situations.* New York: Humanities Press, 1969.

MITCHELL, J. C. Social networks. *Annual review of anthropology,* 1974, *3,* 279-300.

MITCHELL, R. E., & TRICKETT, E. J. Social networks as mediators of social support: An analysis of the effects and determinants of social networks. *Community Mental Health Journal,* 1980, *16,* 27-44.

MOOS, R. H. *The human context: Environmental determinants of behavior.* New York: John Wiley, 1976.

PARKES, C. M. Bereavement: A study of grief in adult life. London: Tavistock, 1972.

RAPPAPORT, J. *Community psychology: Values, research and action.* New York: Holt, Rinehart & Wilson, 1977.

SANDLER, I. Social support resources, stress, and maladjustment of poor children. *American Journal of Community Psychology,* 1980, *8,* 41-52.

SARBIN, T. A role-theory perspective for community psychology: The structure of social identity. In D. Adelson & B. Kalis (Eds.), *Community psychology and mental health: Perspectives and challenges.* Scranton, PA: Chandler, 1970.

SIEBER, S. Toward a theory of role accumulation. *American Sociological Review,* 1974, *39,* 567-578.

TOLSDORF, C. Social networks, support, and coping: An exploratory study. *Family Process,* 1976, *15,* 407-417.

WEISS, R. The provisions of social relationships. In Z. Rubin (Ed.), *Doing unto others.* Englewood Cliffs, NJ: Prentice-Hall, 1974.

WELLMAN, B. A guide to network analysis. Working Paper No. 1A, Structural Analysis Programme, Department of Sociology, University of Toronto. September 1980.

WHITTEN, N., & WOLFE, A. Network analysis. In J. Honigman (Ed.), *Handbook of social and cultural anthropology.* Skokie, IL: Rand McNally, 1973.

Chapter 7

APPLYING NETWORK ANALYSIS TO THE STUDY OF SUPPORT

BARRY WELLMAN

I have written this chapter to urge that we transmute support system analysis into social network analysis. Social network analysis has developed during the past twenty years from a sensitizing metaphor into a comprehensive paradigm. I believe that by using its concepts and techniques, we can transcend the biases and limitations of support system analysis and make our research into social support more powerful.

My first task is to summarize the development and current status of network analysis. I shall then discuss how it can inform the ways in which we formulate research questions, organize data collection, and employ analytic techniques in the study of support. My concrete examples will deal with three key analytic concerns: how we treat the content of ties, whether ties between two persons are considered to be egalitarian and symmetric, and how the structure of social networks can affect the availability of support. Finally, I will suggest some ways in which network analysis can help us to analyze the relationship of interpersonal support to large-scale social phenomena.

Author's Note: The preparation of this chapter has been supported by the Center for Studies of Metropolitan Problems, National Institute of Mental Health (Grant 1 RO1 MH32998-01A1), and the Centre for Urban and Community Studies and the Structural Analysis Programme of the University of Toronto. Several colleagues usefully commented on drafts of the chapter: Christina Black, Benjamin Gottlieb, Barton Hirsch, Leslie Howard, Nancy Howell, Judith Kjellberg, Edward Lee, and Beverly Wellman. Edward Lee assisted greatly in the East York structural analysis.

SUPPORT SYSTEMS

Support system studies have recently advanced community mental health research by demonstrating the importance of supportive interpersonal relations for health. Before the advent of support system research, social studies of health had largely been content to relate the aggregated personal attributes of individuals (e.g., socioeconomic status, ethnicity) to their symptoms and well-being. The result was a raft of sound, but conceptually limited, epidemiological surveys (e.g., Srole et al., 1975).

During the past decade, support system researchers successfully demonstrated that health is related, as well, to the availability of supportive ties: e.g., the number of ties in a social network, the frequency of contact with network members, and the differential presence of kin or friends in these networks. They have shown that such ties provide individuals with significant emotional aid, information, and material resources. Successful support systems seem to foster good health directly, encourage health-related behaviors, provide useful resources in stressful situations, and give participants helpful feedback for maintaining sound behavioral practices (Hammer, 1981).

The analyst's preoccupation with systems of supportive ties is understandable. It is, in part, an assertion of the health-care importance of such ties to epidemiologists accustomed only to think in terms of personal attributes. It is, in part, a reaction to the work of those family therapists who have emphasized the negative effects of kinship ties on mental health. Furthermore, a focus on supportive relations is certainly consistent with the therapeutic goals of health-care investigators.

Yet this focus on supportive ties has had contradictory results. On the one hand, it has been an important analytic step in showing how the nature of social networks is strongly linked to the experience of health and distress. On the other hand, it has weakened and distorted analysis of social support by oversimplifying the nature of ties and networks. This is because when we declare ahead of time that a set of ties constitutes a "support system," we assume in advance precisely that which we want to leave open for study. In order to study the conditions under which individuals do get support, we must allow for the possibility that many of their ties are not necessarily supportive (see also Gottlieb, Chapter 8 in this volume).

We all know intuitively that ties are not always supportive; that support is transmitted in variable, often ambiguous ways; that people often participate in several social networks in different spheres of their lives. However, the "support system" concept negates this sound intuitive knowledge of the complexities of ties and networks by denoting a single system composed only of supportive social relations. Its focus on a simple "support/nonsupport" dichotomy deemphasizes the multifaceted, often contradictory nature of social ties. Its assumption that supportive ties form a separate system isolates them from a person's overall network of interpersonal ties. Its assumption that all of these supportive ties are connected to each other in one integrated system goes against empirical reality and creates the dubious expectation that solidary systems are invariably more desirable. Its assumption that there are no conflicts of interest between "supporters" invokes the false premise of a common good.

To permit our research to catch up to our intuitive knowledge, we must adopt an analytic strategy that takes into account more fully the complexities of ties and networks. Fortunately the switch is simple in conception and sometimes in execution. It entails using a relatively new research strategy in the social sciences: social network analysis. A support system *is* a social network: a set of nodes (e.g., persons) connected by a set of ties (e.g., relations of emotional support). Yet a support system is an analytically constricted social network which only takes into account supportive ties and which assumes that these ties only can form a single, integrated structure.

A switch to a network analytic approach will help remove these constrictions and better enable us to study the complexities of ties and networks. Its concepts and techniques give network analysis several comparative advantages over support system analysis in the study of support:

- It opens up the consideration of supportive ties to anywhere in an individual's social network and does not assume that social support is only available from corporate groups, solidary groups, or specified social categories (e.g., kin).

- It encourages the analysis of supportive ties within the context of the broader range of interpersonal ties that constitute a social network.

- It relates variations in the content, strength, and symmetry of these ties to the availability of different sorts of resources to an individual.

- It provides concepts and techniques to describe the structural patterns of ties and to analyze the effects of different patterns on the flow of supportive resources to individuals.

- It permits the analysis of networks as complex, differentiated structures and not as uniform, unitary wholes, enabling the investigation of how the structure of both the overall social network and its component parts affect the flow of resources.

- It links the study of interpersonal ties to the study of large-scale phenomena, relating social support to the constraints imposed by such phenomena as bureaucratization and capitalism.

THE NATURE OF SOCIAL NETWORK ANALYSIS

The Early Formulation of the Social Network Concept

Social scientists have long used network concepts as partial, allusive descriptions of a social structure (see Radcliffe-Brown, 1940; Simmel, 1908). In the 1950s, anthropologists started developing network concepts more thoroughly in order to study ties that cut across the boundaries of institutionalized groups or social categories (see the reviews in Barnes, 1972; Mitchell, 1973; Wolfe, 1978). For example, Barnes (1954) used the network concept to describe fishing village groups that were organized across both kinship and social class boundaries.

Several scholars started using network concepts to study Third World migrants from rural areas to cities. These migrants were no longer members of their solidary village communities, and conventional modernization theory suggested that they would become rootless, anomic members of urban "mass society" (Kornhauser, 1968). Yet the migrants continued to maintain ties to their ancestral villages as well as forming new urban ties. Their complex social networks, composed of both rural and urban ties, aided them greatly in obtaining resources from the city and the village to cope with the demands of modern life (Mayer with Mayer, 1974; Mitchell, 1961). Scholars became increasingly aware of the advantages of the network approach for the study of how individuals functioned in more than one social world.

Anthropologists usually pay a good deal of attention to cultural systems of normative rights and duties that prescribe proper behavior within such bounded groups as tribes or villages. However, this sort of normative analysis is not easily applied to the study of ties which cut across group boundaries. To study these crosscutting ties, analysts began concentrating on the composition and structure of the networks they formed. They developed the initial sensitizing concept of "the social network" into a series of structural concepts such as *mutual ties* ("to discover how A, who is in touch with B and C, is affected by the relation between B and C. . . . demands the use of the network concept"; Barnes, 1972: 3) and *indirect ties* (A is linked to C through B).

Some anthropologists wondered about how differences in the structures of these networks might be related to social behavior. They, like many social scientists, were preoccupied with questions of social integration. Elizabeth Bott (1957) created the concept of *network density* to measure this by calculating the ratio of observed ties to all theoretically possible ties. She used network density to explain variations in marital role relationships when she could not relate these marital variations to differences in social class. When husbands and wives were involved in separate densely knit networks with their kinfolk, they tended to have more segregated marital relationships than couples who were involved in sparsely knit kin networks.

These studies established the social network concept, developed the practice of studying networks by measuring their structural properties, and produced insightful findings calling attention to the importance of networks in organizing social life. Yet many analysts were somewhat metaphorical in their use of network concepts. Many were content to demonstrate the importance of networks and describe the patterns of ties. They often treated ties as residual, forming only those ties that did not fit within bounded groups and categories. Their structural measurement was usually limited to network density.

Unfortunately, many support system studies refer only to this early work and do not seem aware of more recent network analytic developments. Some invoke "the social network" metaphor to refer to a vaguely defined set of supportive ties (Beels, 1979; Finlayson, 1976; Henderson, 1977; Silberfeld, 1978). To the extent to which these sorts of studies recognize network structure, they deal with it as network density (e.g., Speck and Attneave, 1973).

The Sociological Development of Network Analysis

Sociologists came to the study of networks with somewhat different agendas than did anthropologists (Berkowitz, forthcoming; Mullins, 1973; and Wellman, forthcoming give more detailed accounts). Following Simmel's early lead, they wanted to discover how the structural form of networks constrained individual behavior. Simmel had insisted, for example, that three-person interactions were inherently different from two-person interactions, because group pressure only begins to emerge among three persons. Steeped in American quantitative traditions, these sociologists sought to describe the structure of networks as precisely as possible. They gathered survey and observational data from a variety of settings. They developed "sociometric" techniques for graphically representing these patterns and matrix algebra techniques for finding densely knit clusters in populations.

This work evolved, in part, into the study of *personal networks:* networks of ties defined from the standpoint of a focal individual or, more commonly, a sample of focal individuals. Several urban sociologists, for example, argued that personal networks have supplanted local solidary communities as the principal source of interpersonal support, as the large-scale transformation of industrial social systems fostered the maintenance of far-flung, ramified, specialized interpersonal ties (Fischer, 1976; Wellman & Leighton, 1979).

The personal network approach became directly germane to the study of social support as it focused attention on how the composition, content, and configuration of ties affected the flow of resources to the focal individual. Studies of *personal communities* looked at how an individual's ties fit that person into larger social systems and provided resources for coping with its contingencies (e.g., Fischer et al., 1977; Wellman, 1979). *Search network* studies looked at how individuals mobilized their ties to acquire desired resources (e.g., Bernard & Killworth, 1978; Granovetter, 1974; Lee, 1969).

Rather than studying the effects of personal networks on focal individuals, other sociologists concentrated on studying *whole networks:* all ties of a certain sort among all members of a population. While whole network research is less directly germane than personal network research to the study of support, its concepts and techniques are most useful for describing the underlying structural patterns of a social system. For example, several researchers, dissatisfied with the fuzzy, individualistic probabilities of statistics, have intensively developed mathematical modeling techniques to describe network structures and their changes over time (see the review in Burt, 1980).

Many whole network researchers have been interested in how different structural forms connect or disconnect large-scale social systems. They argue that while densely knit, tightly bounded clusters strongly integrate an individual into a local social system, these clusters simultaneously fragment the large-scale system into a series of disconnected units (see Davis, 1967). Epidemiologists and communication scientists have examined a related problem: how structural form affects the flow of things such as disease and information through a population. They are finding that both tightly bounded clusters and people's biases about the kinds of persons with whom they form ties systematically affect the spread of such things (see Rapoport, 1979; Rogers, 1979).

Network Analyses of Political Processes

In a quite separate research tradition, social scientists used network analytic concepts to explain political processes. Although rarely using network terms or techniques, they have focused on how the pattern of ties in a social system asymmetrically allocates resources.

Some of these researchers have studied contentions for political power within states. In contrast to prevalent "relative deprivation" explanations of the rise of revolutionary movements (Davies, 1962), they emphasize the access of interest groups to resources, the extent to which contending groups mobilize, and the structural possibilities for coalitions and competitive relations (Oberschall, 1978; Tilly, 1979). Other researchers have used network concepts to explain the internal structure of a state in terms of transnational links of dependency between states or interest groups (Friedmann, forthcoming; Wallerstein, 1974). They have effectively argued that it has been such asymmetric relations that have caused Third World underdevelopment, and not backwardness within these states.

Thus all of these researchers argue that the behavior of a unit (be it state or interest group) is significantly structured by its ties with other units. They have shown that such ties are usually unequal bonds of power and dependency, and are rarely equal-status, friendship ties. Hence their work has significant import for the study of support. It demonstrates how network structures constrain the behavior of individual units, be they states or persons. It links political violence, often misattributed to psychological stress, to interpersonal and intergroup ties. It brings into stark relief the ways in which asymmetric ties and hierarchical networks can significantly channel the flow of resources to individuals and states.

Contemporary Network Analysis

The separate network-analytic research traditions have coalesced during the past ten years into a broadly based approach, more comprehensive in its ambitions (see Berkowitz, forthcoming; Wellman, forthcoming). Where early analyses had treated networks as just one among many forms of interpersonal social organization, analyses now treat all social structures as if they were networks. In these analyses, the network's nodes may be groups or organizations as well as persons, and the ties may be dependency relations or flows of resources as well as friendship or kinship ties. Large-scale social systems are considered to be a "network of networks" (Craven & Wellman, 1973).

Network analysts try to study social phenomena strictly in structural terms. They do this by first describing the regular network patterns that underlie the complex surface appearances of social systems, and then by studying how these patterns allocate scarce resources and constrain social behavior. Thus, the analyses focus on the ties between units in a social system and the patterns they form, rather than on the individual units themselves.

At present, sociological network analysis is evolving in two directions. The first is toward a broad "structuralism" that uses network analytic concepts and techniques to deal more powerfully with the same substantive research questions preoccupying most sociologists. The second is toward a more specialized "formalism" that concentrates on mathematically describing network patterns (see Holland & Leinhardt, 1979).

The logic of the network approach in both of these research directions has led analysts to question the categorical, normative, and individualistic assumptions common in other forms of sociological analysis. They have avoided categorical analyses that aggregate individual actors' attributes and internalized norms. Such analyses lump persons together into social categories (e.g., "low SES," "alienated") without directly taking into account their structured social relations. They have criticized normative analyses as nonstructural when they treat persons as individuals responding, compasslike, to internalized norms. Many have eschewed using individualistic statistical techniques that treat persons as independent, unstructured units of analysis. Consequently, network analysts are working now to develop new, relational ways of defining, describing, and analyzing structural data. Many are using graph theory or matrix algebra to describe and analyze structural patterns and their behavioral consequences (see Burt, 1980).

USING NETWORK ANALYSIS
TO STUDY SUPPORT

The development of network analysis is part of the great shift in the physical and social sciences from Aristotelian, categorical analysis to relational, structural analysis (see Bruner et al., 1956). In the study of mental health, support system analysis has been part of this same paradigm shift, moving from explaining distress solely as an individual failing to linking "individual difficulties with characteristics of the social system" (Bloom, 1979: 184). Yet support system research has made an incomplete shift when it looks only for supportive, well-integrated ties and fails to recognize the variegated, ramified ties that form most networks.

Network analysis can facilitate this paradigm shift by emphasizing the asymmetric, multifaceted nature of ties and the importance of structural patterns. By treating the content of these ties as flows of resources, it transforms the study of support into the study of supportive resources, and it links the allocation of these resources to large-scale social phenomena. Several analyses of support have already used such a network approach profitably (see Garrison, 1978; Gottlieb, Chapter 8 in this volume; Hammer, 1981; Hirsch, Chapter 6 in this volume; Ratcliffe, 1978, 1980; Tolsdorf, 1976; Unger & Powell, 1980). I shall use examples from such work and my own research in this section to illustrate some of the ways in which we can move from support system analysis to the study of complex ties and networks.

The Content of Ties

Support and Nonsupport. When one looks only for supportive ties, one finds only supportive ties. This introduces a double distortion. First, it distorts the content of ties by narrowing them to their supportive elements. Second, it distorts the structure of social networks by wrenching these ties out of the larger networks in which they are embedded and which give them meaning.

Yet several support system researchers have entangled themselves among such distorting mirrors. Some have treated all interpersonal ties found as supportive (e.g., Beels, 1979; Finlayson, 1976; Henderson, 1977; Pilisuk & Froland, 1978). It follows, then, that the greater the number of ties a person has, the greater the amount of support available. For example, Silberfeld (1978) counts the number of "close ties" in order to measure the "supports" available for persons experiencing psychological symptoms.

Some researchers deliberately concentrate on studying supportive ties, even while recognizing that other ties exist (see Gore, 1978). They believe that if one wants to study social support, one should look at social support. Fischer's research group, for example, is studying the availability of interpersonal assistance for a variety of contingencies (see Fischer, forthcoming; Jones & Fischer, 1978). Their research gives a clear indication of the kinds of persons and ties that are associated with various types of social support.

Yet by treating support as a variable that *may* occur, and not as a given, we gain more analytic power. We can analyze the circumstances under which a tie will or will not provide support: for example, how the transmission of support is related to the characteristics of individuals, the ties that link them, and the networks that contain these ties. We keep social support as the object of study, but use social networks as the subject of study.

Furthermore, by looking at a broad range of ties, we more accurately treat support as a contingency rather than a fixed relationship. We cannot freeze ties in aspic as supportive or nonsupportive, whatever cross-sectional slices we take of an individuals's life. The contents of ties change over time, as socially and physically mobile persons slough off old ties, gain new ones, and transform existing relationships (see Bell, 1968). New alliances emerge to cope with new contingencies (see Mayer, 1966). Indeed, the supportive ties in one social arena may be those from which a person needs support in another context: Many people turn to their kin as a haven from the marketplace and then turn to the marketplace as a haven from their kin (Howard, 1980). Thus, to look only at support is to underestimate the fluidity of all ties and their complex potential for support and desolation.

It is also clear that supportive ties do not come in separate packages but as parts of networks that also contain nonsupportive ties. The structure of these networks may well affect the quality and quantity of the supportive resources that a focal individual receives. Compare the two four-person networks in Figure 7.1, where A and B often provide support to Ego but C does not. The possibilities for coordinated assistance should be better in I because of the tie between A and B, while the tie between B and C in II may constrain the assistance that B gives to Ego. Yet networks such as II, linking supporters and nonsupporters, are common.

Voluntarism. When we look only at supportive ties, we are apt to make the unwarranted assumption that people only maintain ties because they enjoy their relationships and perceive the benefits to be gained through interaction with their opposite numbers. Evans and Northwood (1979) have formulated this voluntaristic assumption as "mutual aid investment theory" (see also Fischer et al.'s "choice-constraint model," 1977). They assert (1979: 789-790) that

> the mode of interaction [in "natural helping networks"] is egalitarian and reciprocal. . . . [Ties] progress from simple forms of communication and mistrust to security and consummation of relationships. There is a predictable process through which persons pass from pre-affiliation and power struggles to intimacy and role acceptance.

In practice, though, many ties are with persons whom one does not like and with whom one would not voluntarily form a twosome. Such ties are often neither egalitarian nor reciprocal. Nevertheless they are real and significant. They come as an involuntary part of the network membership package. They may be ties to persons with whom the participants have to deal seriously at work or in the neighborhood. They may be part of a solidary kinship group or friendship circle. Or they may be patron-client ties transmitting important resources in both directions. Such nonsupportive ties are often important in terms of the time spent on them, the resources that flow through them (whether the participants desire it or not), the ways in which they constrain other network members' activities, and the indirect access they may give to other, potentially supportive relationships.

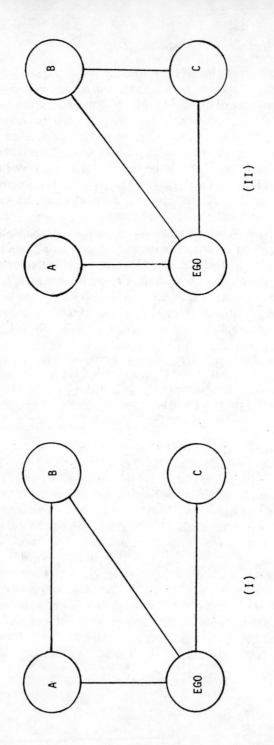

Figure 7.1 Structure and Support

SOURCE: Wellman, B., Black, C., & Lee, E. The East York study: Concepts and procedures. Paper presented at the Sunbelt Social Network conference, Tampa, 1981. Reprinted by permission of the authors.

Finding Social Networks. Many researchers have already taken steps to situate supportive ties within broader social networks by using research designs that gather information about ties defined initially by criteria *other than support.* For example, when our research group wanted to know about the availability of social support to 845 adult residents of East York (an area of metropolitan Toronto), we asked them "about the people outside your home that you feel closest to; these could be friends, neighbours or relatives" (Gillies, 1968). This approach enabled us to discover that only a minority of the close "intimate" ties of East Yorkers are supportive: 30 percent provide support in emergencies and 22 percent provide support in dealing with everyday matters (Wellman, 1979; see also the similar studies of Fischer et al., 1977; Laumann, 1973; Shulman, 1976). While the great majority of East Yorkers have help available from somewhere in their networks, most (86 percent) do not get help from the majority of their intimates. They were most likely to perceive these ties as supportive when the Alter was especially socially close and central in the network, when the tie was between parent and adult child, when both participants lived within metropolitan Toronto (although not necessarily in the same neighborhood), and when they maintained frequent in-person or telephone contact.

Such studies of a small number of intimates may distort information about the amount and nature of support available in a broader network. Most members of Western social systems appear to maintain about 20-50 significant ties and some sort of contact with approximately 1000-1500 persons (see Boissevain, 1974; Pool and Kochen, 1978). In order to study broader networks, my research group has recently reinterviewed a subsample (n = 34) of our original respondents. This time we asked them about all the significant persons with whom they were "in touch" (Leighton and Wellman, 1978); we have found that these networks usually comprise 16 to 35 persons.

Our interviews reveal that many of these ties are neutral, some are clearly harmful, and some are mixed (we are just beginning to analyze these data). East Yorkers often aid a network member without any expectation that this aid will be reciprocated. They do not sue for nonsupport. Instead, they limit the claims for assistance that they make on this relationship because the tie would likely disintegrate if they made the other's lack of helpfulness clear. Yet such nonsupportive ties have often lasted for many years at high levels of intimacy, forming integral parts of networks that, overall, provide substantial support.

Strands of Support. In addition to differentiating between support and nonsupport, we can get fuller and more precise information about the content of ties by treating support as a *set of variables*. Netwsork analysis suggests that ties can be "multiplex" or *multistranded;* i.e., more than one role relationship can link two persons, and more than one type of resource may flow between them (see Nadel, 1957). Each tie may contain a different package of such resources as emotional help, personal service, material assistance, financial aid, social brokerage, and empathetic understanding. Several investigators have developed schemes for recording the different kinds of support that may be present in a tie. Appendix 7.A shows our own recently developed scheme for recording the strands reported in our latest round of interviews (see also Gottlieb, 1978; Jones & Fischer, 1978; Shulman, 1972).

Unraveling the strands of ties can aid research into support in a number of ways. First, consider the "community question" underlying much support system debate. This is the question of how such large-scale social phenomena as bureaucratization, capitalism, industrialization, and urbanization have affected the nature of interpersonal ties (kinship, friendship, and so on) and the extent to which supportive resources are available through them (Wellman & Leighton, 1979). In one sense, the debate has been resolved, as it is clear that most people remain connected in supportive, personal communities. Yet this is just the first round of the debate, for we still must discover if large-scale social transformations have affected the amount and kinds of supportive resources flowing through these ties.

Second, we can determine the types of support that often occur together in a tie. It is possible, for example, that contemporary interpersonal ties are much more specialized in content than was heretofore the case, as a consequence of the move from solidary village life to differentiated urban life. Under such circumstances, are emotional assistance and material aid likely to come from the same or different relationships? Have parent-child bonds retained a broad range of content? We can search out the situations in which interpersonal ties are likely to be narrowly specialized ("single-stranded") or broadly holistic ("multistranded") in content.

Third, we can better relate supportive strands to other components of a tie. Appendix 7.A, for example, records a variety of strands, nonsupportive as well as supportive. While some strands such as sociability do not provide supportive resources directly, their existence affirms self-worth and continued network membership.

However, we are also finding nonsupportive, "structurally embed-ded" strands to be common: In such instances, two persons interact with one another only because the larger work or kinship structure requires it.

Fourth, we can focus on each strand as a tie in an analytically distinct network of, for example, emotional aid. Using this strategy, we might find that emotional-aid ties tend to be reciprocal and egalita-rian, while material-aid ties tend to be asymmetric and hierarchical. This sort of analysis fits nicely with interviewing techniques that ask respondents whom they turned to for assistance in a range of specified situations (e.g., Jones & Fischer, 1978).

We have deliberately asked respondents about significant ties in general, only later inquiring about what sorts of support each of these ties provides. We argue that despite the usefulness of decomposing overall ties into narrower strands, overall ties link persons and not specific strands. The link between Jack and Jill encompasses more than just help in carrying a pail of water, and the specific kind of help given should be interpreted in the context of their overall relationship. The strength and breadth of a tie, and the way in which the tie fits into a larger social network, all affect the flow of specific kinds of support. Indeed too narrow a focus on types of support may obscure the ways in which the strands of a tie can change to fit new situations. For example, many East Yorkers count on their ties to bring help in a wide range of situations without necessarily being able to predict just what these situations will be and what help they will require.

The Inequality of Ties

Strength. Ties vary not only in their content but also in the intensity with which they manifest that content; one tie may provide much more emotional support or financial aid than another. Yet many network and support system analyses have treated all ties as equal in strength, that is, as having the same amount of resources flowing through them. To some extent, this has been a deliberate simplifica-tion, as analysts focused on basic patterns of connectivity. However, some network analysts have recently begun to build information about the strength of ties into their analyses. Unfortunately, I do not know of any study that seriously attempts to measure the amount of supportive resources flowing through ties and strands. For example, in our current East York analyses, we just dichotomize each strand of support as either a "major" or "minor" transfer of resources.

We have done more work in relating the strength of other aspects of a tie to the sheer availability of support. Our research consistently finds that East Yorkers tend to get help from those "intimates" with whom they feel especially close and are in frequent contact. For example, 56 percent of the East Yorkers can get emergency help from their very closest relationships; however, only 16 percent can only get such help from their sixth closest relationships. The stronger the tie, the more likely it is to be supportive and the more assistance that flows through it (see also Wellman, 1979; Fischer, forthcoming).

Strength is not always a virtue in ties. While there is some evidence that stronger ties (however measured) provide more support, weaker ties often provide more diverse support because they access a greater number and variety of social circles. Strong ties link network members to persons of similar backgrounds who travel in the same social circles as they do, and the more ramified weak ties link them to other, dissimilar, social circles. Where close friends tend to hear about the same things at the same time, weaker ties are the source of novel news. Consequently, such weak ties can be unique channels to new, diverse sources of information, often proving more useful than strong ties in providing information about job openings, homes for sale and the like (Boorman, 1975; Gottlieb & Hall, 1980; Granovetter, 1973).

With their links to other social circles, such weak ties can also introduce an individual into these circles as social situations change. For example, movers to new jobs and homes often use such ties to gain an entree into their new surroundings. In such situations, the sponsoring weak ties may well turn into strong ones, and the social support in the relationship, originally limited to the provision of information, may become much more broadly based (see Roberts, 1973).

Symmetry. The strength and symmetry of ties are related. Once we start quantifying the strength of ties, then we can ask if the magnitude of this strength is equivalent in the opposite direction. Early network graphs usually represented ties as symmetric: A tie between A and B was assumed to be equivalent in both directions. Later representations only took simple asymmetry into account; they allowed asymmetric directionality to the ties on a graph. However, the more recent use of matrix representations of networks has encouraged greater awareness of asymmetry, as such matrices record ties from A to B and from B to A separately (see Figure 7.2).

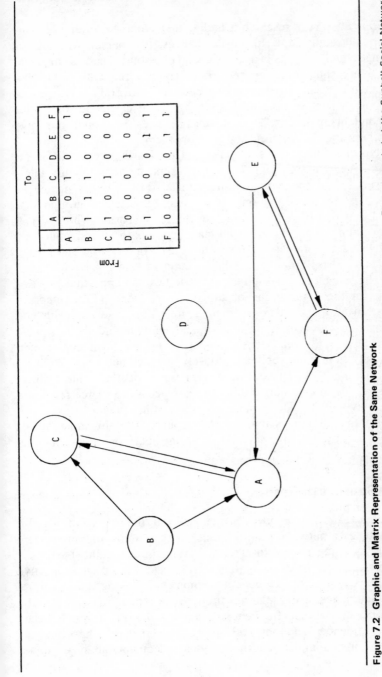

Figure 7.2 Graphic and Matrix Representation of the Same Network
SOURCE: Wellman, B., Black, C., & Lee, E. The East York study: Concepts and procedures. Paper presented at the Sunbelt Social Network conference, Tampa, 1981. Reprinted by permission of the authors.

Our East York research is finding that support is often not symmetrically equivalent. In most instances, two persons do not exchange equal amounts of a specific kind of resource, such as financial aid, over a short- or long-term period. There is frequently not even a symmetric balance between two persons in overall exchanges of support, when we take all kinds of assistance into account. Our respondents make careful distinctions between the support they give to others and the support they get from them.

Norman Shulman's study (1972, 1976) clearly reveals this asymmetry. After interviewing 71 East Yorkers, he subsequently interviewed 198 of the persons whom these East Yorkers named as intimates. He found that only 36 percent of this second group reciprocally named back as an intimate the EAst Yorker who had just named him or her. Their own intimate ties were to others, while they had weaker, asymmetric links to the East Yorkers who had named them (see also Bernard et al., 1981; Hammer, 1980).

The prevalence of such asymmetric ties has important implications for the organization of supportive networks. Contemporary Western interpersonal ties seem rarely to fit into densely knit clusters, permeated with symmetric support, and tightly bounded off from the external world. More often, asymmetric ties, varying in content and intensity, fit into unevenly knit, loosely bounded networks (Wellman & Leighton, 1979). These asymmetric ties link together in hierarchical networks with cumulative differences in access to scarce resources (see Davis, 1970). The result is often a stratified social system, with substantial differences in power and resources. Yet this same form of network structure also serves to give members ramifying, indirect connections to other social circles.

The Structure of Ties

Bundles and Structures. Structural form, the pattern of ties, differentiates a network from a bundle of ties. Some support system analyses disregard structural form, relating the availability of support to the characteristics of the ties themselves. They treat supportive relations as purely two-person phenomena, looking only at those characteristics of the relationship between a focal individual and a "supporter" as their frequency of contact, the travel time between their residences, and their kinship or friendship links. These analysts are making an implicit bet that they can adequately analyze supportive ties in structural isolation, without reference to the nature of other ties in the network or how they fit together (Berkman & Syme, 1979; Gore, 1978).

However, we are accumulating evidence that the structural form of networks does affect the flow of resources through specific ties. For instance, Carrington (1981) has related the structure of intercorporate ties to variations in corporate profit levels. Bott (1957), Hirsch (Chapter 6 in this volume), and Howard (1974) have all shown that the structure of personal networks substantially constrains the behavior of focal individuals. While it is becoming clear that networks are more than bundles of two-person exchanges, it is still much less clear as to which aspects of their structure are most significantly related to the availability of support.

Structure and Density. Studies of support most frequently take network structure into account by calculating the density of ties in a personal network. This is a useful first step. Density has a long history in the network analytic literature. It is easily computed. Most important, it is readily interpreted at high and low values: It is reasonable to assume that high-density networks are well-integrated, solidary groupings, while low-density networks are much more fragmented and uncoordinated.

However, researchers can get into serious trouble if they rely only on density to study network structure. First, density gives ambiguous intermediate-value results because several networks with the same value may have markedly different structural forms. This is because density, as a summary measure of overall network structure, can mask local inhomogeneities in such structures. Figure 7.3, for example, shows the comparative prevalence of fifteen different networks observed in our original East York study, all containing six nodes and five ties. Even when analyzing these small networks, we are finding it useful to supplement density with such other structural indicators as the number of clusters in a network and the extent to which it has a central figure.

The possibilities for structural complexity increase with larger network size. The networks we are now studying have about twenty-five members, creating possibilities for a great many structural forms. Ties are not distributed uniformly or randomly through these networks. Certain patterns recur: For instance, an East Yorker's network often contains three densely knit clusters of about five persons each, plus a scattering of weaker, more sparsely knit ties.

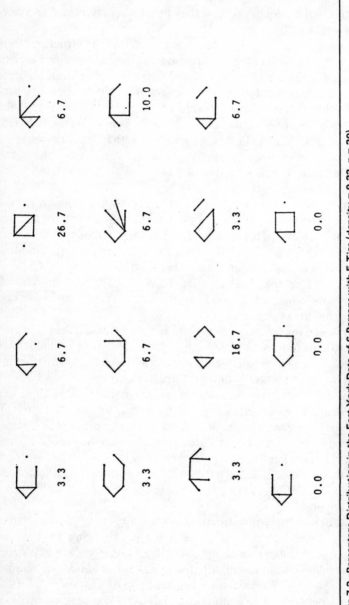

Figure 7.3 Percentage Distribution in the East York Data of 6 Persons with 5 Ties (density = 0.33, n = 30)

SOURCE: Wellman, B., Black, C., & Lee, E. The East York study: Concepts and procedures. Paper presented at the Sunbelt Social Network conference, Tampa, 1981. Reprinted by permission of the authors.

Second, excessive reliance on density often brings on an acute case of "pastoral syndrome," with analysts nostalgically comparing contemporary networks with the well-integrated, solidary networks supposedly prevalent in preindustrial communities (see Bender, 1978; White & White, 1962). Indeed, some "network therapists" make "retribalization" their structural goal (Speck & Attneave, 1973; Trimble, 1980). Such analyses evaluate the focal individual by the extent to which he or she is connected to "*the* social network": a single, solidary, bounded set of interpersonal ties. They unwittingly reproduce the same assumption that network analysts originally critiqued in anthropology — that a person can only be a member of a unitary, corporate group. Yet, only 12 percent of East Yorkers' six-person intimate networks are fully connected, with all intimately linked with all.

Density and Complexity. We need more differentiated conceptions of networks as well as of ties. The norm of a single, densely knit network has too often led analysts to treat complex, ramified networks as tattered residues of defunct solidarities. We do better when we remove the normative idealization of density and inquire into what effects different structural forms have on the availability of supportive resources to network members. The evidence shows that both densely knit and sparsely knit networks have their uses.

Densely knit, bounded, solidary networks seem to enhance the ability of the relatively powerless to conserve and control their existing internal resources; they mobilize help quickly throughout the network. The pervasive interconnections in such networks help members to maintain internal social control. "Urban villagers" (Gans, 1962) often look to such networks as "havens" (Lasch, 1977) against external demands. At the same time, their tight boundaries limit the ability of members to acquire additional external resources.

Sparsely knit, ramified, multiple networks are better structured to acquire additional external resources through direct and indirect ties. This kind of network is quite common in both developed countries (Fischer, 1976) and the Third World (Jacobson, 1973; Ross & Weisner, 1977). For instance, only one-third of an East Yorker's intimates are apt to be intimately tied to one another (Wellman, 1979). Such networks often contain a variegated repertoire of ties: friendship and kinship, local and long-distance, frequent and sporadic. The ramified ties connect network members to more and more diverse social circles, giving them access to a wide variety of resources. In matters of social support, members of such sparsely knit networks have freedom to maneuver and "shop" for appropriate help, at the cost of the sure, coordinated aid available through densely knit networks.

Studying Complex Networks. Network analysts have been developing methods to study such complex structures. We are *clustering* our East York networks, that is, sorting network members into discrete clusters within which there are relatively high densities of ties and across whose boundaries there are few ties (Everitt, 1980; while it would be intellectually desirable to allow individuals to be members of more than one cluster, this is much more difficult to compute). Note that clustering procedures group persons empirically, based on the observed patterns of ties. This avoids the distortions involved in assuming beforehand that kin form one cluster, friends another, and so on. Computer programs for clustering are quite abundant; one is even available in the standard statistical package, SAS.

Clustering has two uses in our study of support. First, it enables us to analyze network members within the social context of those persons with whom they are actually linked. We can discover, for example, whether those persons upon whom an individual relies for emotional support come from the same clusters, whether clusters tend to be homogeneously full of social support or lacking in support, and whether the availability of support is associated with membership in a densely knit cluster or in a cluster predominantly composed of kin. Thus clustering enables the researcher to analyze supportive ties within the broader context of the social networks in which they are embedded.

The second use of clustering is in enhancing our ability to understand the network as a social system. We will be able to examine closely the kinds of groupings that occur among network members and to see how densely knit clusters and more sparsely knit webs fit together and transfer resources.

Blockmodeling is a quite different approach toward describing networks as social systems. Where clustering groups individuals who have many ties among each other and few other ties, blockmodeling groups individuals who are "structurally equivalent" because of their "similarity in ties to third parties rather than by choices of one another" (White et al., 1976: 736; see also Levine & Mullins, 1978; Light & Mullins, 1979). Those in the same block may have no ties to each other, but they all have similar types of ties to others. Better suited to studying whole networks than personal networks, blockmodeling can help us to discover role structures empirically. It can help us discern whether there are regular patterns to supportive ties, and the manner in which supportive resources flow through networks.

Many other methods of studying network patterns are now available (for further leads, see Burt, 1980; Wellman, forthcoming). Measures of *centrality* can identify the extent to which any one person structurally controls the flow of supportive resources through a network (Freeman, 1979). Through their use, the researcher can see whether decentralized or centralized networks better facilitate the flow of supportive resources, or whether certain types of persons (e.g., high-status friends) disproportionately occupy central, dominant positions in personal networks. Studies of *biased networks* can show which sorts of persons are especially likely to form ties and can demonstrate the implications of these biases for the flows of resources through the network (Rapoport, 1979; Taylor & Coleman, 1979).

Transitivity studies indicate the likelihood of triadic clusters to form from two-person ties (Davis, 1979), and how the presence of a third party affects interactions between two persons (Chase, 1980). These and other methods can help make complex networks comprehensible and further enable us to learn how the structural form of ties affects the availability of support to individuals.

BEYOND INTERPERSONAL NETWORKS

I have argues in this chapter for going beyond support systems in order to study support. I have urged a social network approach that, by better comprehending the complexities of ties and networks, would facilitate the study of the circumstances under which focal individuals get support.

I have confined my remarks to interpersonal networks. While we must draw analytic boundaries somewhere, there are dangers in studying interpersonal networks in isolation, as if they are the only relevant social phenomena. We must also realize that such networks are really systems that transport resources to and from individuals, and that the structure of large-scale social systems largely determines the allocation of these resources.

For example, the contemporary social and spatial division of labor — heavily bureaucratic, capitalistic, industrialized, and urbanized — greatly constrains the kinds of networks we form and maintain. Our kin, workmates, neighbors, and friends are often different persons in different network clusters, whatever our wishes might be for holistic, solidary communities. Hence, searches for solidary communities as therapeutically supportive solutions are usually structurally unsustainable.

Indeed, the large-scale nature of our social system means that much social support is intercorporate rather than interpersonal. Corporate entities operate much of the social reproduction business: food, clothing, housing, education, and emotions. Relations among mental health agencies greatly determine the quantity and quality of supportive assistance that referred clients receive (Howard et al., 1979). Personal networks spend much time helping an individual deal with corporate bureaucracies as well as directly providing assistance. Instead of actually feeding or healing their friends, habitués of Tally's Corner work hard to get them food vouchers and connections with a proper clinic (Collins & Pancoast, 1976; Liebow, 1967; Stack, 1974).

This McDonaldization of life, an increasing reliance on corporate resources for reproduction, has important implications for our thinking about social support. People need "brokers" as much as "supporters." The quantity and intensity of ties may matter less than the structure. The densely knit, tightly bounded networks of Boston's Italian American "urban villagers" gave them marvelous interpersonal support, but little means of forming external alliances to stop urban renewal (Gans, 1962; Granovetter, 1973). More ramified networks, on the other hand, might have provided useful connections to deal with bureaucratic pressures.

To date, many support system analyses have been context-free, not taking large-scale phenomena into account. Many neither mention the cities in which their studies were done nor the social classes to which their respondents belong. Yet the analysis of interpersonal support means little unless we are aware of the large-scale pressures that cause the burdens for which individuals need support and the differential distribution of resources upon which they can draw. Further development of the network-analytic approach, from the perspective of the asymmetrically structured allocation of resources, may provide one means of linking such large-scale phenomena to the study of support.

Appendix 7.A
Interactional Strands Used in
East York Analysis

SUPPORT STRANDS

(Each is recorded from Ego to Alter, and from Alter to Ego.)

Doing Things

- Gave help with small household jobs (such as minor repairs to house, car, cottage; small amount of help with housework).

- Did other small services (such as driving person to doctor, occasional child care, errands).

- Gave help with big household chores (such as major repairs, regular help with housework).

- Did big service that took a lot of time or effort (such as regular day care, looking after a sick person for a long time).

- Helped out in dealing with organizations, agencies, the government (such as helping with an application for government benefits).

Giving and Lending Things

- Gave or loaned household items (such as food, tools, washing machine, lawn mower).

- Gave or loaned small amount of money.

- Gave or loaned money for a mortgage, down payment, large home improvement.

- Gave or loaned large amount of money (but not for a mortgage or down payment).

SOURCE: Wellman, B., et al., East York interview codebook. Resource paper, Centre for Urban and Community Studies, University of Toronto, 1981. Reprinted by permission of the authors.

Help with Personal Problems

- Gave advice about getting along with family members (such as marriage problems, raising children).

- Gave other emotional support during routine or minor upset.

- Gave emotional support during major crisis or long-lasting problem.

Information Help

- Gave information about possible job openings, promotions for other person.

- Made important job contact for other person (such as telling an employer about him/her).

- Gave information about house or apartment for rent or sale.

OTHER STRANDS

(These are coded symmetrically in terms of strength of strand.)

- informal shared activities

- formal group shared activities

- shared values and interests

- sexual interaction

- sociability (consummatory, nonsexual enjoyment of one another)

- structural embeddedness (interaction with other because larger structure obligates it; e.g., work, kin group, friendship circle)

REFERENCES

BARNES, J. A. Class and committees in a Norwegian island parish. *Human Relations*, 1954, 7, 39-58.

BARNES, J. A. *Social networks*. Reading, MA: Addison-Wesley, 1972.

BEELS, C. C. Social networks and schizophrenia. *Psychiatric Quarterly*, 1979, *51*, 209-215.

BELL, C. *Middle-class families*. London: Routledge & Kegan Paul, 1968.

BENDER, T. *Community and social change in America*. New Brunswick, NJ: Rutgers University Press, 1978.

BERKMAN, L. F., & SYME, S. L. Social networks, host resistance, and mortality. *American Journal of Epidemiology*, 1979, *109*, 186-204.

BERKOWITZ, S. D. *An introduction to structural analysis*. Toronto: Butterworths, forthcoming.

BERNARD, H. R., & KILLWORTH, P. A review of the small world literature. *Connections*, 1978, *2*, 15-24.

BERNARD, H. R., KILLWORTH, P., & SAILER, L. Research on informant accuracy in network data, and on the small world problem. *Connections*, 1981, *4*, 2.

BLOOM, B. Prevention of mental disorders: Recent advances in theory and practice. *Community Mental Health Journal*, 1979, *15*, 179-191.

BOISSEVAIN, J. F. *Friends of friends*. Oxford: Blackwell, 1974.

BOORMAN, S. A. A combinatorial optimization model for transmission of job information through contact networks. *Bell Journal of Economics*, 1975, *6*, 216-249.

BOTT, E. *Family and social network*. London: Tavistock, 1957.

BRUNER, J. S., GOODNOW, J. J., & AUSTIN, G. A. *A study of thinking*. New York: John Wiley.

BURT, R. Models of network structure. *Annual Review of Sociology*, 1980, *6*, 79-141.

CARRINGTON, P. *Horizontal co-optation through corporate interlocks*. Ph.D. dissertation, University of Toronto, 1981.

CHASE, I. Social process and hierarchy formation in small groups. *American Sociological Review*, 1980, *45*, 905-924.

COLLINS, A. H., & PANCOAST, D. L. *Natural helping networks*. Washington: National Association of Social Workers, 1976.

CRAVEN, P., & WELLMAN, B. The network city. *Sociological Inquiry*, 1973, *43*, 57-88.

DAVIES, J. C. Toward a theory of revolution. *American Sociological Review*, 1962, *27*, 5-19.

DAVIS, J. A. Clustering and structural balance in graphs. *Human Relations*, 1967, *20*, 181-187.

DAVIS, J. A. Clustering and hierarchy in interpersonal relations. *American Sociological Review*, 1970, *35*, 843-852.

DAVIS, J. A. The Davis/Holland/Leinhardt studies. In P. W. Holland & S. Leinhardt (Eds.), *Perspectives on social network research*. New York: Academic Press, 1979.

EVANS, R. L., & NORTHWOOD, L. K. The utility of natural help relationships. *Social Science and Medicine*, 1979, *13A*, 789-795.

EVERITT, B. Cluster analysis. *Quality and Quantity*, 1980, *14*, 75-100.

FINLAYSON, A. Social networks as coping resources. *Social Science and Medicine*, 1976, *10*, 97-103.

FISCHER, C. S. *The urban experience*. New York: Harcourt Brace Jovanovich, 1976.

FISCHER, C. S. *Little worlds*. Chicago: University of Chicago Press, forthcoming.

FISCHER, C.S., JACKSON, R.M., STEUVE, C.A., GERSON, K., JONES, L.M., with BALDASSARE, M. *Networks and places.* New York: Free Press, 1977.

FREEMAN, L.C. Centrality in social networks. *Social Networks,* 1979, *1*, 215-239.

FRIEDMANN, H. The political economy of food. *American Journal of Sociology,* forthcoming.

GANS, H. *The urban villagers.* New York: Free Press, 1962.

GARRISON, V. Support systems of schizophrenic and nonschizophrenic Puerto Rican migrant women in New York City. *Schizophrenia Bulletin,* 1978, *4,* 561-596.

GILLIES, M. *The construction and content of a questionnaire for the 1968 Yorklea Study Social Environment Survey.* Unpublished paper, Community Studies Section, Clarke Institute of Psychiatry, 1968.

GORE, S. The effect of social support in moderating the health consequences of unemployment. *Journal of Health and Social Behavior,* 1978, *19,* 157-165.

GOTTLIEB, B.H. The development and application of a classification scheme of informal helping behaviours. *Canadian Journal of Behavioral Science,* 1978, *10,* 105-115.

GOTTLIEB, B.H., & HALL, A. Social networks and the utilization of preventive mental health services. In R. Price, R. Ketterer, B. Bader, & J. Monahan (Eds.), *Prevention in mental health.* Beverly Hills, CA: Sage Publications, 1980.

GRANOVETTER, M. The strength of weak ties. *American Journal of Sociology,* 1973, *78,* 1360-1380.

GRANOVETTER, M. *Getting a job.* Cambridge, MA: Harvard University Press, 1974.

HAMMER, M. Reply to Killworth and Bernard. *Connections,* 1980, *3,* 14-15.

HAMMER, M. *Impact of social networks on health and disease.* Paper presented at the meeting of the American Association for the Advancement of Science, Toronto, January 1981.

HENDERSON, S. The social network, support and neurosis. *British Journal of Psychiatry,* 1977, *131,* 185-191.

HOLLAND, P.W., & LEINHARDT, S. (Eds.). *Perspectives on social network research.* New York: Academic Press, 1979.

HOWARD, L. *Industrialization and community in Chotangapur.* Ph.D. dissertation, Harvard University, 1974.

HOWARD, L. Personal communication, November 1980.

HOWARD, L., ROSES, S., WAXLER, N., & WELSH, J. *Environmental constraints, occupational conflict, and patient definitions in three psychiatric settings.* Paper presented at the meeting of the Canadian Sociology and Anthropology Association, Saskatoon, June 1979.

JACOBSON, D. *Itinerant townsmen.* Menlo Park, CA: Cummings, 1973.

JONES, L.M., & FISCHER, C.S. *Studying egocentric networks by mass survey.* Working paper No. 284, Institute of Urban and Regional Development, University of California, Berkeley, January 1978.

KORNHAUSER, W. Mass society. *International Encyclopedia of the Social Sciences,* 1968, *10,* 58-64.

LASCH, C. *Haven in a heartless world.* New York: Basic Books, 1977.

LAUMANN, E.O. *Bonds of pluralism.* New York: John Wiley, 1973.

LEE (HOWELL), N. *The search for an abortionist*. Chicago: University of Chicago Press, 1969.

LEIGHTON, B., & WELLMAN, B. *Interview schedule/aide-mémoire: East York Social Networks Project – Phase IV*. Resource paper, Centre for Urban and Community Studies, University of Toronto, 1978.

LEVINE, J. H., & MULLINS, N. C. Structuralist analysis of data in sociology. *Connections*, 1978, *1*, 16-23.

LIEBOW, E. *Tally's Corner*. Boston: Little, Brown, 1967.

LIGHT, J. M., & MULLINS, N. C. A primer on blockmodeling procedure. In P. W. Holland and S. Leinhardt (Eds.), *Perspectives on social network research*. New York: Academic Press, 1979.

MAYER, A. The significance of quasi-groups in the study of complex societies. In M. Banton (Ed.), *The social anthropology of complex societies*. London: Tavistock, 1966.

MAYER, P., with MAYER, I. *Townsmen or tribesmen* (2nd ed.). Capetown: Oxford University Press, 1974.

MITCHELL, J. C. The causes of labour migration. In *Migrant labour in Africa south of the Sahara*. Abidjan: Commission for Technical Cooperation in Africa South of the Sahara, 1961.

MITCHELL, J. C. Networks, norms and institutions. In J. Boissevain & J. C. Mitchell (Eds.), *Network analysis: Studies in human interaction*. The Hague: Mouton, 1973.

MULLINS, N. *Theories and theory groups in contemporary American sociology*. New York: Harper & Row, 1973.

NADEL, S. F. *The theory of social structure*. London: Cohen & West, 1957.

OBERSCHALL, A. Theories of social conflict. *Annual Review of Sociology*, 1978, *4*, 291-315.

PILISUK, M., & FROLAND, C. Kinship, social networks, social support and health. *Social Science and Medicine*, 1978, *12B*, 273-280.

POOL, I., & KOCHEN, M. Contacts and influence. *Social Networks*, 1978, *1*, 5-51.

RADCLIFFE-BROWN, A. R. On social structure. *Journal of the Royal Anthropological Society of Great Britain and Ireland*, 1940, *70*, 1-12.

RAPOPORT, A. Some problems relating to randomly constructed biased networks, In P. W. Holland & S. Leinhardt (Eds.), *Perspectives on social network research*. New York: Academic Press, 1979.

RATCLIFFE, W. D. Social networks and health. *Connections*, 1978, *1*, 25-37.

RATCLIFFE, W. D. Social networks and health: A bibliographic update. *Connections*, 1980, *3*, 15-16.

ROBERTS, B. R. *Organizing strangers*. Austin: University of Texas Press, 1973.

ROGERS, E. M. Network analysis of the diffusion of innovations. In P. W. Holland & S. Leinhardt (Eds.), *Perspectives on social network research*. New York: Academic Press, 1979.

ROSS, M. H., & WEISNER, T. S. The rural-urban migrant network in Kenya. *American Ethnologist*, 1977, *4*, 359-375.

SHULMAN, N. *Urban social networks*. Ph. D. dissertation, University of Toronto, 1972.

SHULMAN, N. Network analysis: A new addition to an old bag of tricks. Acta Sociologica, 1976, *19*, 207-323.

SILBERFELD, M. Psychological symptoms and social supports. *Social Psychiatry,*
      1978, *13,* 11-17.
SIMMEL, G. Group expansion and the development of individuality. In D. Levine
      (Ed.) and P. Albares (Tr.), *Georg Simmel on individuality and social forms.*
      Chicago: University of Chicago Press, 1908 [1971].
SPECK, R. V., & ATTNEAVE, C. L. *Family networks.* New York: Pantheon, 1973.
SROLE, L., LANGNER, T. S., MICHAEL, S. T., KIRKPATRICK, P., OPLER,
      M. K., & RENNIE, T. A. C. *Mental health in the metropolis,* 2 vols. (rev. &
      enlarged ed.). New York: Harper & Row, 1975.
STACK, C. B. *All our kin.* New York: Harper & Row, 1974.
TAYLOR, D. G., & COLEMAN, J. S. Equilibrating processes in social networks,
      In P. W. Holland & S. Leinhardt (Eds.), *Perspectives on social network research.*
      New York: Academic Press, 1979.
TILLY, C. Collective violence in European perspective. In H. D. Graham &
      T. R. Gurr (Eds.), *Violence in America; Historical and Comparative Perspectives*
      (rev. ed.). Beverly Hills, CA: Sage Publications, 1979.
TOLSDORF, C. C. Social networks, support, and coping. *Family Process,* 1976, *15,*
      407-417.
TRIMBLE, D. A guide to the network therapies. *Connections,* 1980, *3,* 9-21.
UNGER, D., & POWELL, D. R. Supporting families under stress. *Family Rela-
      tions,* 1980, *29,* 566-574.
WALLERSTEIN, I. *The modern world-system.* New York: Academic Press, 1974.
WELLMAN, B. The community question. *American Journal of Sociology,* 1979, *84,*
      1201-1231.
WELLMAN, B. Network analysis: From method and metaphor to theory and
      substance. *Sociological Theory,* forthcoming.
WELLMAN, B., BILLINGSLEY, B., BLACK, C., KIRSCH, S., & LEE, E. *East
      York interview codebook.* Resource paper, Centre for Urban and Community
      Studies, University of Toronto, February 1981.
WELLMAN, B., BLACK, C., & LEE, E. *The East York study: Concepts and
      procedures.* Paper presented at the Sunbelt Social Network Conference, Tampa,
      February 1981.
WELLMAN, B., & LEIGHTON, B. Networks, neighborhoods and communities.
      Urban Affairs Quarterly, 1979, *15,* 363-390.
WHITE, H. C., BOORMAN, S. A., & BREIGER, L. Social structure from multi-
      ple networks: I. Blockmodels of roles and positions. *American Journal of
      Sociology,* 1976, *81,* 730-780.
WHITE, M., & WHITE, L. *The intellectuals versus the city.* Cambridge, MA:
      Harvard University Press, 1962.
WOLFE, A. The rise of network thinking in anthropology. *Social Networks,* 1978, *1,*
      53-64.

Chapter 8

PREVENTIVE INTERVENTIONS INVOLVING SOCIAL NETWORKS AND SOCIAL SUPPORT

BENJAMIN H. GOTTLIEB

Much of what we now know about the nature and effects of social support is an extension of the ideas which the late epidemiologist, John Cassel, advanced in 1974 in a keystone paper entitled "Psychosocial Processes and 'Stress': Theoretical Formulations." Recent studies have lent further support to his proposition that some deficiency in people's primary-group ties is associated with increased vulnerability to disease, both medical and psychiatric (Brown et al., 1975; Hammer et al., 1978; Henderson, 1977; Tolsdorf, 1976), and several investigations have illuminated the nature of those psychosocial processes that Cassel classified as health-protective in their effects (Gottlieb, 1978; Weiss, 1974). However, while we can now speak with greater confidence about the empirical relations between stress and support, and despite the greater precision we can bring to our

Author's Note: This chapter is a refined and elaborated version of a paper presented at the symposium, "Helping Networks and the Welfare State," in May 1980. The symposium was organized by the University of Toronto Faculty of Social Work, Toronto, Ontario.

measurement of social support, we have not progressed very far toward the goal of bending our new knowledge to the purpose of designing health promotion programs in the community. We have tended to neglect Cassel's (1974: 480) injunction to find ways of "identifying families and groups at high risk by virtue of their lack of fit with their social milieu and determining the particular nature and form of the social supports that can and should be strengthened if such people are to be protected from disease outcomes."

Some might argue that this is as it should be; basic research should precede and inform action, especially where that action involves efforts to restructure the social world people inhabit or to alter fundamental social processes. On the other hand, there are those who believe that action research, in the form of carefully planned and controlled social experiments and demonstration projects, yields a very different order of knowledge, one that can inform theory while also answering practical questions concerning, for example, the characteristics of those who benefit most and least from the program, the untoward side effects of the program, the effects of the program's setting, and the effects produced by different levels of exposure to the intervention. These latter questions are certainly among those being asked by community mental health workers who are eager to know whether and how current work on the topic of support systems and social networks can be translated into concrete preventive strategies within the catchment areas they serve.

Hence, my purpose in this chapter is to review several action-research studies that have attempted to mobilize social support on behalf of contrasting groups. I have organized these planned interventions into two major classes based on the distinction between studies that have concerned themselves with the *quality of support* available to people and those concerned with providing people with *access to meaningful social ties*. Equally important, this chapter offers a critique of these interventions and, in so doing, draws extensively on social network analysis. Since network analysis is a relatively new approach to the study of social support, I will briefly review it and point out its advantages over other approaches that have been used to date. Throughout this chapter, my purpose is to consolidate existing knowledge and to propose directions for future action research and interventions involving the mobilization of social support for health protection.

THE SOCIAL NETWORK APPROACH:
SOCIAL CONNECTEDNESS AND HEALTH

The social network is a unit of social structure that includes all of an individual's social contacts. The network can be studied from the point of view of a single member or it can be studied as a whole. Its composition can be broken down in a number of ways, based on formal sociological classifications (such as nuclear family, extended family, and peers), based on psychological dichotomies (such as intimate versus casual ties), or based on the settings from which ties originate (such as neighbors, workmates, domestic relations, voluntary associations, and the community's health, welfare, and educational institutions). Any given network can, in addition, be analyzed in terms of such structural features as size, density, clustering, and dispersion. When the individual is the focus of analysis, the character of his or her linkages to others can be specified along such dimensions as the frequency, intensity, duration, and source of the tie; the "multiplexity" of the tie, a term that refers to the number of different role relations subsumed by the tie (e.g., a tie to a brother-in-law who is also a business partner, a neighbor, and a close friend); and the symmetry (sometimes referred to as reciprocity) of the tie, which refers to the extent to which resources are equally exchanged between the partners.

By way of illustration, these network dimensions have been invoked by Hammer et al. (1978: 535) to characterize the social world in which persons diagnosed as schizophrenic participate. The composite picture they present, based on their review of several network studies, reveals that

> the networks of schizophrenic individuals tend to be smaller than those of normal individuals, particularly with respect to both number and proportion of non-kin connections. The non-kin subsets in these networks are internally less interconnected than in normal networks and they seem to have fewer connections with the kin clusters. Schizophrenic individuals also tend to have more asymmetric and fewer multiplex relationships than nonpsychotic controls.

The link between this sort of network analysis and the topic of social support is that networks may be structured in such a way as to leave individuals with many or few channels of communication, and with a large or small fund of social resources that can be mobilized in the coping process. Network analysts maintain that the structure of the social environment can be shown to affect people's access to the sort of ongoing feedback and guidance needed in everyday life.

Social network analysis thus represents the most complex of three avenues investigators have explored in their search to identify the social conditions associated with healthy human functioning. The other two approaches eschew detailed analysis of the social ecology in which the individual is embedded, preferring instead to mark social support in terms of simple measures of social integration or in terms of indexes of access to intimate, confiding relationships. I will provide one example of research that epitomizes each of the latter two approaches to operationalizing the social support construct. I will also argue that both of these approaches yield little useful information about social support; at most, they have generated hypotheses that can best be examined through the use of network analysis.

A recent epidemiological study by Berkman and Syme (1979) provides a classic illustration of the kind of knowledge the social integration approach to the study of social support can provide. It serves equally well as an example of the limits of this approach. In that study, the age-adjusted mortality rates of a stratified random sample of Alameda County residents were collected over a period of nine years, and were then examined in relation to a set of items, originally collected from this sample, that inquired about the amount of social contact in their lives. Specifically, respondents were originally surveyed about members' marital status, about their extent of contact with close friends and relatives (later partitioned into three levels of contact), whether they participated in both formal and informal group associations, and whether they belonged to a religious congregation. The researchers created a "social network index" by aggregating these data and found that, for every age group and for both sexes, people with the lowest level of social contact had mortality rates from 2 to 4.5 times greater than those with many social contacts. Furthermore, this index continued to predict mortality even when statistical controls were introduced for the initial state of health of the respondents, their socioeconomic level, their use of health practices known to increase risk status, and their use of preventive health services. In short, this study and others that adopt equally molar measures of social embeddedness (Myers et al., 1975; Lin et al.,

1979) document the proposition that "social factors" are capable of altering health states. While this is important information, providing support for Cassel's (1974) hypothesis that social contact is capable of moderating stress, these data tell us nothing about the number and kind of social contacts associated with low-risk status, or about the interpersonal processes that may lie at the heart of social support. Certainly, these data provide none of the details necessary to inform the design of preventive programs involving the mobilization of social support, but they do suggest a series of hypotheses that might be investigated through the sort of detailed research on the organization of the social environment being undertaken by network analysts.

The counterpoint to these macroscopic studies of social support is set by a cluster of studies showing that access to at least one intimate, confiding relationship is vital to health protection. These studies concentrate on what Weiss (1974: 23) has called "attachment providing relationships," and reflect the belief that social support is founded upon the most profound of social ties, the dyadic bond. There are two lines of research testifying to the importance for mental health of intimate ties. On the one hand, there is much evidence to show that loss of a loved one, either through separation and divorce (Bloom et al., 1978) or through death (Kraus & Lilienfeld, 1959; Parkes, 1972; Raphael, 1977), is a life event associated with a general predisposition to morbidity; on the other hand, there is evidence that persons who maintain contact with at least one confidant, even in the face of reduced social contacts with others over time, report more positive mood states, greater life satisfaction, and better health status than those without these ties (Lowenthal & Haven, 1968; Bunch, 1972; Miller & Ingham, 1976; Conner et al., 1979). Lowenthal and Haven (1968: 22), for example, asked a sample of elderly persons whether there existed "anyone in particular you confide in or talk to about yourself or your problems," and related this and conventional measures of social interaction to three indicators of adaptation. While their data analysis revealed that high social interaction and increased social contact over time were each associated with more positive ratings of psychiatric status, they did not find a significant association between low access to social ties and psychiatric impairment. However, this anomaly in their data was clarified when the authors assessed the morale of their respondents as a *joint* function of these conventional measures of social contact and the presence or absence of a confidant. Here, they found that access to an intimate, even in the face of sudden decrements in social contacts brought on by widowhood and retire-ment, was vital to health protection.

When we consider Lowenthal and Haven's (1968) findings, which are consistent with the results of other studies equating social support with social intimacy, together with the findings characteristic of the "social integration" approach, we can conclude only that (a) there is something about social contact that is important to health mainte-nance, and (b) the distinction between social isolation and access to at least one confiding relationship may be of greatest importance in the study of social support. However, by simply defining social support in terms of extensive or intensive social contact, these studies al-together ignore processes occuring in human transactions, and they are blind to situational and social structural factors mediating the expression of social support. In short, they provide no information about the substance of social support or about the context in which it arises. How can we understand social support without knowing something about what transpires in the course of human dialogue? Surely, the broader social environment shapes the norms people hold about the occasions on which it is appropriate to provide help, about their right to help from others and their duty to help others (Schreiber & Glidewell, 1978), and about what constitutes help. Further, it is likely that the social orbits people inhabit differ in their capacities to render support in response to different types of life events and tran-sitions. Hence, intuition alone makes it difficult to swallow the propo-sition that one confiding relationship is capable of buffering the stresses associated with events as diverse as job loss, a death in the family, a move to a new city, and the birth of a first child. Indeed, Lowenthal and Haven (1968) found that access to a confidant was *not* capable of moderating the depression experienced by those elderly who fell seriously ill during the two-year period prior to follow-up. They signal their understanding of the fact that social support must be assessed in relation to specific adaptive challenges when they state that "a social support — such as an intimate relationship — may serve as a mediating, palliative, or alleviating factor in the face of social losses, but one should not expect it to cross system boundaries and serve a similar role in the face of physical losses" (1968: 27).

The fact of the matter is that people must have connections with other people in order to receive social support, but social connected-ness is not equivalent to, nor is it a guarantee of access to, social support. Other factors must come into play, and social network analysis offers a promising method of extracting details about how the configuration of the social environment and the norms shared by its members determine its potential for providing help at times when individuals face particular life crises and transitions (Gottlieb & Hall, 1980). Network analysis is capable of sampling the norms people subscribe to concerning the occasions on which informal help, as opposed to professional resources, ought to be extended; it is capable of gauging the quantity of support to which people have access on the basis of their ability to maintain reciprocal ties to others; it takes into account how networks of the same size, but differing in their internal structure of connections, have different consequences for the support they are able to generate. Some examples may help to illustrate the advantages network analysis brings to the task of unraveling the relationship between social connectedness and health protection.

In his research on the intimate ties of Toronto's East Yorkers, Wellman (1979) found that even though the majority of respondents (61 percent) had at least 5 intimate ties, only 30 percent of these intimates were reported to be sources of help in emergency situations, and only 22 percent were perceived as helping with everyday needs. While this is ample demonstration of the fact that knowledge of people's social contacts says little about their access to support, Wellman's application of social network analysis to these data helped him to illuminate the structural basis for this pattern of support. By examining the density of his respondents' networks, he learned that the constituent kin and kith sectors were not well connected — there were few cross-connections between the members of these sectors. Only one-fifth of the networks had a density greater than 50 percent. More dense or close-knit networks would probably have furnished greater quantities of support due to a high level of communal solidarity. Loose-knit networks are structurally segmented, and therefore information about the distress of a member or about a member's need for support would not circulate among all parties and would not prompt as many parties to respond as in a cohesive network. So here, knowledge of one aspect of the structure of the social environment systematically predicts its capacity as a support system. Furthermore, while dense networks may furnish a greater quantity of support, they may also, paradoxically, place greater constraints on members' behaviors, in the same way that any highly cohesive group places greater conformity pressures on its members than does a noncohesive group. This point is made by Hirsch (1979) in his study of the social support rendered to students facing the pressures of final exams. He found, with Wellman (1979), that dense social networks furnished considerably more social support than loose-knit networks, but that there was an inverse relationship between density and satisfaction with the quality of support received. Hirsch (1979) interprets this pattern in terms of the greater variety of norms and roles that exist in low-density networks, making them capable of offering a greater range of helping resources. More variegated and loose-knit social networks may constitute more potent support systems for people because

> as one's interests or needs change, there will be a higher probability of finding individuals to satisfy one's changing requirements [and] if varied input can result in the formulation of superior coping strategies . . . then having access to diverse role partners may enhance one's ability to cope with change [Hirsch, 1979: 275].

In a similar vein, Laumann (1973) has hypothesized that interlocking (close-knit) networks are capable of exerting a higher level of social influence and control over any given member's attitudes and behavior than are radial (loose-knit) networks. In the former structure, the interconnected members communicate with each other about a common associate's situation, forming alliances and coalitions with one another for the purpose of influencing his or her attitudes and behavior. In radial networks, members have lower affective involvement and commitment to one another because they share fewer common interests and concerns and because there is less similarity in their social positions. Hence, Laumann (1973: 115) agrees with Hirsch (1979) that "radial networks are in some sense more flexible and, consequently, more adaptive to the demands of a modern industrial society that is undergoing continuous social change and in which many of its personnel are likely to be highly mobile, both geographically and socially."

A second study by Hirsch (1980) provides empirical evidence for the superiority of loose-knit social networks as supportive milieux for persons undergoing abrupt life transitions. In that study Hirsch focused on two sets of women who were attempting to involve themselves in new spheres of activity requiring that they surrender their former social identities, which were largely based on their domestic involvements. One group was composed of recent widows, while the other was made up of women over the age of 30 who were returning to full-time university studies. All but 5 of the total sample of 34 women were facing life events requiring considerable social readjustment. Hirsch again found that participation in close-knit social networks, here defined as networks in which family ties tended to be connected with friendship ties, was significantly associated with higher levels of psychiatric symptomatology, poorer mood states, and lower self-esteem scores. He also found that more detailed knowledge about the character of these women's friendship ties was useful in distinguishing between those making better and those making worse adaptations to their life transitions. Women with a greater number of multidimensional friendships — friendships based on at least two types of shared activities which are important to the focal individual — had higher levels of self-esteem and were more satisfied with the support they received from others in the forms of "socializing" and "tangible assistance." In short, women who participated in loose-knit social networks and who maintained multidimensional ties to friends were embedded in the most supportive social milieux, given the life transitions they were facing. This is so because women with multidimensional friendships could enlarge those spheres of activity they pursued with others that did not depend exclusively on their former roles as spouse and homemaker; a loose-knit network exerted less uniform pressure to stay within these old roles. As Hirsch (1980: 18) concludes,

> the greater access to salient non-family roles and activities provided by low-density, multidimensional NSS allows for a smoother and less drastic reorganization of their lives. Women in such networks may merely have to change the extent of their already existing commitment or identification with particular activities or relationships, rather than having to develop entirely new ones.

To summarize, I have used these examples of network analysis to point out that simple measures of network size, frequency of contact, and access to close attachments yield information that is so general as to be useless in distinguishing between more and less potent support systems. These gross measures are also misleading to the extent that they fail to make distinctions between the capacity of people's social contacts to help them withstand different types of life crises and transitions. Third, the studies using these simple measures neither inform our understanding of the substance of social support — the help that helpers extend — nor illuminate the term "system" in their treatment of the support system construct. In contrast, network analysis promises to yield an ecologically sound, though complex, portrait of how the social environment is structured and of how this structure is capable of radiating supportive functions to its members. While it may err in the direction of reductionism, network analysis nevertheless renders a multidimensional account of the social system surrounding the help seeker and considers how the sociocultural norms of this social aggregate influence the expression of social support between any two constituent actors. More of the kinds of fine-grained analyses that Wellman and Hirsch have initiated ought to be undertaken with the aim of identifying the sort of network structures that are associated with successful social readjustment across a variety of stressful life events and transitions. These analyses should also help us to identify which network dimensions or properties constitute the subset determining the supportive character of the whole. Ultimately, it is these sorts of analyses that promise to yield insights about the relationship between patterns and processes of social connectedness and health protection.

SOCIAL NETWORKS AND THE DESIGN
OF PREVENTIVE INTERVENTIONS

From all that I have said so far it is reasonable to conclude that those who are at risk of ill health are certainly those few people who are socially isolated, plus the much larger number of people whose networks of ties are not structured in such a way as to form socially supportive milieux capable of generating the "resistance resources" (Antonovsky, 1979) necessary for health maintenance. It follows logically that primary preventive interventions designed on behalf of the general population ought to focus either on restructuring social networks so as to enhance people's access to supportive social ties, or on boosting the quality of support available from people's existing ties. Those who are persuaded that primary prevention ought to be directed toward specific populations at risk might be more inclined to stage these interventions among those who are undergoing life crises and transitions that deplete their social contacts or render these contacts less meaningful or resourceful. Here I am referring to life events entailing important social losses (through death, separation, divorce, geographical moves, and retirement) and events that stimulate needs for new, more appropriate reference-group contacts (such as the transition to parenthood, entry to a new social status accompanying certain chronic illnesses and physical handicaps, and entry to a social position that confers a deviant or minority status on the occupant).

In what follows I will review and critique two types of planned interventions intended to improve the adequacy of the social support available to people: interventions aimed at improving the quality of support expressed within existing dyadic bonds and interventions aimed at heightening the salience of particular social ties, new or existing. The studies I will review in the former category have aimed to *promote the health* of their intended beneficiaries (without regard to specific stressors these beneficiaries may face), while those reviewed in the latter category have aimed to *protect the health* of populations undergoing specific life events and transitions: populations at risk. In my review of each type of intervention, I will bring to bear ideas and new initiatives that are suggested by social network analysis.

Interventions to Improve the Quality of Support

One type of preventive intervention that involves the mobilization of informal resources focuses on *improving the supportive quality of network contacts*. Recognizing that people undergoing stressful experiences typically initiate their help-seeking strategies by unburdening themselves to sympathetic figures in their social orbits, researchers have tried to find ways of optimizing the quality of help these associates provide. While a campaign using bumper stickers that flash the question, "Have you hugged your kid today?" represents one way of nudging people to think about the quality of support they provide as parents, more focused strategies of teaching helping skills have been extended to categories of people who are known to be approached frequently as informal helping agents, as well as to ordinary citizens. The former, "natural caregivers," are persons whose work roles bring them into repeated contact with large numbers of citizens who come to trust them and to open up to them about their problems and worries. Family physicians, divorce lawyers, the clergy, and teachers typically make up their numbers.

A classic illustration of how programs can be designed to enhance the support caregivers provide has recently been reported by Wiesenfeld and Weis (1979). In this study, hairdressers were involved in a ten-week group consultation and training program which included pre- and posttests of their helping strategies. The program was predicated on data revealing that "approximately one-third of the time hairdressers spent talking to customers was devoted to discussion of moderate-to-serious problems and that the hairdressers wanted professional consultation in their roles as helpers" (Wiesenfeld & Weis, 1979: 786). The hairdressers attended at least seven training sessions that concentrated on teaching three core helping skills: empathic listening, reflecting feelings, and presenting behavioral alternatives. In addition, the consultants discouraged the trainees from using two helping responses to which they had become accustomed, on the grounds that these strategies were not conducive to constructive change: the provision of specific advice and a response called "count your blessings." The hairdressers were asked to read a counseling text, they were invited to present "case vignettes," videotapes were shown, lectures were given, and time was set aside for "troubleshooting." The results, comparing these trainees' preferred helping responses to a set of hypothetical client problems, with a control group's responses (hairdressers who had no time to participate), revealed that the trainees dramatically increased their use of the "reflecting feelings" response and decreased the frequency with which they offered specific advice. The control hairdressers did not change their manner of responding in the directions deemed desirable by the trainers.

A second project, also intended to improve the quality of support available in people's social networks, has been described by D'Augelli et al. (forthcoming), and I will outline its thrust before offering my critique of these two strategies of strengthening natural support systems. The Community Helpers Project, which D'Augelli and his colleagues initiated at Pennsylvania State University, aimed not only to enrich the process of natural caregiving within two nearby rural communities, but also to "expand local help-giving" (D'Augelli et al., forthcoming: 2). Adopting a life development perspective, which emphasizes the importance of equipping people with the personal and social resources necessary for coping with normative and unexpected life events, and influenced also by Warren's (1978) and Wellman's (1979) sociological research on community helping networks, these researchers began with a community survey intended to identify patterns of informal help-seeking and help-giving in the two locales, the norms governing the expression of these behaviors, and local patterns of social participation. These data were then used as a basis for choosing among alternative approaches to enhancing the effectiveness and the reach of local helping networks. D'Augelli and Ehrlich (1980) report that the approaches considered fell into two categories: strategies involving modification of certain structural properties of local networks, and training interventions intended to enhance the helping skills extended by informal caregivers within their established networks. The former approach was rejected for reasons I will discuss later; instead, the project proceeded with the tasks of identifying citizens in each locale who were interested in and appropriate candidates for training in several kinds of helping skills. In fact, the training included not only the sort of helping skills Wiesenfeld and Weis's (1979) hairdressers received, but also offered life development and crisis intervention skills. Those among the first generation of trainees were expected to return to their communities of origin and extend their learning to local residents who, in turn, would be more effective sources of support within their own natural networks. Through this chain of training, the project staff hoped to radiate more effective helping skills throughout the target locales.

I want to draw special attention to the strategy initially used to recruit the first and second generations of trainees, since progress toward the goal of expanding or radiating local help-giving hinged on this element of the program's design. The original set of trainees included a large proportion of people already involved in some aspect of the formal human services system in each locale; this was so because they were known to the members of the advisory boards that the project established in each locale, who were themselves involved in the communities' professional help-giving network. These sorts of people made up two-thirds of the trainees in one locale that had more human services than the other, more rural locale, where only 40 percent of the trainees were already in professional helping roles. The rest of the trainees from the latter community were informal caregivers, such as clergymen and agricultural extension agents, and ordinary citizens. As a group, the first-generation trainees were described by Danish (1978) as relatively high in socioeconomic status and for the most part having some college education. The second-generation trainees (those to be trained by local residents who had learned how to train others) were recruited in three ways: through the personal contacts of the original group of trainees, through a field liaison person who was hired to do this and who was chosen because of his wide contacts in the community, and through direct advertising in the mass media and in public places. Finally, the project used a variety of pre- and posttest measures to assess the training program's effectiveness in teaching helping skills to both generations of trainees, and to assess the helpers' helping activities.

While the hairdresser study and the Community Helpers Project aimed to improve the interactional quality of network contacts, both collected data concerning only the proximal goal of teaching helping skills to trainees, not concerning the ultimate goal of creating more effective support systems in the community. To do this, they ought to have examined the reactions of those who had been helped by the trainees, or to have tapped their perceptions of the adequacy of the support available to them prior to and following the trainees' attendance at the workshops where they enhanced their helping skills. However, even had they collected these outcome data, they would not have been able to identify the factors contributing to positive and negative results without information about two critical aspects of the helpees' social networks: (1) the norms and expectations their helpees held about informal support; and (2) the position occupied by the trainees in the structure of their helpees' networks, positions that determined the trainees' relative influence on the helpees' emotional lives. In short, *both action-research studies failed to recognize that the reactions and perceptions of their intended beneficiaries were strongly conditioned by the sociocultural context in which they participated and by the character of their ties to those offering help*. In what follows, I elaborate on these network issues as they apply to the two studies.

In the hairdresser study insufficient attention was paid to the goodness of fit between the helping skills that were disseminated and the norms about helping that prevailed among the hairdressers and among those who approached them for support. In particular, Wiesenfeld and Weis (1979) did not probe the meanings that the parties to informal helping exchanges attached to their dialogues. For example, they discounted their hairdressers' use of a helping response the authors called "count your blessings," on the grounds that it cuts off further problem exploration. However, from the viewpoint of the parties to this exchange, this tactic may help them to gain a more balanced perspective on their situation, it may encourage them to engage in some relieving social comparisons, or it may help them to restore some confidence in their abilities to draw on other personal or social assets in dealing with their situations. Wiesenfeld and Weis (1979: 792) are, in fact, fully cognizant that they imposed their own values on their trainees, and that they risked adverse outcomes in the process:

> If one were to imagine the situation of discussing a personal problem with a long-known hairdresser, and if, in the past, this person generally seemed to hold strong opinions about most matters, one would likely feel uncomfortable were the hairdresser to change his or her style to a stereotyped client-centered psychotherapeutic technique. . . . Steps must be taken to ensure that any type of training can be easily and constructively integrated into any existing support network.

They go on to suggest that more knowledge about the functioning of informal support systems ought to precede the planning of programs to improve them, but they provide no details about the sort of knowledge needed.

As I have pointed out, the authors have already collected some information about the informal support expressed between hairdresser and client, and this information illuminates certain aspects of the norms and expectations the parties hold concerning informal support. Rather than building on these accepted ways of relating, or even assessing their impact at the outset, the authors dismissed the hairdressers' tactics on the grounds that they departed from expert knowledge (e.g., the counseling literature's preference for "continuing responses"), and introduced that knowledge into the training program. Hence, in the act of extinguishing the hairdressers' native helping responses — those responses expected and potentially valued by their clients — Wiesenfeld and Weis also disregarded their own injunction to consider carefully how training programs could be integrated into existing support networks.

Network analysis draws attention to a second issue pertaining to the impact of the hairdressers on their clients. Some exploratory assessment of the social networks of the hairdressers' clients may reveal that the hairdressers do not occupy central positions in these networks, that they have little influence (relative to the client's first-order contacts) upon the client's problem-solving efforts or emotional state, and that they are not at all tied into the more dense social fabric in the client's life. They represent weak links in the client's network, and as such, they may be more important as sources of information about ideas, influences, and resources that are socially distant from the client. I credit Granovetter (1973) for this latter idea about the

functions of weak ties, an idea that was empirically supported by data
he collected documenting the relative importance of people's
second-order contacts in helping job changers find new employment.
Hence training programs might concentrate more profitably on shar-
pening the referral skills of hairdressers, since this is one type of
helping behavior for which they are best suited, given their
hypothesized position in the structure of their clients' networks. To
make my point differently, I am arguing that knowledge of the position
of hairdressers, relative to other actors in the clients' social networks,
might suggest what specialized helping functions they play in those
networks. Since they are not psychologically close to their clients, no
amount of tinkering with their counseling skills will show up in an
impact on their clients' feelings or coping behaviors. Their first-order
(strong) ties have the greatest power in this domain. The hairdressers'
structural position does, however, make them important links to the
outside world and its resources, and they therefore ought to be
targeted for programs like that mounted by Leutz (1976), which focus
on improving the referral knowledge and accuracy of informal community caregivers.

Although the Community Helpers Project began with a survey
that sampled the helping norms and patterns of social participation in
the two locales, it too culminated with a uniform training intervention
whose impact on the helpees was not determined. D'Augelli (1980)
argues that these survey data did *not* suggest that this training
intervention, which the project staff had used predominantly with
professional and paraprofessional workers in the past, would be in-
congruous in the local contexts. Unfortunately, this conclusion was
based on respondents' answers to two questions asking them to rank
order or check eight categories of help that they typically extended to
others and that they "liked to get" from others. These questions were
so global in nature and the response categories so limited as to
preclude analyses that might have been capable of differentially in-
forming decisions about the compatability of the training program
with local patterns of helping. More important, that the respondents
were presented with eight categories of help, predefined by the project
staff, calls into question whether local norms and meanings affecting
the expression of social support were tapped at all. A survey approach
that adopts closed-ended response categories may not be adequate to
the task of sampling network norms about helping. Instead, a variety
of field research methods typically practiced by anthropologists who

have conducted network analyses (Barnes, 1972; Kapferer, 1971; Sokolovsky et al., 1978) might be more capable of generating the sort of qualitative data necessary for achieving a more "ecologically valid" understanding of local helping preferences. However, even these anthropological studies have not yet yielded the sort of analytic precision needed to inform decisions about alternative methods of enhancing the functioning of social networks. Hence, my critique of the Community Helpers Project only highlights an area of network research that is much underdeveloped. The project's designers did, indeed, take steps to determine the goodness of fit between the helping skills to be disseminated in the community and the helping norms that prevailed among citizens, but they lacked the empirical tools to gauge this relationship.

I have argued that the survey data collected during the developmental phase of the CHP were too limited and too global to inform the staff's decisions about how to tailor their training interventions in a fashion congruent with local sociocultural contexts. But apparently these survey data also formed the basis for a prior decision, namely, whether the project would attempt to improve the reach and effectiveness of natural helping networks via a training intervention or via structural modifications of existing networks. Here, important questions arise about the staff's interpretation of the network data they collected. D'Augelli and Ehrlich (1980: 3) report that the approach involving structural modification of networks was rejected because the survey data

> did not indicate that alteration of the density, range, pathways, location, frequency and duration of helping networks was needed. Extensive networks already existed and a substantial amount of informal help was available. Second, initiating structural modifications would not necessarily be desirable and could be quite risky. For example, anecdotal reports were that some informal care givers in the areas already [had] a heavy "caseload" and felt overburdened. Others feared losing their anonymity.

Network analysis suggests that these two reasons may contradict one another and that a structural approach would have been warranted. The fact that there existed "extensive networks" offering a "substantial amount of help" does not guarantee that they were structured in a way that optimized the likelihood that all existing members had access to support and that others outside the networks' boundaries could become integrated within these support networks. On the contrary, the survey's finding that certain informal caregivers "felt overburdened" by the large number of people who approached them for help suggests that in these networks there may be undue reliance on a limited number of help sources, and that if these contacts are lost (through death, geographical relocation, sickness, or the like), the support available in these networks would be severely attenuated. For example, it may be that these networks approximate a wheel in which the whole is held together by each of the spoke's attachment to the hub, not to each other. In the language of network analysis, there may be insufficient cross-connections among the individuals in these networks (low density), or too few clusters or connected sets of ties; or too many of the connections that do exist may be dependent on (mediated by) a single close connection. Any of these structural configurations, which reflect unsupported links in a network, may account for the finding that some informal caregivers are overtaxed. More important, these structural configurations are not the sort associated with robust networks that are capable of radiating support on behalf of members in the future. Their fragility stems from their centralization in a limited number of ties which, if severed, would result in a marked reduction of support in the network. Lacking in cross-connections, the remaining members would shift their dependence to another central figure or seek support outside their informal social contacts, and the network itself would be increasingly at risk of dissolution.

If my inferences about aspects of the density of the respondents' networks are tentatively accepted, what are the implications for structural modification? In short, what can be done to increase the density of the respondents' networks, to create more clusters, to strengthen the members' embeddedness in a social aggregate? The overall goal, of course, is to bring more individuals into meaningful relationships with one another, and this can be accomplished by collaborating with these central figures and encouraging them to "sponsor" linkages among their own connections. Collins and Pancoast (1976) have described this approach in some detail. Furthermore, they argue that the goal of such work should be to extend the reach of the network once it becomes more dense, so that new members are brought into relationship with those whose ties are of longer duration. Alternately, Todd has described a social network workshop approach capable of accomplishing this same end (Gottlieb

& Todd, 1979), and Fairweather et al. (1969) have aimed to provide
ex-mental patients with a highly connected cluster of social ties by
means of a structured team approach to community living.

There is nothing in what I have said thus far that suggests that
training per se is inappropriate as a way of strengthening social
support networks. However, healthy support system functioning is
not only predicated on the members' perceptions of the adequacy of
the help they give and get, but also on their perceptions of whether
this help is available when needed, whether relationships are reciprocally helpful, and whether these helping relationships are likely to
persist over time and are to some extent substitutable. A training
intervention can focus on network-building skills — learning how to
develop ties to others, learning how to help others form new connections, and learning how to reciprocate help — *and* on help-giving
skills. Indeed, one crucial topic for future study and action on the
promotion of potent support networks centers on the identification of
those circumstances that dictate which of these two approaches or
what combination of them would have greatest impact.

Finally, I wish to comment briefly upon the manner in which the
CHP set about the work of recruiting its trainees, since here, too, the
project attended too little to matters of social structure in the two
locales, a deficiency that seriously undermined its much hoped-for
"spread of effect" in the community. Recall that the original cohort of
trainers were selected by members of the project's local advisory
boards and tended to come from the ranks of the more educated,
higher-income strata. In the more populated locale, many of the
trainers worked in the human services field, while in the rural area,
more informal caregivers were represented. But presumably, the logic
behind training these people to train others, rather than having the
project's professional staff directly train the "grass-roots" people,
was predicated on the proposition that the original set of trainers
would be drawn from diverse local social networks and therefore
would have the sort of natural entree to citizens that professionals
lacked. As the project's directors argue,

> if fellow citizens are engaged in recruiting helpers, more helpers will
> be interested in joining. In addition, the experience can proceed
> more rapidly since the trainer has fewer problems of acceptance.
> Finally, since the trainer can use local examples, notions of helpful-
> ness, and typically experienced dilemmas, the training can be more
> personally engaging and involving. The end result is that the process

of skill acquisition can occur with far fewer barriers than if outside professionals were the trainers [D'Augelli et al., 1979: 6].

My point is that the project's methods of selecting the original set of trainers did not ensure that these trainers would not also face the same number of barriers to the social networks existing in the project's sites as the professionals might encounter. To the extent that these trainers did not penetrate the "grass roots," the skills taught would be *concentrated* in a limited number of social networks, not *radiated* through these locales. More effective outreach based on a more comprehensive initial sampling of diverse social networks might have corrected this problem. Without such an early assessment of local networks, the project's effects might only have spread to *helpees* in one stratum of the community, not to *networks* existing in diverse local social strata.

I have argued that these and other action-research projects falling into the category of preventive interventions that seek to enhance the supportive quality of existing social ties, ought to pay more heed to the norms governing the expression of helping behavior among the intended beneficiaries. There is no single, universal standard for judging social support; instead, meanings arise from prevailing sub-cultural norms and from specific interactional contexts. Efforts to enhance the quality of support ought to begin by assessing the existing forms and impact of social support, and use this information as a guide to subsequent action. Second, more attention ought to be paid to the structural properties of networks so as to ensure that those whose helping skills are to be developed do, in fact, play an important part in the emotional lives of citizens, to ensure that the intervention spreads to a significant proportion of a given network's members, and to gauge the appropriateness of this overall approach to the enhancement of support (as opposed to others involving the restructuring of the network itself).

Interventions That Foster Contact with Similar Peers

The second type of preventive intervention involving the mobilization of informal resources focuses on *efforts to bring people into contact with similar peers* who are either already in their network of social ties or who can be grafted onto their network. This approach is based on information drawn from reference-group theory (Hyman, 1942), studies of affiliative and social comparison processes (Gerard,

1963; Schachter, 1959), and crisis theory (Caplan, 1964), which indicates that when people experience the emotional and cognitive uncertainties accompanying life crises and transitions, they have a need to share and compare their own reactions and beliefs with others', preferably with persons currently or recently experiencing similar events. When they have opportunities to do so, there is a moderation in the amount of stress they experience. In what follows, I will restrict my discussion to initiatives taken by practitioners and researchers to structure meaningful reference-group contacts for people facing stressful life events and transitions.

There are a number of reports of support groups that have been established by professional health practitioners who saw some value in bringing together clients/patients in similar potentially stressful circumstances. Messinger et al. (1978: 264), for example, convened "remarriage preparation groups," which they felt could "help the participants with this transitional process through increased awareness of their situations, encouragement to communicate and renegotiate their contracts (with their spouses), the learning of new information and techniques, and the opportunity for some role modeling." This is only one example of several kinds of groups that Schwartz (1975) classifies under the heading, "situation/transition groups" and that differ from mutual-help groups only in that they are moderated by a trained leader and are time-limited. It is noteworthy that many of the members of these groups become integrated within one another's social networks; the ties that germinate within the more structured group setting are transplanted to the natural social environment of the members. Barrett (1978) has, in fact, documented how effective support groups are in maximizing "treatment gains." She found that participants in all three types of support groups she established among widows continued to interact with each other after the groups' formal terminations, and maintained their gains at follow-up, fourteen weeks after the last group sessions. Her experimental design also allowed her to document the health gains made by support groups in comparison to control groups composed of widows waiting to enter groups.

A second experimental study of support groups merits detailed attention because it not only included measures of the groups' impact on the participants' subjective reactions and attitudes toward a stressful life event, but also included objective measures of the intervention's impact on those behaviors of the participants known to be associated with *future* competence. Minde et al. (1980) established hospital-based support groups among parents of premature infants. The sixteen couples assigned to the groups met once weekly for 7 to 12 weeks and were encouraged to share their feelings about giving birth to a small baby, provided with information about neonatal care, and helped with certain concrete needs (e.g., babysitting, housing referrals) by the project staff. The sessions were attended by other parents of premature infants, by a nurse who served as the project coordinator, and by a "veteran mother" who acted as the "official animator" of the group. Parents assigned to the control group received the routine care offered by the premature nursery. Pre- and posttest measures included observations of twelve infant behaviors and ten caretaker behaviors (parent-child interaction), clinical interviews probing the parents' experience and attitudes toward their caretaking role during the postpartum period, and ratings of their caretaking competence. In addition, a record was kept of the number of weekly hospital visits made by the mothers.

The results revealed that mothers in the support groups visited their infants more frequently, expressed a greater understanding of their infants' conditions, felt more comfortable with their role as caretakers and, commencing three weeks after the group sessions began, interacted more with their infants in general and, in particular, significantly increased three types of maternal behaviors compared to control-group mothers. Since it has been found that these early maternal caretaking patterns predict later desirable maternal behaviors and aspects of child development, support groups among this population represent a promising approach to primary prevention. At the same time, it was clear that the groups were of immediate benefit in ameliorating the parents experience during this stressful life event. As Minde et al. (1980: 6) observe,

> their relief about "not being alone in such a state" was usually quite dramatic and led to a great feeling of intimacy among group members. . . . Although not documented by empirical data, we felt that only after these feelings had been shared was it possible for the parents to . . . understand the implications of topics related to the treatment and care of premature infants such as the meaning of positive and negative pressure ventilators, oxygen levels, respiratory monitor or tube feedings.

The Minde et al. (1980) study also reveals that community caregivers such as pediatricians are in a particularly strategic position to identify people facing similar stressful events and to convene them as support groups. The groups can serve as temporary reference communities (Powell, 1975) activated only during the early stage of a life crisis and when there is a need to supplement the support available in an individual's social network; or active attempts can be made to weave group members into the social fabric of one another's lives by encouraging extragroup contacts, holding meetings in the natural environment of the participants, and urging support-group members to introduce one another to their respective family members and friends, thus increasing their network embeddedness. One way of integrating similar peers into an established network is to populate the support groups themselves with both family members and "fellow sufferers." This strategy has been used among cancer patients who have been brought together in support groups attended also by their families (Corder & Anders, 1974), and it has proved effective not only as a way of modifying the patient's emotional stress, but also as a means of mobilizing support on behalf of the patient's family.

So far, I have limited my attention to preventive interventions that enlarge people's social networks to include new peer contacts whose common life experiences empower them as sources of support. These peers help one another better to understand the circumstances surrounding the life events or transitions they are facing; they exchange problem-solving strategies; they support one another's efforts at behavioral and attitudinal change; and, through the process of social comparison, they reduce feelings of uniqueness regarding their problems and establish new norms to support one another's revised social identities. New reference-group supports are likely to be needed when old social contacts either reinforce undesirable behaviors, as in the case of the alcoholic's drinking companions, or when they have not experienced the sort of life transition or event that is occurring, and therefore lack influence as sources of support. For example, when the life event at hand is not a developmental crisis like those most people face, but a rarer situational stressor — such as the diagnosis of a chronic or life-threatening disease — it is likely that existing network contacts will be insufficient sources of support. It follows that the normative life transitions can be addressed by mobilizing existing network contacts who have some personal experience with the transition, so that here, the task of preventive interventions is to reorient people to those members of their network whose life experiences qualify them as similar peers. Instead of grafting new supportive ties onto the network, intervention focuses on increasing contact with network members who share a similar social role or who have faced a similar stressful life experience. One final example of a preventive intervention directed toward achieving this aim — among couples experiencing the transition to parenthood — follows. This example also will be used to identify several issues that must be more fully explored in programs mobilizing social support for health protection.

The transition to parenthood represents a life experience that has an impact on a couple's social network, both in terms of an overall, temporary reduction in social support and a relinquishing of specific ties to peers who no longer constitute a meaningful reference group (Duvall, 1971; White, 1974). Richardson and Kagan (1979) found that, on the average, new mothers reported that the birth of their first child was accompanied by undesirable changes in their patterns of peer socializing, chiefly involving an alienation from old ties, and that, while some mothers were able to adjust to this shift in their relationships, others were left with feelings of anger and resentment. Access to similar peers in the network distinguished between mothers who were more and less capable of maintaining network integration:

> For those whose circle of friends were parents themselves or interested in parenting, the natural and temporary pre-occupation with a new child facilitated a reintegration of the friendship including self as parent. Responses to experienced distance from old friends, most likely not parents themselves, ranged from anger, an almost philosophic acceptance and detachment from old ties, to active attempts to maintain and repair ties with old friends [Richardson & Kagan, 1979: 7].

The researchers also found that the onset of parenting effected closer ties to the couples' parents, making these family ties more important to them and more active as sources of support. Considered together, these findings imply that it might be useful to plan interventions that assist new parents in reorienting themselves to those members of their social networks who can provide support for the parenting role. If new parents could be identified and brought together in a group context that encourages them to engage in the process of social comparison, they might benefit in the short term from the immediate support provided, and, in the long term, from the lessons this group experience teaches about utilizing supports in their own social networks. It was the latter lesson we attempted to emphasize in the support groups described below.

This study (Mc Guire & Gottlieb, 1979) was undertaken in collaboration with two family physicians who wanted to initiate some sort of educational program for parents with a first child. They were prompted to do so because they felt that these parents were overly anxious about relatively minor child-care matters and child behaviors, and that this anxiety expressed itself in the form of a disproportionately high rate of using the physicians' services. While the physicians' goal was to impart information and know-how to these parents so as to increase their self-care skills, their ideas were compatible with our notions regarding the potential benefits of social support. Hence, they agreed to participate in an experimental project that would provide a service and test our hypotheses about the role of support groups in moderating the parents' stress and fostering greater reliance on peer supports. Thus, half of each physician's new parent-couples were randomly assigned to what we called a "cognitive guidance" condition, which involved sending them written educational materials on various aspects of infant development, nutrition, and care, while the other half also received these materials but, in addition, were randomly assigned to seven weekly social support group sessions convened by the physician and his spouse. The couples were *not* selected on the basis of any known risk factors or on the basis of their rates of utilizing the physicians' services. Twelve couples with a first and only child between the ages of 1 and 24 months were assigned to the support groups, and twelve were assigned to the comparison condition.

The parent groups were structured to maximize three conditions conducive to the expression of social support: contact with similar others, opportunities to engage in social comparisons regarding areas of emotional and cognitive uncertainty, and exposure to a broad range of problem-solving strategies for parenting concerns. All 48 parents independently completed the identical questionnaire once before either attending their first group session or before receiving the educational materials, and again, five weeks after attending the final group session. Since we wanted to know about both the health and the social consequences of the interventions, the questionnaire included measures of stress, well-being, knowledge of diverse ways of dealing with child-related concerns, and it measured the social effects via four variables, inquiring into the couples' use and evaluation of members of their own social networks as sources of support for the parenting role. Specifically, we probed the number of people with whom they discussed personal child-rearing matters, the number with whom them discussed child-rearing problems in particular, the frequency of these discussions during the prior two weeks, and their satisfaction with the social support available to them.

We found that the couples in both support groups significantly increased their frequency of discussing child-rearing matters with members of *their own* social networks and that couples in only one of the groups enlarged the number of network members whom they engaged in these discussions. Those in the cognitive guidance condition did not change in these ways. However, the trend toward increased social support following the group sessions was *not* accompanied by lower levels of reported stress or by more positive ratings of their subjective sense of well-being, an outcome we attributed to the lack of empirical tools that are sensitive to changes in the health of respondents who are not chosen on the basis of known risk, that is, the absence of health indicators in primary prevention research. Nevertheless, we could not conclude that the support groups were health-protective, only that they engendered the social sequelae cited above. In short, our results provided partial confirmation of our hypothesis and service intention, namely, that the group experience would convince the participants of the value of informal support and social comparison, and that this conviction would generalize to the natural networks in which they participated.

In retrospect, several caveats must be sounded about this type of preventive intervention. First, programs that attempt to heighten the salience of informal resources in people's networks could backfire on health promotion if it turns out that those who populate the network are not equipped to offer support or that they recommend unproductive or self-defeating coping strategies. What if it turns out that other parents in our participants' networks recommend frequent corporal punishment, or what if these new parents are exposed to peer models who neglect their children or administer home remedies that are unsafe? We know, for example, that one of the predictors of child abuse and other forms of maltreatment is having been raised in an abusing household, and if the immediate family of child-abusing parents is indeed more salient as a source of informal support than the more distant subnetworks of peers and workmates, then we would want to ensure that the immediate family's influence is neutralized or that there is reduced contact with this sector of the network or that this sector itself is pinpointed as the target of change. In short, we need to know more about the structural properties and the norms of social networks and assure ourselves of their prosocial character before we can safely encourage greater reliance on them. Furthermore, we will probably find that there is no such thing as a "network for all seasons," just as it is rare to find individuals who are highly adaptive in multiple challenging contexts. Instead, we should begin by asking more detailed questions like, "What sort of network structure and what sort of network norms are best suited to the adaptive tasks of these people facing this type of life transition?" and "Can we mobilize existing, prosocial sources of support during this period of social readjustment, or should we graft a temporary, new reference community onto the network?" Moreover, we may find, with the network therapists (Speck & Attneave, 1973), that alterations in the network itself may be required to promote more competent social responses to members who are seeking help.

Second, the data from our study raise questions about whether some parents were *personally* better disposed than others to this sort of intervention. Some parents contributed more to the group discussions than others and were more enthusiastic about the entire enterprise of comparing notes and disclosing feelings about the joys and anxieties of parenting. It is likely that people with certain personalities, with certain orientations toward engaging peers for help, and with better social skills might gain more than others from this sort of social intervention. Some people have a greater need for affiliation than others, and some have a stronger commitment than others to an ethic that dictates that self-reliance, not mutual help, is the sine qua non of coping. Moreover, people who are not sensitive to their feelings or who are unaccustomed to disclosing them — people who my clinical colleagues call "repressors" rather than "sensitizers" — would probably not be suitable candidates for social interventions that rely on the open expression of unhappy feelings as the basis for mutual help. In fact, there is some evidence that when these sorts of people are encouraged to ventilate their fears about imminent and threatening events — when, for example, they face major surgery — they fare much more poorly psychologically and medically than their counterparts with the same repressive style who have been left to their own devices. Similarly, there are some people who simply do not have the interpersonal skills that go into the work of building and maintaining a network of satisfying social ties. It is more apt to say *mutually* satisfying social ties, since people who are forever asking others for help, and who therefore do not live up to the fairly pervasive norm of reciprocity in our society, develop reputations as social albatrosses and tend to become isolated. In sum, our study suggests that there may be some important personalogical variables concerning people's coping styles, attitudes toward help-seeking, and social skills that ought to be assessed in order to determine the prime candidates for interventions that amplify social supports during stressful life transitions.

CONCLUSION

Cassel's (1974) epidemiological formulations regarding the role of social support in moderating stress, and Caplan's (1974) subsequent elaboration of these ideas in terms of types of support systems with which professionals can collaborate, have spawned numerous empirical investigations and action projects directed toward assessing and promoting the health-protective functions of social support. The original excitement generated by the pioneering work of these two scholars has given way to more critical analyses of the social support construct, and there is now a recognition of the fact that the concept of a support system has undergone considerable reification, since there is no evidence pointing to the material existence of a social aggregate that is unconditionally prosocial in its behavior and comprehensive in its ability to meet members' needs. Instead, there is a growing recognition of the fact that most people are embedded in a network of social ties that has the power to provide support *and* to exercise constraints. (See, for example, Eckenrode and Gore's chapter in this volume.) This revised, more balanced perspective on the functions of social networks suggests that the social environment is capable of radiating both stress and support, and that individuals differ also in their receptivity toward and skillfulness in using social supports in their lives. Most important, recent research has reframed the question to be asked about the nature and consequences of social support. The global question of whether social support is health-protective has now been replaced by the more specific query, "Which people with what skills on what occasions ought to be mobilized on behalf of persons with what skills and help-seeking preferences?"

In this chapter I have traced several lines of basic research on the relation between social support and stress, and I have characterized and critiqued two types of preventive interventions directed toward mobilizing social support in the face of stressful life events and transitions. I have argued that social network analysis represents the most useful and ecologically valid approach to the study of social support, and that preventive programs have suffered because they have not given sufficient attention to the social structure and the social norms surrounding the populations they intend to serve. Further action research should be directed toward exploring how social networks arise and take shape in the community, and how their influence on matters of health, both positive and negative, can be modified.

REFERENCES

ANTONOVSKY, A. *Health, stress and coping.* San Francisco: Jossey-Bass, 1979.

BARNES, J. Social networks. *Addison-Wesley Module in Anthropology,* 1972, *26,* 1-29.

BARRETT, C. J. Effectiveness of widows' groups in facilitating change. *Journal of Consulting and Clinical Psychology,* 1978, *46,* 20-31.

BERKMAN, L. F., & SYME, S. L. Social networks, host resistance, and mortality: A nine-year followup study of Alameda County residents. *American Journal of Epidemiology,* 1979, *109,* 186-204.

BLOOM, B. L., ASHER, S. J., & WHITE, S. W. Marital disruption as a stressor: A review and analysis. *Psychological Bulletin,* 1978, *85,* 867-894.

BROWN, G., BHROLCHAIN, M., & HARRIS, T. Social class and psychiatric disturbance among women in an urban population. *Sociology,* 1975, *9,* 225-254.

BUNCH, J. Recent bereavement in relation to suicide. *Journal of Psychosomatic Research,* 1972, *16,* 361-366.

CAPLAN, G. *Principles of preventive psychiatry.* New York: Basic Books, 1964.

CAPLAN, G. *Support systems and community mental health.* New York: Basic Books, 1974.

CASSEL, J. Psychosocial processes and "stress": Theoretical formulations. *International Journal of Health Services,* 1974, *4,* 471-482.

COLLINS, A., & PANCOAST, D. *Natural helping networks.* Washington, DC: National Association of Social Workers, 1976.

CONNER, K. A., POWERS, E. A., & BULTENA, G. L. Social interaction and life satisfaction. An empirical assessment of late-life patterns. *Journal of Gerontology,* 1979, *34,* 116-121.

CORDER, M. P., & ANDERS, R. L. Death and dying: Oncology discussion group. *Journal of Psychiatric Nursing and Mental Health Services,* 1974, *12,* 10-14.

DANISH, S.J. *Facilitating natural caregiving as a means of improving a community's quality of life.* Paper presented at the meeting of the American Psychological Association, Toronto, Canada, August 1978.

D'AUGELLI, A. Personal communication, September 1980.

D'AUGELLI, A., & EHRLICH, R. *Evaluation of a community-based system for training natural helpers II. Effects on informal helping activities.* Unpublished manuscript, Pennsylvania State University, College of Human Development, 1980.

D'AUGELLI, A., VALLANCE, T., DANISH, S., YOUNG, C., & GERDES, J. The community helpers project: A description of a prevention strategy for rural communities. *Journal of Prevention,* forthcoming.

D'AUGELLI, A. R., VALLANCE, T. R., YOUNG, C. E., & DANISH, S. J. *The community helpers project: A description of a prevention strategy for rural communities.* Paper presented at the meeting of the American Psychological Association, New York, September 1979.

DUVALL, E. *Family development.* Philadelphia: J. B. Lippincott, 1971.

FAIRWEATHER, G., SANDERS, D., MAYNARD, H., & CRESSLER, D. *Community life for the mentally ill.* Chicago: Aldine, 1969.

GERARD, H. B. Emotional uncertainty and social comparison. *Journal of Abnormal and Social Psychology,* 1963, *66,* 568-573.

GOTTLIEB, B. H. The development and application of a classification scheme of informal helping behaviors. *Canadian Journal of Behavioural Science,* 1978, *10,* 105-115.

GOTTLIEB, B. H., & HALL, A. Social networks and the utilization of preventive health services. In R. Price, R. Ketterer, B. Bader, & J. Monahan (Eds.), *Prevention in mental health.* Beverly Hills, CA: Sage Publications, 1980.

GOTTLIEB, B. H., & TODD, D. Characterizing and promoting social support in natural settings. In R. Munoz, L. Snowden, & J. Kelly (Eds.), *Social and psychological research in community settings.* San Francisco: Jossey-Bass, 1979.

GRANOVETTER, M. The strength of weak ties. *American Journal of Sociology,* 1973, *78,* 1360-1380.

HAMMER, M., MAKIESKY-BARROW, S., & GUTWIRTH, L. Social networks and schizophrenia. *Schizophrenia Bulletin,* 1978, *4,* 522-545.

HENDERSON, S. The social network, support and neurosis. *British Journal of Psychiatry,* 1977, *131,* 185-191.

HIRSCH, B.J. Psychological dimensions of social networks: A multimethod analysis. *American Journal of Community Psychology,* 1979, *7,* 263-278.

HIRSCH, B.J. Natural support systems and coping with major life changes. *American Journal of Community Psychology,* 1980, *8,* 159-172.

HYMAN, H. H. The psychology of status. *Archives of Psychology,* 1942, No. 269.

KAPFERER, B. Norms and the manipulation of relationships in a work context. In J. C. Mitchell (Ed.), *Social networks in urban situations.* Manchester, England: Manchester University Press, 1971.

KRAUS, A. S., & LILIENFELD, A. M. Some epidemiologic aspects of the high mortality rate in the young widowed group. *Journal of Chronic Diseases,* 1959, *10,* 207-217.

LAUMANN, E. O. *Bonds of pluralism.* New York: John Wiley, 1973.

LEUTZ, W. The informal community caregiver: A link between the health care system and local residents. *American Journal of Orthopsychiatry,* 1976, *46,* 678-688.

LIN, N., SIMEONE, R. S., ENSEL, W. M., & KUO, W. Social support, stressful life events, and illness: A model and an empirical test. *Journal of Health and Social Behavior,* 1979, *20,* 108-119.

LOWENTHAL, M. F., & HAVEN, C. Interaction and adaptation: Intimacy as a critical variable. *American Sociological Review,* 1968, *33,* 20-30.

McGUIRE, J. C., & GOTTLIEB, B. H. Social support groups among new parents: An experimental study in primary prevention. *Journal of Clinical Child Psychology,* 1979, *8,* 111-116.

MESSINGER, L., WALKER, K. N., & FREEMAN, S. J. Preparation for remarriage following divorce: The use of group techniques. *American Journal of Orthopsychiatry,* 1978, *48,* 263-272.

MILLER, P., & INGHAM, J. G. Friends, confidants, and symptoms. *Social Psychiatry,* 1976, *11,* 51-58.

MINDE, K., SHOSENBERG, N., MARTON, P., THOMPSON, J., RIPLEY, J., & BURNS, S. Self-help groups in a premature nursery: a controlled evaluation. *Journal of Pediatrics,* 1980, *96,* 933-940.

MOOS, R. H. The social climate scales: An overview, Palo Alto, CA: Consulting Psychologists Press, 1974.

MYERS, J., LINDENTHAL, J., & PEPPER, M. Life events, social integration, and psychiatric symptomatology. *Journal of Health and Social Behavior,* 1975, *16,* 121-127.

PARKES, C. M. *Bereavement: A study of grief in adult life.* London: Tavistock, 1972.

POWELL, T. J. The use of self-help groups as supportive reference communities. *American Journal of Orthopsychiatry,* 1975, *45,* 756-764.

RAPHAEL, B. Preventive intervention with the recently bereaved. *Archives of General Psychiatry,* 1977, *34,* 1450-1454.

RICHARDSON, M. S., & KAGAN, L. *Social support and the transition to parenthood.* Paper presented at the meeting of the American Psychological Association, New York, September 1979.

SCHACHTER, S. *The psychology of affiliation.* Stanford, CA: Stanford University Press, 1959.

SCHREIBER, S., & GLIDEWELL, J. Social norms and helping in a community of limited liability. *American Journal of Community Psychology,* 1978, *6,* 441-454.

SCHWARTZ, M. D. Situation/transition groups: A conceptualization and review. *American Journal of Orthopsychiatry,* 1975, *45,* 744-755.

SOKOLOVSKY, J., COHEN, C., BERGER, D., & GEIGER, J. Personal networks of ex-mental patients in a Manhattan S.R.O. hotel. *Human Organization,* 1978, *37,* 5-15.

SPECK, R., & ATTNEAVE, C. *Family networks.* New York: Pantheon, 1973.

TOLSDORF, C. Social networks, support and coping: An exploratory study. *Family Process,* 1976, *15,* 407-418.

WARREN, D. *The multiplexity of urban social ties*. Paper presented at the meeting of the Ninth World Congress of Sociology, Uppsala, Sweden, August 1978.

WEISENFELD, A. R., & WEIS, H. M. Hairdressers and helping: Influencing the behavior of informal caregivers. *Professional Psychology*, 1979, *7*, 786-792.

WEISS, R. S. The provisions of social relationships. In Z. Rubin (Ed.), *Doing unto others*. Englewood Cliffs, NJ: Prentice-Hall, 1974.

WELLMAN, B. The community question: The intimate networks of East Yorkers. *American Journal of Sociology*, 1979, *84*, 1201-1231.

WHITE, R. W. Strategies of adaptation. In G. Coehlo, D. Hamburg, & J. Adams (Eds.), *Coping and adaptation*. New York: Basic Books, 1974.

Chapter 9

MUTUAL AID AND PROFESSIONAL SERVICES
Opposing or Complementary?

PETER B. LENROW
ROSEMARY W. BURCH

This chapter asks whether and how the work of professional helpers can be related to the mutual aid that is provided by laypersons in intentionally created social networks. By "mutual-aid networks" we mean both resource-exchange networks, such as food co-ops, day-care co-ops, and neighborhood improvement associations, and more personally oriented "self-help" groups that support their members' efforts to (a) control their own problem behaviors (e.g., overeating, alcohol abuse, or child abuse); (b) cope better with stressful conditions that they do not expect to change (e.g., loss of a loved one, a physical handicap, terminal illness); (c) cope with the crises of transitions in their lives (e.g., career change, first baby, retirement); or (d) explore new interests and learn to take charge of their lives in more fulfilling ways. By "professional helpers" we mean professionals in the human services, including the fields of health care, mental health, law, and education.[1]

We start from the tensions that often exist between professional helpers, on the one hand, and laypeople in mutual-aid networks, on the other. We explore the mutual perceptions that contribute to these tensions. We then examine and reject the prevailing and polarized views about whether professional helping can be compatible with mutual aid among laypeople. Instead, we offer an alternative view focused on interdependence as an aspect of all helping relationships. We argue that while interdependence of the participants is obvious in mutual aid, its importance in effective professional helping has been neglected, obscured, or denied in most training and practice. Our argument holds that where professional helpers and their clients take seriously their interdependence, the professional-client relationship has much in common with mutual aid among laypeople. In both cases, the participants learn to collaborate as partners with different but equally important resources to contribute to their common task. We hypothesize that when professional helping has these qualities, professionals and laypeople in mutual-aid networks can learn much from each other's experiences. We identify factors that interfere with the development of these qualities. And we indicate currents of social change that provide some hope that these factors can be overcome.

PROFESSIONAL INTEREST IN MUTUAL AID AMONG LAYPEOPLE

The increasing number, variety, and visibility of mutual-aid networks among laypeople have awakened many professionals to the importance of such social support systems in promoting psychological and physical health (Gartner & Riessman, 1977; Katz & Bender, 1976; Levy, 1976). As they come to recognize that such networks are resources in community mental health, increasing numbers of professionals also become interested in how their own resources and those of lay networks might be related (Collins & Pancoast, 1976). Because such networks seem to have a powerful influence on the behavior and well-being of their members, they prompt the professional to ask, "Can I increase the effectiveness of my helping efforts by becoming linked in some way with lay groups that provide mutual aid among their members?" Because many of the mutual-aid networks are made up of people who rarely use the services of professional helpers, they prompt the professional to ask, "Can I enlarge the population that I and my colleagues serve by linking in some way with such groups?" Because little is known about what makes for a more health-enhancing network as compared to one that is less health-enhancing or even in some ways destructive of its members health, the growing interest in such groups prompts the question, "Can I help to sort out which features of these networks are particularly important in promoting their members' best interests?"

All three questions have self-interested and more altruistic aspects: "If I can increase the degree and the range of my effectiveness through a link to such groups, my job security, my departmental budget, the administrative support I get in my agency, my agency's support from the community, and my own sense of competence and importance will probably increase. At the same time, if I can promote the use and effectiveness of such networks, it will increase the number and variety of 'at-risk' populations that receive help. This will reduce needless individual suffering and promote a healthier community."

As this mix of self-serving and public-spirited interests galvanizes professional helpers to approach such groups of laypeople or initiate new groups, they are typically met with very mixed, emotionally charged reactions, if not outright rejection (Kleiman et al., 1976). Conversely, when professionals are approached by such lay groups for sponsorship, training, or consultation, they often find themselves in the midst of a confusing web of tensions.

MUTUAL PERCEPTIONS THAT GENERATE TENSIONS

The tensions and mixed reactions are expressions of the ways in which the laypeople and professionals perceive each other. Among the individual differences, two patterns can be discerned among many laypeople in mutual-aid networks. Some laypeople have a mixture of respect and mistrust toward professionals, based on beliefs that professionals (a) are expert in dealing with specific problems and should take charge when people seek help with those problems, (b) are no more competent (and sometimes less competent) than laypeople in dealing with other problems and should not take charge in dealing with these problems, (c) have some knowledge and skill that laypeople could learn to use in mutual aid, and (d) will use lay requests for such knowledge and skill as opportunities to try and take charge of how laypeople deal with matters outside the professional's area of expertise. The main themes here are the sense of dependence on the professional's perceived power and resentment about being vulnerable to the professional's possible abuse of that power.

Other laypeople experience more intense mistrust, based on beliefs that professionals (a) are essentially exploitative, being more concerned with their economic interests and privileges than with the well-being of laypeople and the community as a whole; (b) are not competent to apply their specialized knowledge and skill to the lives of most laypeople because their understanding is limited by their academically cloistered, bureaucratically oriented, or socially privileged positions; and (c) have such limited knowledge that they frequently produce unintended and undesirable side effects, even when they are using their expertise with people whose life situations they can understand. These laypeople advocate avoiding contacts between their mutual-aid networks and professionals, except where the group needs a narrowly defined technical service in order to survive in a society that is dominated by bureaucratic organizations (e.g., when they need a legal opinion, an engineering opinion, or a health certificate). They express less sense of dependence on professionals' power and more determination to control the unavoidable interactions that they do have with professionals.

It is tempting for professionals to think that the tensions they encounter are generated only by laypeople's preconceived ideas, based on stereotypes or on personal conflicts about dependency. However, the apprehensions of many laypeople are based not on hearsay but on their own firsthand experiences with a variety of professionals in agencies and private practice. And their mistrust may result not from fantasies but from attitudes shown by professionals when they are face to face with laypeople. At best, the inevitable mix of self-serving and public-spirited interests that professionals bring to lay networks is likely to evoke confusion and suspicion on the part of their members. The extent to which professionals can reduce this mistrust depends in part on their underlying attitudes toward the laypeople. (Even such things as where — i.e., on whose turf — the professional is prepared to meet are taken as indicators of the professional's underlying attitudes.) And professionals have a variety of attitudes that interfere with their arriving at a differentiated and affirmative view of the laypeople and their networks.

Some professionals regard lay groups as having potential resources but presume that they would be more effective if they were more efficient and if they learned technical skills that the professional can teach. Without realizing it, they may be approaching these groups as raw materials to develop in their own image, rather than discovering health-enhancing characteristics that are peculiar to these groups.

Other professionals seem to approach lay mutual-aid groups as cults that need to be converted to accept the professionals' values.

They may regard most laypeople as simplistic, irrational, and/or irresponsible, and selectively attend to behavior that fits with these expectations. Not surprisingly, this leads them to the conclusion that such groups need to be regulated in some manner by professionals.

Still other professionals initially romanticize the knowledge and skill of laypeople, become disillusioned by their limitations, and withdraw after a period of intense involvement. They expect lay groups to be endowed with special "folk wisdom" that is not available among professionals, overgeneralize about the members' perceptiveness or healing capacities, and underestimate their limitations. When the lay groups turn out to have at least as much internal conflict, self-defeating behavior, and defensiveness as professional groups and bureaucratic services, the professionals who were drawn to lay groups as a relief from conflicts on their own turf may lose interest. This leaves the laypeople confused, hurt, and more mistrustful of professionals than ever.

All three of these orientations toward lay networks are ethnocentric, stemming primarily from stereotypes held by the professionals rather than based on open-minded dialogue, experience with more than one or two such groups, and a willingness to accept the groups on their own terms. Because these orientations do not take seriously what the networks mean to their members, such views are experienced as condescending by network members and contribute to the tensions between professionals and laypeople.

ARE PROFESSIONAL HELPING AND LAY MUTUAL AID COMPATIBLE?

What do these tensions imply about the possibility of constructive relations between professionals and lay networks of mutual aid? Professionals seem to move toward one of two polarized positions on this question. One position holds that the tensions and distorted mutual perceptions are due primarily to defensiveness in a situation where both professionals and laypeople feel vulnerable and where each interest group is concerned to protect its own sphere of influence. In this view, the defensiveness can be overcome by identifying resources that are unique to professionals and needed by lay networks, other resources that are unique to lay networks and needed by professionals, and then rationally coordinating an exchange of resources. The problem is seen as primarily a matter for rational problem-solving and efficient coordination of resources.

A second position holds that there is an inherent antipathy between the nature of professional helping and the nature of lay mutual aid. The former is hierarchical in its essential structure and the latter is equalitarian. The mutual mistrust between professionals and laypeople in mutual-aid networks is not due primarily to *mis*understanding of each other's basic priorities, but to an accurate perception that their values are in fundamental conflict. This means that the form of helping that each uses is more effective when isolated from, rather than coordinated with, the other. And it means that each interest group will inevitably undermine the credibility and effectiveness of the other.

If the essential structure of professional helping is incompatible with the structure of mutual-aid networks, then the idea of rationally coordinating the two forms of helping in complementary roles would be wishful thinking. But we believe that these two polarized positions obscure possibilities in professional helping which, when developed, make professional helping similar in important respects to mutual aid.

INTERDEPENDENCE AS AN UNDERDEVELOPED
ASPECT OF PROFESSIONAL HELPING

To assess the claim that there is an inherent conflict between these two forms of helping, we need an analysis of the full range of variations in helping relationships. We might then identify generic forms of helping of which various kinds of lay and professional helping may be special cases. This would let us check whether or not the main structural distinctions are necessarily between lay and professional helping. One such study (Lenrow, 1978a) has identified two generic forms of helping: *long-term social exchange* and *aid to strangers in distress*. The former refers to exchange that is mutually beneficial when considered over long periods of time. It is characteristic of people in enduring social networks that involve reciprocal obligations and common purposes. The latter refers to interaction in which one participant has greater power and uses it in the service of what he or she perceives as the other participant's interests under circumstances that provide no prospect of reciprocation by the person helped. The participants are strangers in the sense that they are not members of each other's networks of everyday mutual obligations. But these two large classes of helping relationships are not differentially related to lay mutual-aid groups and professional work. Rather, aspects of long-term social exchange and aid to strangers in distress can be found in both lay and professional helping (Lenrow, 1978a: 271-273).

Professional-client relationships in urban, mass society do have far more in common with aid to strangers in distress than with long-term social exchange (Lenrow, 1978b). However, virtually all forms of helping involve *interdependence between the participants*. That is, in order for the resources of one person to be effective in contributing to the interests or well-being of another person, the second person must make use of some of his or her own resources. The second person must actively indicate what his or her interests are, whether the efforts of the first person are meeting those interests, and, if not, what is getting in the way. Even a relatively helpless infant must give signals of distress when hungry and actively suck and/or protest in order for the mother's attention and milk to be effective in serving the infant's needs. Erikson (1959), in particular, has emphasized the mutual regulation between mother and infant that is essential for the well-being of each. The more complex the life situation, the more fully the resources of the second person must be used in order for the first person's resources to be effective on the second person's behalf.

In the case of mutual aid, whether we consider a single planned exchange or the long-term, informal balancing-out of favors in an enduring network, the interdependence of the participants is obvious: If we are trying to serve each other's interests, each of us has to be active in guiding how the other uses his or her resources on our behalf. However, in the relationships of professionals and the people whose interests they are supposedly serving, it has become difficult to see such interdependence. The dependence of the client on the professional is clear, but it is not immediately apparent that the professional is also dependent on the resources of the client (i.e., resources other than fees). In fact, the exchange of money for services seems to make the professional-client exchange appear to be just like any other commercial transaction: A merchant needs a customer; a professional needs a client. This obscures an important distinction. In purely commercial exchanges, each party is understood to be serving his or her own interests, but when professionals sell services, it is understood that they are supposed to serve the clients' interests at least as much as their own. In order to be effective in using their resources to serve the clients' interests, professionals must depend on the clients' active exercise of their own resources.

What are some examples of interdependence in a professional-client relationship? In order for a trial lawyer to serve a client's interests when accused of a crime, the lawyer needs the client's fullest, most accurate description of "what happened" and "what he was doing at the time." Without careful recall and disclosure by the client, the lawyer cannot prepare a defense that anticipates and addresses possible testimony from other witnesses. In order to negotiate a business contract for a commercial client, a lawyer needs the client's judgments about goals, priorities, and the trade-offs in various possible compromises. He or she needs the client's perceptions about what the effects of various possible outcomes will be on the client's business, and perhaps on the client's home life.

In order to make a diagnosis, a physician needs the client's reports of how he or she feels, what hurts, what sort of pain, how long it has been going on, what the client has been doing about it so far, what stresses he or she is currently experiencing, whether there is a family history of this sort of problem, and so on. In order to make recommendations that the client is likely to carry out, the doctor also needs the client's perceptions about what impact various possible plans will have on his or her daily life, who else will be affected, and how the client expects to manage the changes (Innes, 1977; Stone, 1979). In following the course of a client's treatment, the doctor or nurse depends on the client to understand the professional's instructions about how to observe his or her own condition and cope with changes as they occur. They depend on the client to make these observations and to communicate about them to the professionals. Even in responding effectively to emergency situations when an ill or injured person is unconscious, health professionals depend on the client's resources in the form of relatives or friends who can report how the emergency occured, provide emotional support to the client, and provide hours of attention and observation that the professional staff does not have the manpower to supply.

While such resources of clients are important in order for professionals to use their resources effectively in the client's interests, there is something about conceptions of professional roles that leads both professionals and laypeople to overlook the fact that they are interdependent. What contributes to this misperception?

FACTORS THAT INTERFERE WITH
PERCEPTION OF INTERDEPENDENCE
IN PROFESSIONAL HELPING

Several factors make the professional's resources seem all-important and efficacious through unilateral action. One is that professionals are presumed to have very scarce resources. A second is that only other professionals are believed to be able to understand these resources. A third is that this special knowledge is regarded as entitling them to much independence in making decisions. And a fourth is that their special knowledge and general prestige are regarded as entitling them to set the ground rules about how they will relate to clients. The unilateral exercise of their power is presumed to be justified on the grounds that it is necessary for efficient and effective use of their special technical resources (Hughes, 1971).

When such conceptions are widely held by both professionals and laypeople, it is no wonder that professionals give little thought to what resources their clients might contribute and that clients typically take a passive role in relating to professionals. When professionals make unilateral decisions about what will serve the client's interests, they can rationalize this by reminding themselves that they have special resources that the client needs, have the training to know what they are doing, and are too busy with their special work on behalf of clients to pay a lot of attention to the views of individual clients. Ironically, when clients feel belittled and irritated by such unilateral actions, they often use the same view of professionals to talk themselves into resuming their passive, compliant roles.

This view of professional helping tends to be a self-perpetuating set of ideas. In the absence of opposing forces, it might persist on its own. However, unlike a perpetual motion machine, it does not operate in a vacuum. Indeed, there has been much criticism of professional practice from both consumer groups and some professionals (Gartner & Riessman, 1977; Szasz & Hollender, 1956). Yet professional-client relationships have changed very little. The fact that the old views about professional helping are so hard to change suggests that they are based on (a) more general beliefs that are deeply embedded in the culture, (b) nonrational aspects of interpersonal relationships, and (c) social structures that institutionalize a and b.

One basic belief in our culture that has such an effect is an uncritical view of science. This is a belief that, first, science is the best resource for solving human problems, and second, professionals base their decisions and actions on science. By not recognizing the limitations of science in addressing human problems and the limited uses of science in professional practice (Lenrow & Cowden, 1980), this belief creates an exaggerated view of professional resources. The power that is ascribed to professionals on the basis of such beliefs permits them to wrap their work in mystery and act unilaterally.

This brings us to the nonrational processes that contribute to the unilateral actions of professionals: Rationally, professionals derive status from the fit between their specialized competencies and human problems objectively defined; but nonrationally, they derive status from the wish that everyone has for an external source of relief from distress — a wish for omniscient and omnipotent helpers. In our highly secularized society, scientific and technical expertise is regarded as the prime source of such relief. Such felt needs for the protective authority of rational experts tend to flatter professionals, render them uncritical about how indispensable they are, and encourage them to elaborate their roles in ways that make sure they are indispensable (Lenrow & Cowden, 1980).

This is not something that professionals simply impose on laypersons, nor something that laypersons make professionals do. Rather, it is a nonrational process that they enter into mutually. It draws on generalized patterns that individuals have developed for dealing with feelings of vulnerability. Such patterns in adults are built on patterns that persist from childhood. These patterns center on the paired images of a child in distress — feeling helpless, alone, and overwhelmed by dangers that are embellished by imagination — wishing for the presence of a parent with power to make things right. When adults feel vulnerable, they often behave partly on the basis of these old expectations that distress is a condition from which we need to be rescued by powerful, parental figures. When adults react in this way to distressing circumstances and appear helpless and frightened in the client role — analogous to the vulnerable child — the professional also reacts partly on the basis of old images and often tries to take the role of all-powerful rescuer. It follows naturally from such an image of a helper that the professional engages in unilateral action that presumes the client has little to contribute on his or her own behalf.

It is important to recognize, however, that the psychological connection between childhood images and professional-client relationships is not simply a remote or unconscious one transferred from the context of the family. Rather, our society introduces children firsthand to what is expected of professionals and clients. This introduction comes in the form of visits to the pediatrician and the first school setting. Doctors and teachers typically teach children and their parents that the professional is in charge, is the expert, and has routines that they are expected to follow in return for the professional's commitment to protect the child's health and transmit academic skills. So the child's reality as well as his or her fantasy lays down expectations of a passive, compliant role for the client and an all-powerful role for the professional.

This has the unintended side effect of ascribing to the professional an unrealistic amount of responsibility for the solution of the client's problems. It is a burden of responsibility that professionals cannot realistically expect to meet through unilateral actions, given the interdependence that is involved whenever anyone undertakes to help another person meet his or her needs. When they do not elicit or understand the client's perceptions, ideas, or choices, professionals increase the risks of not solving the problem. Then, when they do not succeed, they tend to rationalize in terms of the mysteries of scientific expertise and/or to blame the clients and call for more thorough compliance with their decisions. But the definition of professional and client responsibilities remains as unrealistic as ever, setting the stage for another round of disappointment, mystification, and blame. While this situation is unfair to both professionals and clients, they mutually maintain the cycle by enacting reciprocal roles based on a shared conception of who has the important resources in the helping relationship, namely, the professional.

The beliefs about professionals' scientific expertise and the nonrational transfer of childhood expectations to adult roles do not influence professional-client relationships in some random way. Rather, they are systematically reinforced (i.e., institutionalized) by the structure of human service settings and professional training. The key aspects of social structure appear to be bureaucratic organization and norms for professional work that are dominated by male sex-role stereotypes.

Bureaucratic organization of hospitals, clinics, schools, social service agencies, and legal services reinforces the presumption that hierarchy and rational control are the most effective approaches to human problems. Bureaucracy routinizes reliance on hierarchical and impersonal modes of dealing with people, and it encourages specialization of functions in the name of efficiency. The result is typically a fragmentation of services that works against the individual's need to be recognized as a whole person and to find coherence in his or her life (Lenrow & Cowden, 1980).

Moreover, by putting clients in positions where they can exercise little control over decisions, bureaucratic organizations induce clients to take roles that are childlike in their passivity and dependence on authority. In situations where they can exercise so little control, hospital patients (Taylor, 1979), students (Chessler, 1971), and clients in other bureaucratized settings either struggle actively to gain greater influence or become very passive. Professionals observing this behavior typically interpret it not as situation-induced but as evidence that the clients are "immature," that is, have "trouble controlling their impulses," have "hang-ups with authority," or are "too passive and dependent." They readily conclude that clients have few resources to contribute on their own behalf. This is then seen as justification for procedures that give clients little control over decisions. In this way, bureaucratic services build in a self-fulfilling view of the incompetence of clients and rationalize professional control over them.

A second structural factor that institutionalizes blindness to interdependence in professional-client relationships is male dominance of professional norms. In the dominant values of this industrialized, urbanized society, work is conceived of in impersonal, utilitarian terms, and contrasted with caring relationships. By utilitarian terms, we mean the evaluation of work on the basis of its efficiency as an impersonal instrument in achieving some predefined goal. The goals are defined primarily in terms of the accumulation of power in a hierarchy of people competing for a limited supply of material rewards or prestige. In terms of utilitarian values, even when cooperation or mutually rewarding interactions among people are promoted on the job, they are conceived of as means that may be useful to the organization in reaching a favorable position in relation to other, competing organizations (Lenrow, 1978b). By caring, we mean one person's nuturing of another person's potential resources. This involves respect for people's strivings for a sense of competence in shaping their own lives (Smith, 1974; White, 1960) and for a sense of participating in something larger than their own most narrow or immediate interests (Bakan, 1966). In the dominant, utilitarian conception of work, people are tools and relationships are means to some impersonal end. In caring relationships, the well-being of people is valued as an end in itself, not as a means to some other end.

The dominant belief in this society is that caring must be suppressed on the job in the interests of utility and controlled competitiveness. In this widely held stereotype, caring is for the home and is thought to be an appropriate concern for women (Block, 1973; Broverman et al., 1972). This traditional belief that work and caring are mutually exclusive is violated when work is defined as helping or human service. Such a hybrid form of work generates tension because no one is clear about how to deal with the contrast between utilitarian values and caring.

In professional training, there is a tendency to deal with these tensions by regarding professional work in thoroughly utilitarian terms. This means ignoring or denying the idea that promoting people's well-being involves treating their potential resources as central in the relationship. When professionals ignore the resources that clients can contribute, such a mind set limits thinking about the range of alternatives that might be adopted in developing a relationship to serve a client's interests. When professional training encourages such a mind set, there is a danger that professional helping will not only neglect caring, but will neglect so much important information about people that it will not serve utilitarian values either (Stone, 1979).

An important factor in reinforcing utilitarian values in the professions to the exclusion of caring is the domination of the professions by men. Men are generally socialized in this society to be more comfortable with impersonal relationships on the job. Moreover, the job in the helping professions requires responding constantly to people who are in distress. Men are typically socialized to deal with distress — their own and others' — by being detached, controlling their emotional expression, trying to gain control over the situation, and suppressing wishes for nurturance, protection, or other forms of dependency. With this sort of emotional conditioning, they are often very uncomfortable about the prospect that a professional might display emotions such as concern, tenderness, and appreciation in the face of a client's distress, or might admit to depending on the client's resources. At the prospect that such feelings might be expressed, men often talk as if this would open the floodgates to uncontrolled emotions and "hurt professional standards," such as detachment, rationality, and impartiality.

Women in the helping professions may be more comfortable exploring how caring relationships with clients can be integrated with work roles (Howell, 1975). But there is strong resistance because men still control the definition of professional norms. And men in the professions, like most other men, are less ready to depart from the traditional separation of work and caring. Even in fields where women outnumber men (e.g., nursing and some specialities in social work), there is a tendency for the leadership to be preoccupied with proving that their fields measure up in terms of the utilitarian standards of the rest of the male-dominated professions.

TAKING INTERDEPENDENCE SERIOUSLY IN PROFESSIONAL-CLIENT RELATIONSHIPS

Despite these institutional, cultural, interpersonal, and intrapsychic obstacles, there are individual professionals whose modes of helping take seriously the interdependence of professional and client. What are the hallmarks of such professional helping? How do these professionals deal with the interdependence? How do they deal with tensions between work and caring? In addressing these questions, we describe such professional helping in terms of dilemmas, problem-solving, and the promotion of health.

As soon as professionals recognize their interdependence with clients, they face dilemmas: How can I take initiative and use my own best judgment when the effectiveness of my skills and judgments depends on what the client is willing and able to contribute in the way of knowledge and skills? And how can I behave in keeping with my own values when a client's willingness to contribute his or her own resources will depend on that person's perception that I am acting in ways consistent with the client's values? Since the professional does not initially know what values he or she has in common with the client, it is not clear how to take initiative without inadvertently discouraging the client from taking initiative or without presuming too much about what working relationship will fit the client's values as well as one's own (Lenrow, 1978b).

Professionals who open themselves to such dilemmas by taking interdependence seriously seem to deal with them by giving careful attention to the perceptions and priorities of the client from the outset, proposing provisional ground rules for their working relationship, and encouraging the client to propose changes in the ground rules in order to make them more consistent with his or her values: "Would you tell me a bit about how you decided to see me? What led you to be concerned about this? The way I usually like to work is. . . . Does it make sense to you that we start out that way and decide together as we go what ways of working fit us best?" Similarly, the professionals we are describing rely heavily on the clients' perceptions (as well as their own) in formulating the problem and a range of options for dealing with it. They encourage the client to critique these judgments, to ask for explanations, and to offer alternative ideas based on their own perceptions and values.

These professionals do not only solicit the client's opinions and show respectful interest when they are offered. They also ask the client to help them check to see if the professional's impression corresponds with what the client intended. In this way, professionals demonstrate that (a) they do not want to presume to know what the client's comments mean, and (b) they are prepared, and need, to learn from the client's perceptions and judgments. They need to learn not only about specific matters on which the client has expertise — such as the prior history of the problem, people who can be called on to help with the problem, and responsibilities that affect how it is feasible to deal with the problem — but also about what the client's views and concerns are in every phase of their work together.

These professional helpers proceed with a mix of confidence and humility: confidence that, as people who are initially strangers to their clients, they can bring fresh and varied perspectives to the clients' problems; humility in that they cannot initially know whether or to what extent these perspectives will be suited to the life situations of the clients. They can have confidence that they bring ideas and skills that have been useful to other people; but they must have humility about whether or not they will be able to enlist the resources of a given client enough to help generate a useful range of options for that client.

Professionals who take interdependence seriously seem to proceed from the premise that in promoting another person's well-being, it is essential that the person use and strengthen his or her skills in decision-making. Most professionals regard good decision-making skills as a central part of their own expertise. They often guide or critique their own work in terms of an idealized model of systematic decision-making. The model typically includes such processes as clarifying the problem; identifying factors that contribute to the problem; generating the widest range of possible solutions; attaching weights to the risks involved in each option; selecting an option; assigning responsibility for implementing the option; evaluating the effectiveness of the implementation; and cycling back to check prior steps if the results are not satisfactory. Professionals who take interdependence seriously not only critique their own decision-making in such terms, but also proceed on the assumption that at every step in this process, they need information that only the client can provide (Stone, 1979). In addition, they see it as crucial for the long-term well-being of clients that the clients use such processes of decision-making. They consciously try to model good decision-making as they collaborate with clients in dealing with their specific problems. But, in addition to applying good decision-making to problems *after* they have arisen, they coach their clients in how to make decisions that are likely to *prevent* problems from becoming serious. The assumption here is that by becoming more effective in recognizing the consequences of their everyday choices, clients can learn not just to reduce problems, but to make choices that promote their health, i.e., their sense of competence, coherence, and mutually satisfying relationships (Antonovsky, 1979; Smith, 1974).

This coaching includes encouragement and information about how clients can approach other professionals and service agencies in ways that enhance the clients' self-respect rather than leaving them feeling defeated or degraded. It includes adding to their information about how to find resources that will be useful in making good decisions and resources that will be useful in implementing them. And it includes providing them with information about what contributes to healthy bodily and psychological functioning.

Hypothetically, the fact that these professionals engage clients as active participants in decision-making itself contributes to their self-esteem as respected collaborators (Haan, 1979). To the extent that the decisions in which they participate are effective in dealing with their specific problems, they experience self-esteem through a sense of competence (White, 1960). And to the extent that they learn how to make health-promoting decisions, they experience a greater degree of direction over their own lives.

What does it look like when professionals approach clients from such a perspective? Some vignettes:

A fifth-grade teacher is correcting written assignments in her classroom while her students are supervised on the playground by other staff. She notes that the writing of most students shows many careless errors and a minimum of effort. A group of students bursts into the room and reports that there is a new aide on the playground who would not let them play where they always have before. As the rest of the class returns from recess, the teacher gathers them all in a circle to hear the complaints: "What happened? What made that so upsetting? What do you think you might be able to do about it? Do you think the new aide knows how you feel about it? Do you think she knows what upset you? Would you like her to know? What might be some ways to let her know? Yes, I could talk to her or ask the prinicpal to, but are there ways *you* could let her know? Yes, you tried to tell her. How did that work? Are there other ways you could tell her? Yes, when you are not mad any more. Yes, you could write it. What do the rest of you think about this? Who saw and heard what happened? Could you pair off and talk about what you would want to tell the aide? How about having pairs with one person who was right there and one person who was not there? Will that work? Then how about groups of two or three? OK? Does that work out right? Now, you know we have been talking in class about how writing can be a good way to tell people things. After you come up with suggestions about what you would want to tell that aide, do you think you could write a letter to let her know? Yes, a real letter to give to her. You can see whether it helps to write down your ideas and put them the way you want them. Let's have each group of two or three write a letter as an example. And when we get back together in the circle, you can read the examples and choose which ideas and which ways of saying things you might want to put in a final letter. What do you think about that idea? Sounds good, huh? Let's try it out and see what you come up with. After you see what the groups come up with, you can decide what to do next about this problem. Now, in the small groups, how about taking turns writing the ideas and checking the spelling and punctuation? Then you will get the ideas and the writing skills of each person and wind up with letters that will be clearer for the group to read. By working together, you can check each other's work. Ready to try it? Do you all remember where to look up spelling and punctuation? Let's see if every group has a book handy. OK, let's all get back in the circle in twenty-five minutes. Then those of you who are upset about what she did can decide what would be a good thing to do about it."

A lawyer sits down in his office with a new client who is buying a condominium and wants an evaluation of the purchase and sale contract that has been provided by the seller: "Well, generally, I like to see whether or not a client has any questions or concerns about the purchase before I go over a contract, even a routine one. That way, when I'm checking on whether it is properly drawn in terms of the legal technicalities, I can evaluate whether there are terms in it that are likely to give you problems in the areas that you are especially concerned about. It does not cost you any more for me to check that out while I am reading the documents. It also protects me, so you do not call me after I have said the contract is OK and tell me you are upset that it does not accomplish something you wanted. So what sort of a condominium is this? And how are you planning to use it — rent it out, live there, office, or what? Can you give me an idea of what you have at stake in this purchase; that is, does this represent a risky financial venture where you cannot afford to have anything go wrong or you will lose your shirt, or is this an investment that does not represent much of a financial worry to you? So you will be deeply in debt and want to guarantee that you will have no further costs besides the ones you listed? Well, from what you have heard about the city ordinances, we had better check out what the rent commission is ruling these days about buildings that are being converted from rental apartments. You can save yourself some money by going down to city hall yourself and asking for copies of these documents [*Writes down their technical names.*]. Let me explain what these are and why we need them. If I go down and get that information, I will have to charge you for the time. Or, if I write and request the documents in order to save the trip down there and the additional costs to you, it will take at least a week. And from what you said, it sounds like you are in a hurry to settle this. Is that right? Now when you are down there, sometimes those clerks give you a hard time and say that these papers are not available. If they do, just say that your attorney advised you to pick up those papers. For some reason, that seems to get them to be more cooperative. They probably figure that lawyers know what their clients have a right to see. I will keep a copy of this contract, and if you drop the other papers off in the next couple of days, I will read all of this and call you at the end of the week. In the meantime, if you have any questions, call me."

A psychologist meets in his office with a thirteen-year-old boy and his parents: (*To the boy*) "When did you first hear that your folks had made an appointment for all of you to see me? . . . Whose idea was it to do that? Do you know why they set up this appointment?" (*The parents explain.*) "So he has been good in school until this year and now he is getting Cs and 'talking back to teachers.' " "Would you say more about 'talking back to teachers.' What did you mean by that? So you received 'poor work slips' from two teachers and on one it said that he talked back to the teacher. *(To the boy)* Can you give me an idea of what the teacher is talking about? You were telling that kid to stop throwing spit balls, and the teacher yelled at you. And when you tried to explain, the teacher thought you were being a wise guy." *(The parents explain that the misunderstanding with that teacher has been settled and the son and teacher now are getting along fine. But they cannot get him to do his homework.)* "You say 'He always was so cooperative up until now.' Would you say a little more about that? So compared to his older sister, he has been no trouble, but now he is not doing his homework when you want him to? When did you start to feel that you needed to talk to someone like me about this? The guidance counselor said he did not know what more he could do? Do you remember what led you to talk to the guidance counselor? So you had been after him to stop watching television and do his homework, and when you were screaming at him, you almost belted him? It sounds like that was pretty upsetting for you. So you figured that things were getting out of hand and you could use some advice? Well, it is not at all unusual for parents to get so frustrated that they feel like belting their kids, but it can be scary." *(To the boy)* "Do you remember how you felt when that happened? Do you have any ideas about what got things so heated up? You think that your dad was upset about the way your sister had screamed at your mother and ran out of the house? And you are in junior high now, but you feel they treat you like a baby?" *(To the parents)* "What do you think about that? So you think he has a point there. It sounds like you would like to find ways of dealing with each other that work better for you all."

A nurse meets with ten four-year-olds in a preschool as part of a health education program: "Hi. How are you?" ("Fine." "Good.") "You know when someone says, 'Hi. How are you?' and you say, 'Fine,' what does that mean — 'I am fine?' " ("I am feeling fine." "I am good.") "Yes, and what is another word for that? What is another way you could say that?" ("OK." "I am feeling OK." "Healthy!") "Yes, you could say all of those things. When we say, 'I am healthy,' what is that like? What can you do when you are healthy?" ("Go outside." "Jump high.") "Yes, and when you are healthy and you sit quietly by yourself, how do you feel?" ("You feel good.") [*Listens to stories about times they were sick and times they felt good.*] "Who helps you stay healthy?" ("The doctor." "Nurses, like you!" "My mommy." "My aunt." "Daddy.") "Yes, those people are all part of your 'Keep-Healthy Team.' What do you think that is?" [*Listens to children's ideas about staying healthy.*] "What is a 'team?'" ("Like a baseball team." "They play together." "A football team." "My daddy is on a bowling team." [*Discussion about people they know on teams.*] "Yes, when people work all together, they are a team. And people like doctors, nurses, mommies, and daddies work together to help you stay healthy. So they are a team. Doctors and nurses know things to help you stay healthy. Mommies and daddies are important on the team because they are with you a lot and can see that you eat things that help you stay healthy. And they are with you a lot and can see how you feel." [*Listens to stories about things their mommies gave them to eat that were "good for them."*] "But who are you with all the time?" ("My mommie.") "Who else are you with even more of the time?" ("My brother." "My dog sleeps on my bed.") [*Listens to ideas about pets.*] "OK. But besides mommies, daddies, brothers, and pets, who are you with *all* the time?" ("Me!" "Myself.") "Yes, you are with yourself all the time. And when you are all by yourself, without your mom and dad around, it is important for you to know some things about how to help keep yourself healthy. But usually you can call your mom or dad to help. And that is important because teams work best when people work together." [*Listens to stories about working together.*] "Who is the *most important* member of your 'Keep-Healthy Team?'" ("The doctor." "Mommie." "Daddy.") "They are important, but there is someone else who is even more important on your team. Who is that?" ("Me!") "Yes, you! What do you think about that?" [*Listens to ideas about how they help the rest of the team.*]

In all of these vignettes, the professionals are approaching their clients (or students) as collaborators, whose active contributions the professionals depend on in order to be able to use their own skills effectively. They all provide information about how the system of formal and informal helping works and how the individual can take a central role in it. They encourage clients to be confident that it is *appropriate* for them to expect to participate as an active collaborator with a professional and that it *benefits both* the professional and the client for them to participate as equals.

When a professional combines these characteristics with coaching the client to be an active participant in decision-making with other professionals (as well as in informal support networks such as family and friends), this begins to transform their relationship. After an initial collaboration, the professional and client are no longer complete strangers to each other. They know what values they have in common and can appeal to in order to keep the working relationship collaborative. So long as there is an expectation that they may work together again after an initial collaboration, they begin to experience themselves as part of an ongoing network, or team, that is committed to certain common values concerning health and well-being.

Approaching clients as active participants on a team serves the professionals' utilitarian values: They will get better cooperation, be trusted on a more realistic basis, have more information on which to base effective decisions, and find that clients are more effective in implementing decisions. But such a mode of working with clients also serves nonutilitarian values: health in the positive sense of fulfillment, rather than only the absence of disorder; respect for the resources of all participants; and a sense of community as well as a sense of competence. This mix of utilitarian and nonutilitarian values has much in common with the values of laypeople in mutual-aid networks.

INTERDEPENDENCE AND RELATIONS BETWEEN PROFESSIONALS AND LAY NETWORKS OF MUTUAL AID

When professionals recognize their interdependence with clients, it has the effect of equalizing their power. The process that ensues is a form of mutual aid between professional and client. For these professionals, there is little dissonance between the ways they work with clients and the ways laypeople help in mutual-aid networks. Consequently, when they try to work with mutual-aid lay groups, these professionals are more able to establish credibility as collaborators who have as much to learn as to teach. They are perceived as using their power *with* and not *over* people (Howell, 1980; Szasz & Hollender, 1956). But such professional helpers are still very rare. What are the prospects for changes that will nurture the development of more of them?

We have identified formidable obstacles to taking interdependence seriously in professional helping. What possibilities are there of reducing the obstacles or surmounting them? In this chapter, we do not propose a strategy for change. Elsewhere one of us (Lenrow & Cowden, 1980) has proposed a combination of short-term reforms and long-term efforts at promoting mutual-aid networks and raising consciousness about the beliefs that obscure professionals' interdependence with clients. Here we simply point to developments in the society that offer some hope that the interdependence of professionals and clients will become a first principle in professional helping — a principle modeled in professional training and exemplified in professional practice.

There are promising currents of change in both values and knowledge. In the domain of values, there is the *community movement,* recognizing the importance of a sense of belonging to a community, where there is mutual respect, mutual aid, and commitment to common goals. The *ecology movement* gives central place to the interdependence of living things. It also emphasizes that the settings in which people live and work are the places where resources must be directed in order to reduce stress and promote healthy conditions. This deemphasizes the idea of remedying human problems by providing services in large bureaucratic institutions. These movements are joined by the *consumer movement,* which encourages users of human services to organize and become well-informed in order to hold the providers of services accountable for the quality of their services (Sunderland, 1976). It attempts to raise consciousness about the myths that have made services so hard for citizens/consumers to influence.

The *self-help movement* draws on these other three movements and adds important currents of its own. It emphasizes the importance of nonprofessional, nonbureaucratized, informal helping through enduring social networks, rather than lone, unusually skilled, individual helpers. It also emphasizes help on the basis of mutual self-interest rather than altruism (Sarason & Lorentz, 1979). There is the *women's movement,* which exposes falacies, stereotypes, and discriminatory practices that perpetuate male control over work roles and arbitrary definitions of acceptable expressive styles. It emphasizes, as does the *civil rights movement,* that such stereotypes and practices stunt the full psychological development of men and women. Finally, there is the *preventive health movement,* which focuses on learning to cope with stress, on the one hand, and promoting "wellness," on the other. Part of this latter idea is an emphasis on suiting health care to the whole person — in particular, to the individual's need for a sense of coherence (Antonovsky, 1979). In contrast to narrowly specialized and largely isolated services, it encourages modes of health care that are integrated into the person's everyday life.

In the areas of substantive concern to each of these movements, there has been impressive development of new knowledge. For example, in the field of sex-role learning, so fateful for attitudes toward dependency, nurturance, emotional control, and competitiveness, there has been a major growth of social science research (Block, 1973; Broverman et al., 1972; Rebecca et al., 1976). In relation to health care, there has developed a whole new field, health psychology, which attempts to conceptualize how health care is being provided, on what beliefs it is based, with what effectiveness it is administered, and how it could be made more effective (Haan, 1979; Kagan, 1979; Stone, 1979). Promising techniques have also been developed for training interested professionals to be more sensitive to the views of their clients (Kagan, 1979).

All of these currents are transforming the domain of health education. They are making it a field for integrating and applying all of these values and all of this knowledge, in schools, continuing education, health care settings, and mass-communication media. As such educational programs expose more and more people to the themes of these movements, laypeople, especially young people, may indeed come to believe, "I am the most important member of my health-care team."

We hope that this essay can contribute to these important currents so that eventually laypeople will be able to count on being active and valued participants in all decisions that affect their well-being. In the meantime, we hope that our analysis can guide both laypeople and professionals in deciding which professionals are compatible with the values and self-interests of mutual-aid networks. We propose that the crucial test is how seriously the professional takes the interdependence of participants in any helping relationship.

NOTE

1. By "help," we mean interaction between two or more people that is (a) uncoerced, (b) intended to benefit at least one of them, (c) unambiguous as to who is intended to benefit, and (d) experienced by the intended beneficiary as enhancing his or her well-being (i.e., bodily integrity, efficacy, belonging in a network of supportive relationships, and/or sense of coherent purpose).

REFERENCES

ANTONOVSKY, A. *Health, stress, and coping.* San Francisco: Jossey-Bass, 1979.

BAKAN, D. *The duality of human existence.* Boston: Beacon Press, 1966.

BLOCK, J. H. Conceptions of sex role: Some cross-cultural and longitudinal perspectives. *American Psychologist,* 1973, *28,* 512-526.

BROVERMAN, I. K., VOGEL, S. R., BROVERMAN, D. M., CLARKSON, F. E., & ROSENKRANTZ, P. S. Sex-role stereotypes: A current appraisal. *Journal of Social Issues,* 1972, *28,* 59-78.

CHESLER, M. A., & LOHMAN, J. E. Changing schools through student advocacy. In R. A. Schmuck & M. B. Miles (Eds.), *Organization development in schools.* Palo Alto, CA: National Press, 1971.

COLLINS, A. H., & PANCOAST, D. L. *Natural helping networks: A strategy for prevention.* Washington, DC: National Association of Social Workers, 1976.

ERIKSON, E. H. Growth and crises of the healthy personality. *Psychological Issues,* 1959, *1*(Monograph 1), 50-100.

GARTNER, A., & RIESSMAN, F. *Self-help in the human services.* San Francisco: Jossey-Bass, 1977.

HAAN, N. G. Psychosocial meanings of unfavorable medical forecasts. In G. C. Stone, F. Cohen, & N. E. Adler (Eds.), *Health psychology: A handbook.* San Francisco: Jossey-Bass, 1979.

HOWELL, M. C. *Helping ourselves: Families and the human network.* Boston: Beacon Press, 1975.

HOWELL, M. C. *Separatism and sex-role change.* Paper presented at a symposium, Competence and Caring: Working out the balance. Lincoln School, Providence, Rhode Island, April 1980.

HUGHES, E. *The sociological eye: Selected papers on work, self, and the study of society, II.* Chicago: Aldine, 1971.

INNES, J. M. Does the professional know what the client wants? *Social Science and Medicine,* 1977, *11,* 635-638.

KAGAN, N. Counseling psychology, interpersonal skills, and health care. In G. C. Stone, F. Cohen, & N. E. Adler (Eds.), *Health psychology: A handbook.* San Francisco: Jossey-Bass, 1979.

KATZ, A. H., & BENDER, E. I. Self-help groups in Western society: History and prospects. *Journal of Applied Behavioral Science,* 1976, *12,* 265-282.

KLEIMAN, M. A., MANTELL, J. E., & ALEXANDER, E. S. Collaboration and its discontents: The perils of partnership. *Journal of Applied Behavioral Science,* 1976, *12,* 403-410.

LENROW, P. Dilemmas of professional helping: Continuities and discontinuities with folk helping relationships. In L. Wispe (Ed.), *Altruism, sympathy, and helping.* New York: Academic Press, 1978. (a)

LENROW, P. The work of helping strangers. *American Journal of Community Psychology,* 1978, *6,* 555-571. (b)

LENROW, P., & COWDEN, P. Human services, professionals, and the paradox of institutional reform. *American Journal of Community Psychology,* 1980, *8,* 463-484.

LEVY, L. H. Self-help groups: Types and psychological processes. *Journal of Applied Behavioral Science*, 1976, *12*, 310-322.

REBECCA, M., HEFNER, R., & OLESHANSKY, B. A model of sex-role transcendence. *Journal of Social Issues*, 1976, *32*, 197-206.

SARASON, S. B., & LORENTZ, E. *The challenge of the resource exchange network.* San Francisco: Jossey-Bass, 1979.

SMITH, M. B. Normality for an abnormal age. *Humanizing social psychology.* San Francisco: Jossey-Bass, 1974.

STONE, G. C. Patient compliance and the role of the expert. *Journal of Social Issues*, 1979, *35*, 34-59.

SUNDERLAND, S. C. *Citizen empowerment manual.* New York: College of Human Services, 1976. (Mimeo)

SZASZ, T. S., & HOLLENDER, M. H. A contribution to the philosophy of medicine: The basic models of the doctor-patient relationship. *Archives of Internal Medicine*, 1956, *97*, 585-592.

TAYLOR, S. E. Hospital patient behavior: reactance, helplessness, or control. *Journal of Social Issues*, 1979, *35*, 156-184.

WHITE, R. W. Competence and the psychosexual stages of development. *Nebraska Symposium on Motivation.* Lincoln: University of Nebraska Press, 1960.

Chapter 10

LINKING FORMAL AND INFORMAL SUPPORT SYSTEMS

CHARLES FROLAND, DIANE L. PANCOAST,
NANCY J. CHAPMAN, and PRISCILLA J. KIMBOKO

The debate about the role of the state in providing for the welfare of its citizens is at least as old as the Poor Laws. In moving from a residual to an institutional concept of the role of the public sector in the Western industrialized countries, those of us involved as professionals in the delivery of human services may at times have lost sight of the substantial role that informal caregiving still plays in the daily lives of our clients and those who manage not to become clients (Gladstone, 1979).

Considerable interest has been shown recently both by policy makers and mental health agencies in understanding how informal caregiving fits into the contemporary view of human services and in examining ways of combining professional, voluntary, neighborhood, and family sources of support in a more deliberately articulated pattern (President's Commission on Mental Health, 1978; National Commission on Neighborhoods, 1979). While this new interest in informal caregiving offers the possibility of more and better services, it raises many questions that must be resolved in linking formal and

Authors' Note: "Natural Helping Networks and Service Delivery," Grant 18-P-00088, Office of Human Development Services, Office of Policy Development, HHS. For a description of the sample of thirty agencies and a further description of the study, see Froland, Pancoast, Chapman, & Kimboko, 1980.

informal support. For example, what is the appropriate division of responsibility between the care that should be provided under public or professional auspices and that which people should be expected to provide for themselves? Is there a risk that the promotion of mutual help and the mobilization of informal sources of support will provide a political justification for reduced expenditures for statutory services? How does the quality of care provided informally compare to that provided by professionals? If informal care is desirable, how is it possible for mental health workers to support informal helping systems without drastically changing either the nature of informal care or the accepted role of the professional practitioners?

These questions are important to all human services practitioners and policy makers. In mental health specifically, emphasis on deinstitutionalization and the development of catchment-based services have focused attention on the role of community members in the provision of mental health care (Gershon & Biller, 1977). The current interest in community support systems for the chronically mentally ill (Turner & TenHoor, 1978) is a more recent expression of concern for including informal caring in a broad conception of community mental health.

As the interest in developing mutually beneficial connections between professionals and various informal helpers moves to the stage of identifying strategies for action, theory and ideology must come to terms with the realities of practice. Confusion often results. This confusion stems from the difficulties of trying to reconcile the fundamental differences between formal and informal ways of providing support and is felt both by practitioners and program administrators. In everyday practice, professionals and informal caregivers have to grapple with differing assumptions and expectations about what "support" means and how it should be provided. Program policy makers must try to reconcile different purposes for involving informal networks of support in service delivery (Darvill, 1975). In many ways, trying to combine the efforts of professional service providers with those of family members, concerned neighbors, and devoted friends is like trying to link two cultures in which very different beliefs, customs, and norms of exchange prevail (see, for example, Lenrow and Burch's chapter in this volume). Both practitioners and policy makers in the formal service system are presented with a number of choices for attempting to relate to informal systems of support. The choices that are made can easily lead to tensions when representatives of the two systems have different ideas about who should be involved and in what way.

This chapter examines what some of these tensions are, where they can occur in programs and practice, and how they might be resolved. We will consider the difficulties these tensions can create for agencies and professionals, and we will describe their implications for program design and implementation. Our intent will not be to point out why the task of combining the efforts of professionals and informal helpers should be undertaken, or to provide a comprehensive picture of what the task entails. Rather, we direct our discussion to those who consider the task worth while but wish to avoid some of the potential conflicts that can occur in the development of program policies and in the course of professional practice. Our purpose in this regard will be to suggest points for consideration rather than to prescribe solutions.

We divide our discussion of considerations for program design into three areas. First, we discuss some of the major differences between the support provided by professionals and the support rendered by informal helping systems in order to provide a basis for understanding how the relationship between the two systems can produce tensions. Second, we consider some of the issues involved in defining a role for informal sources of support and in identifying the program purposes that might be served by these roles. Finally, we examine a range of factors that have implications for modifying the traditional role of the professional.

Our examination of the foregoing issues will draw upon the findings of a study we have conducted of thirty agencies in which professional staff have developed working partnerships with informal support networks within the communities they serve. The study represents an exploratory effort to understand how human service agencies can strengthen the role of existing networks of informal helping or foster new sources of informal support in dealing with different types of client problems or target populations. We will make use of observations by the staffs of these agencies in order to illustrate what difficulties were encountered and to suggest how they might be handled. Before we consider the three major issues, it will be useful to provide a brief overview of the ways in which agency staff in our study were combining their efforts with those of informal helpers.

OVERVIEW OF PROGRAM STRATEGIES

The programs we visited included a wide array of agencies reflecting a diversity in target populations and problems being served, staff size and available resources, and community settings. Table 10.1 displays the five general program strategies we identified among the thirty agencies (Froland et al., 1979). The first strategy listed, *personal network intervention,* focused on an individual client's support system. Here, agency staff were concerned with providing consultation and assistance to sustain and reinforce the informal efforts of family, friends and neighbors known to a client. The second strategy, *volunteer linking,* was adopted in situations where existing sources of personal support were limited, and involved matching lay helpers to clients in order to provide companionship, support, and advocacy. A third strategy, *mutual-aid networks,* was the most common approach utilized by the agencies in the sample, and involved the development of links between individuals with common problems, interests, or backgrounds for the purpose of sharing resources and reducing social isolation. The last two strategies were directed at a neighborhood or community. The *neighborhood helper* strategy involved identifying central figures in a neighborhood who were performing key helping roles informally, and developing a consultative relationship to support existing patterns of help and to prevent the need for formal services. The last approach, *community empowerment,* involved the development of ties among informal opinion leaders within a community in order to plan improvements in services and to identify existing resources for meeting needs. These five approaches were frequently combined in a coordinated strategy for working with informal sources of help, and most often were employed in conjunction with backup services within the agency or available in other agencies.

DIFFERENCES BETWEEN FORMAL AND INFORMAL CARE

The boundary between professional services and informal systems of support is in many ways a line between the bureaucratic and the communal, a distinction between "the public world of the bureaucrat and the private world of mothers" (Abrams, 1978). Briefly, we define formal care as governmentally mandated or sponsored professional services, whether state-administered or provided

TABLE 10.1 Overview of Program Strategies

APPROACH	STRATEGY	ACTORS
Personal network	• consult with client's significant others; support existing efforts • convene network of providers and family, friends, and others to resolve problems. • expand client's range of social ties	• family members, friends, neighbors, service providers
Volunteer linking	• provide lay therapists for counseling • establish companionate relationships • recruit and link volunteer advocates to clients	• citizen volunteers • people with skills, interests relevant to client's needs • people with similar experience
Mutual aid networks	• establish peer support groups • consult with existing groups and support activities	• local religious associations • clients with similar problems • people with shared concerns
Neighborhood helpers	• establish consultative arrangement with neighbor to monitor problems • convene neighbors to promote local helping	• neighbors • clerks, managers in local businesses • religious leaders
Community empowerment	• establish local task forces for meeting community needs • provide for community forums to have input into local policies	• opinion leaders in local business, religious institutions • members of local voluntary associations • neighborhood leaders

through chartered intermediaries, such as private nonprofit organizations. As such, formal care also includes some private practice when controlled by either regulation or reimbursement, as well as services provided by voluntary organizations that receive governmental financial support either directly or indirectly through tax transfers. Informal care includes those sources of care and assistance provided by kin, friends, and neighbors; indigenous or natural helpers; and informal self-help or mutual-aid activities found within networks or groups, usually on an unorganized or spontaneous basis (Wolfenden Report, 1978).

Informal networks of support are a realm of care that is highly pluralistic and differentiated in the types of people involved, what they do, and why (see Pancoast and Chapman, forthcoming; Curry and Young, 1978). Helpers in ongoing relationships include family members, trusted friends, and new acquaintances who are willing to help out. People who offer to help strangers as volunteers or members of a mutual-aid group may be individuals who have a special concern about particular problems because they experienced them in their own lives or are close to someone who has; people who want to try out a role analogous to a professional helping role; or people who have time and skills that are underutilized. Neighborhood or community helpers may have some special talent; they may be particularly resourceful in getting things done, or they may simply take an interest in local concerns and get involved with a wide range of people.

These different types of people can and do perform essential roles as part of a support system for others. Some are specialists in the sense that they have a particular knowledge or skill that is well suited to specific tasks. Others are generalists and help in a variety of ways. Some are more interested in helping those they know or those who are neighbors, while others offer help in a wide number of circumstances, often with people who are initially strangers. For many, what they do is an integral part of their life and may be a consequence of family background, a particular job or position, or other personal experience. Looked at more broadly, these types of individuals make up an ecological system of everyday helping in which people play interrelated or complementary roles in helping each other, providing support, or getting things done in the neighborhood or community. Informal helping is not a one-way activity but a mutual flow, involving the receipt and donation of help. Help is provided as part of a continuing set of mutual exchanges that constitute a larger system of rights and obligations within a primary group, neighborhood, or culture (for elaboration, see Lenrow, 1976; Riessman, 1976).

In contrast, formal services operate under a system of explicit categories for assessing need or eligibility; formal rules of procedure; specialization and formal coordination among helping roles; definitions and expectations associated with client or consumer status; consistency of standards for treating problems independent of personal characteristics or situations; and objectively stated criteria for what constitutes success or progress. Expressed in the terms of classical sociology, the distinction between the world of lay helpers and the world of professionals lies in the contrast drawn by Weber between bureaucratic and primary-group relations (see Litwak, 1978), or by Parsons in his discussion of pattern variables characterizing action based, for example, on universalistic versus particularistic criteria (see Abrams, 1978).

As more theoretical representations of the differences between formal and informal support, these contrasts suggest that attempts to combine the efforts of each type of support will encounter basic conflicts (Froland, 1980b). On the face of it, an attempt to link formal and informal modes of support would seem to result in a clash of two different cultures: one seeking the reliability of formal rules and routine procedures, the other emphasizing the privacy of unspoken rules and spontaneous activity (Abrams, 1978). Norms of exchange, conceptions of problems and solutions, and matters of authority and responsibility are considerably different and potentially at odds. It might be argued that such different systems of support are perhaps alien to one another, and that the best relationship one may hope for is peaceful coexistence.

By and large the two worlds of care are separate and independent most of the time. People generally meet most of their daily needs through informal relationships and expect to "play by the rules" when they choose (or are forced) to rely on formal sources of help. However, there are also many instances in which these distinctions are blurred and where the need arises to achieve a blend of the characteristics of the two types of care: when a local group of priests requests family life education sessions from a family service agency for parishioners; when an agency providing home-based services for the elderly receives a request for a homemaker but does not want to disturb the web of informal caring already in place; when a mutual-help group decides to seek funding from the United Way in order to hire a staff person and publicize its activities; when a settlement house decides it has lost touch with a neighborhood and wants to reestablish a presence.

Clearly, it is not impossible for formal and informal sources of support to complement each other; indeed, as Litwak (1978) has argued, exchange between both types is necessary in dealing with the various tasks of care. The difficulty of establishing such a complementary exchange stems from the task of balancing the tensions arising from often contradictory values and assumptions regarding how care should be provided (Litwak & Meyer, 1974). Given these tensions, what is the appropriate role of informal helpers in the delivery of agency services?

ROLE OF INFORMAL SUPPORT IN PROGRAMS

The impetus to incorporate volunteers, indigenous helpers, self-help resources, and other informal, nonprofessional sources of care into the context of mandated or publicly sponsored service agencies has traditionally had a number of alternative rationales (Litwak, 1978). One stems from a concern about the costs of trained professional providers, attendant shortages of skilled personnel, and projected increases in demand or needs for formal services. These concerns have launched a debate about the feasibility of substituting nonprofessional for professional services with the hope of meeting demand while reducing the expense of using scarce public resources (Gershon & Biller, 1977). This *cost effectiveness* thesis argues that there are certain tasks that can be performed by untrained lay helpers with little or no pay, thus obviating the need for more expensive and scarce professional resources. Evidence of a declining GNP, citizen tax revolts, and burgeoning demands for services have combined to lend an urgency to the cost effectiveness thesis (Davies, 1980).

A second rationale for involving informal helpers in the human services is often based on a critique of professional services. It is argued that professional services are inaccessible or unresponsive to clients, insensitive to different cultures or special needs, or unlikely to allow a meaningful participatory role for clients and citizens. Nonprofessional or indigenous helpers are seen as providing a "bridge" between providers and consumers, one that is likely to improve the acceptability of services to local groups. This *social participation* thesis suggests that, because indigenous helpers are integrated into a client culture and share similar values with that culture, they will be better equipped to identify needs and to relate professional services to clients more appropriately (Levine et al., 1978).

A third orientation, characterized as an *organizational effectiveness* rationale, forms a wider backdrop for deciding on the role of informal helpers in service delivery. Similar to the cost effectiveness orientation in that it views the formal sector as having overarching responsibility for seeing that care is provided, it is different in viewing informal caregiving as inherently better suited to certain tasks than formal agencies, not just less expensive. Assuming that rationalistic structures with universalistic criteria, routine procedures, and formalized systems of management offer a way to provide greater equity, reliability, and efficiency in the delivery of services (Wilensky & Lebeaux, 1958), the role of the formal sector is to find the best way to organize the tasks of care. Tasks requiring, for example, technical knowledge or the routine administration of resources can best be handled by formally organized professional services. Practical tasks with many unexpected contingencies should be handled by families, friends, and other informal sources of support (see Litwak, 1978). Since most tasks require both uniform and nonuniform activities, there will be a need to combine efforts. In theory, the resulting role defined for informal helpers depends on how much of each kind of activity is required.

While not exhausting the possibilities, these rationales prompt diverse responses to the question of how and why the community might be involved in the delivery of public services. Since each orientation has attractive elements, we may wish to adopt all at the same time. In practice, however, these orientations may be incompatible, since "action taken to promote [one] will create conditions and circumstances inimical to the development of the other[s]" (Tucker, 1980). For example, emphasizing the cost effectiveness rationale, we may opt to involve informal helpers only where they may efficiently substitute for professionals. Adopting a social participation rationale, we would likely design a program that encourages informal helping for its own sake and that is highly sensitive to the individual abilities of the helpers. The organizational effectiveness rationale may lead to role definitions for informal helpers that are either fairly restrictive or more expansive, depending on a judgment of who can most effectively perform the task.

Thus, depending on the rationale to which we subscribe, we could develop programs with conflicting roles for informal sources of support. For example, earlier attempts to train indigenous helpers for quasi-professional roles have met with the criticism that such helpers begin to take on a professional frame of reference and lose the ability to relate effectively to their indigenous reference groups (Levine et al., 1978; see also Chapters 8 and 11, this volume). What started as an effort to provide more responsiveness to needs at less expense has sacrificed the unique qualities of the paraprofessional for the sake of efficiency. The social participation rationale was abandoned in favor of cost effectiveness. While we are not suggesting that efficiency, effectiveness, and participation are always incompatible, the lesson that can be drawn is that different orientations toward the purposes to be served by involving informal helpers in services implicitly define different helping roles, some of which may be in conflict.

In addition to these orientations, other program goals may be mutually exclusive because of the choices they imply (Froland, 1980a). For example, the goals of preventing the need for services and improving the accessibility and responsiveness of care are not always compatible. Professional collaboration with informal sources of care for the purpose of serving one of these objectives may counteract efforts of other staff in the agency who are trying to meet a different objective. For example, some staff may be working with informal helpers in order to facilitate the identification of unrecognized needs and to increase the rate of referrals to professional services, thereby increasing the demand for formal services. Other staff may work with informal caregivers to support and reinforce existing patterns of helping so as to reduce the need and consequent demand for professional intervention. In both instances, the types of helpers identified may be similar, but the roles defined for them by agency staff are markedly different. In our study, these two examples come from different agencies, but should the programs be combined, staff would clearly be working at cross purposes.

The tension between conflicting purposes and their potential consequences in role ambiguity and strain for informal helpers, requires that we make tradeoffs to find some balance among competing expectations. Difficulties may be minimized or avoided by taking stock of the appropriate roles and responsibilities of professionals and informal caregivers in making decisions that seek to promote collaborative arrangements. Each program purpose will define a role for informal sources of support that implicitly emphasizes only *some* of the skills and attributes of informal helpers, offers only *some* of a broad range of possible opportunities for participation, and provides incentives that encourage only *some* of a wide range of informal helping activities. In short, whom we choose to involve, what we ask them to do, and what we are prepared to contribute are the major questions that underlie what we can expect to gain from informal sources of support.

IMPLICATIONS FOR THE PROFESSIONAL ROLE

When we are clear about the role of informal support systems in programs, we can begin to move toward the goal of developing mutually beneficial relationships between informal helpers and professionals. Because of the dynamic and spontaneous character of informal systems of support, professional staff may also have to reconsider their traditional practice roles. As a start, attention should be given to what staff and helpers can reasonably expect of each other and how the stresses and strains that will inevitably result can be worked out (Froland, 1980b).

There are a number of factors that influence the development of mutually beneficial helping roles. Some of these pertain to attitudes of individual staff on matters of professional ideologies, training, and standards of responsibility. Others stem from the very nature of informal support systems.

Of the set of factors pertaining to staff attitudes, a professional's philosophical orientation to practice provides an overarching influence on the relationship that will be developed with informal helpers. Among program staff in the agencies in our study, there was widespread commitment to the principles of self-determination, self-reliance, and mutual aid. These principles served as a frame of reference for staff in the help they provided. In working with clients, staff emphasis on these principles was expressed by building on an individual's abilities and strengths, by seeing how people may be helped by others or how they may help themselves, by ensuring that people take responsibility for choosing how they will be helped, and by identifying ways for individuals who share problems to share solutions as well. In working with the community at large, staff may express more political conceptions of helping by emphasizing ways whereby the community might recognize and mobilize its own strengths and resources, and by advocating for individual rights and community control over programs. Throughout, there is a belief that "people do best when they're in charge," and it is this belief that directs staff to look at natural support networks, self-help efforts, and informal helpers.

A second major influence on the development of a professional role concerns professional ideologies and attitudes toward training and knowledge. Orientations toward training and clinical experience and, particularly, the degree to which this is believed to confer a superior status or authority in determining who is best able to lead or to make decisions about client problems heavily influence staff relationships with informal helpers. To the extent that differing ideologies about care are confronted, an exclusive reliance on professional frames of reference will undermine the development of a collegial relationship with informal helpers.

Staff members must develop a sensitivity to the norms of informal helping systems if they are to develop partnerships with informal sources of support. Informal helpers may not define problems in the same way as professionals do. They see individuals in the context of a natural setting or set of personal relationships rather than as clients or target populations. They are concerned with meeting their own needs as well as those of the person being helped. This can create a dilemma for staff, since seeing an individual's problems one way may imply taking sides with one set of individuals as opposed to others in the network. For example, in working with the networks of frail elderly persons, staff may find that some relatives see the need for institutionalization while friends who are providing daily assistance disagree. While staff may be working to prevent institutionalization of the client, taking too strong a position on the subject may alienate certain parts of the elderly person's network and may close off access to potential sources of help.

Professional standards of responsibility and accountability represent another source of influence on the manner in which professionals relate to lay helpers. A staff member is often required to weigh the advantages and disadvantages of being an expert and stepping in, versus being a colleague and standing back. Members of a client's personal network may consider themselves responsible but may exercise this responsibility differently than would a professional, whether more forcefully and with apparent violation of privacy or less directly and with apparent unconcern for the welfare of a particular individual. For example, friends of a chronically mentally ill client may respond to the clients' hallucinations with little distress, since they know that they are only short-lived and abate when the client is left alone. In contrast, the professional is likely to react with alarm and feel a responsibility to hospitalize the client. The professional standards of staff who enter the informal system may be in conflict with members' norms and thus may cause considerable strain or tension if a collaborative relationship is sought. Community subcultures where alcoholism is a way of life provide another illustration of a situation that can pose this sort of difficulty.

Because of the ambiguities and tensions that can arise in questions of ideology and responsibility, staff of several programs have identified the need for a staff support group to air frustrations, provide consultation on problems, and help define strategies. Further, the availability of a support system to staff who are working with informal helping networks can serve to encourage them to continue their efforts. Without peers who provide support or needed feedback, staff can easily fall back into traditional direct-service professional roles. In contrast, staff who spend a great deal of time in the community and who have little contact with other agency staff often become unfamiliar with or even alienated from agency activities. In either case, an important aspect of sustaining work with informal helping systems is for staff to remain integrated with and supported by the agency.

A second set of factors influencing the development of a professional role pertains to the nature of informal systems of support. A major factor here concerns the types of demands that can be made on informal systems of support. Where and how an agency taps into the informal system has far-reaching implications, not only for the kind of partnership that can be developed but also for the future direction the informal helping will take. People's sense of obligation to one another and confidence in their ability to be helpful will be influenced by professional interventions. For example, one faction in a community may be given added resources and legitimization through their contact with staff, with the effect of changing the local balance of power.

Informal helpers may encounter role expectations in their contact with agency staff that are different from what they are used to in their daily lives. An essential part of the professional's relationship with the helper is to understand the helper's readiness or ability to take responsibility for aiding others. For example, just because parents have adjusted to having a developmentally disabled child does not mean that they are ready to support other parents during their adjustments. Likewise, that a person has been active in developing social or recreational opportunities for the elderly does not mean he or she is ready to advocate for low-income housing for the elderly. Staff must be sensitive to a helper's willingness and ability to take on new or expanded helping roles; otherwise there is a risk that helpers will become disenchanted or frustrated with what they feel others expect of them or what they come to expect of themselves.

Agency staff must be alert to changes that occur within the informal helping network and they must be prepared to modify their efforts accordingly. Many of these changes may occur because of staff contact with informal helpers. For example, some helpers become increasingly identified with the agency in which staff are working, as the way staff involve them in their work begins to instill in them some professionalized conceptions of helping. Some helpers come to be seen as informal leaders and are requested to serve on task forces and commissions in an advisory capacity. Similarly, some mutual-aid networks continue indefinitely on an informal and spontaneous basis, while others become increasingly more formalized and develop the independent status of a legally constituted organization with elected leadership. Changes such as these are not necessarily positive or negative events, although the character of the helping may lose or gain certain attributes. The question for staff is whether these changes are appropriate in the context of program objectives; whether they are beneficial, or at least not harmful to the helping process; and whether new or additional efforts need to be undertaken.

Staff relationships with helpers also need to remain flexible in the face of changes in the personal circumstances of informal helpers or the helping network. Such changes come about because helpers go through transitions that decrease their ability to provide help. People move, change jobs, or simply change their interests. These changes can be disruptive to informal helping relationships. Staff responsibilities also change, either within an agency or as the result of turnover. These sorts of changes occur to varying degrees in all programs and are inevitable. Because they can create difficulties in sustaining links with informal helping networks, programs need to identify ways to mediate their impact. Often this is done by continually trying to identify and involve new helpers and by giving new staff careful orientation and phasing them in slowly.

Staff roles are also influenced by the growth and development of the informal systems during the course of collaborative efforts. Some programs have the aim of fostering an independent or self sufficient helping network. Initially, staff may act as a catalyst or organizer among clients and helpers. While the network is developing a sense of purpose or identity, members may look to staff to provide direct assistance. As the network develops further and members begin to take ownership of activities, staff may move to a less active role, providing consultation or backup support. Staff must also be alert to changes that signal a need for additional efforts. For example, one program was involved in developing a mutual-aid network for the frail elderly but found that elderly in boarding homes were increasingly being excluded as the group became more formalized. Additional efforts had to be undertaken separately to provide a support system for the institutionalized elderly. The important lesson from program experience is that successful collaboration with informal helping networks is not a stable venture in which staff simply follow routine steps and can expect consistent results. It is a dynamic process in which approaches are modified as relationships grow, as new relationships are sought out to enrich activities, and as activities and roles are continually reevaluated to assure their appropriateness.

CONCLUSION

However difficult the task of combining formal and informal support, one should not conclude from our discussion that it is impossible. Our intent has been to clarify the difficulties by pointing out the differences between the two systems of support, by identifying some of the potential conflicts that can occur in the roles defined for informal helpers, and by describing where staff may need to reconsider their professional roles in relating to informal sources of support. As we learn to respect the differences between informal and formal support and as we recognize the possible conflicts that blending them may engender, we can combine the efforts of professionals and informal support networks to mutual benefit in a more planned and focused way. The staff in the agencies we have studied have highlighted the tensions in their work and they have taught us about how informal networks of support need to be accommodated both by professional staff in practice and by policy makers in making decisions about program goals and objectives. These lessons do not, by any means, provide a comprehensive blueprint for action, but they do suggest a number of strategies that have been successfully implemented.

Combining formal and informal sources of support is certainly not an easy process, nor may it be desirable or possible in many instances. But it does provide a perspective and a direction that can be pursued in providing more comprehensive services. It also provides a new opportunity to forge a more equal partnership with informal, voluntary sources of caring, one that is in sharp contrast to traditional perspectives that at times have seen informal caregivers as handmaidens of professionals or as unruly nuisances. The difficulty of the choice it presents to us as professionals is that it asks us to renegotiate the balance between public and private responsibilities for care. We must be prepared to question whether public or professional assumption of responsibility also implies an assumption of control over the process of caring. The perspective provided by our study of agency experience is that responsibility and control can be shared with citizens to a greater extent than it has been in the past, and that a partnership between formal and informal support provides a way that a comprehensive community mental health system can become a reality. Such a partnership is best served when the parties in mental health care participate on an equal footing.

REFERENCES

ABRAMS, P. *Neighborhood care and social policy: A research perspective.* Berkhamsted, England: The Volunteer Centre, June 1978.

CURRY, R., & YOUNG, R. *Socially indigenous help: The community cares for itself.* Paper presented to the American Psychological Association, Toronto, September 1978.

DARVILL, G. *Bargain or barricade?* Berkhamsted, England: The Volunteer Centre, April 1975.

DAVIES, B. *The cost-effectiveness imperative, the social services and volunteers.* Berkhamsted, England: The Volunteer Centre, March 1980.

FROLAND, C. *Some costs and consequences of interweaving professional and informal sources of care.* Portland, OR: Regional Research Institute, June 1980. (a)

FROLAND, C. Formal and informal care: Discontinuities in a continuum. *Social Service Review,* December 1980. (b)

FROLAND, C., PANCOAST, D., CHAPMAN, N., & KIMBOKO, P. *Professional partnerships with informal helpers: Emerging forms.* Paper presented to the American Psychological Association, New York, September 1979.

FROLAND, C., PANCOAST, D., CHAPMAN, N., & KIMBOKO, P. *Expanding human services with informal helping resources.* Portland, OR: Regional Research Institute, April 1980.

GERSHON, M., & BILLER, H. *The other helpers.* Lexington, MA: D. C. Heath, 1977.

GLADSTONE, F. J. *Voluntary action in a changing world.* London: Bedford Square Press, 1979.

LENROW, P. Dilemmas of professional helping. In L. Wispe (Ed.), *Sympathy, altruism and helping.* Cambridge: Harvard University Press, 1976.

LEVINE, S., TULKIN, S., INTAGLIATA, F., PERRY, J., & WHITSOM, E. *The paraprofessional: A brief social history.* Unpublished manuscript, Department of Psychology, SUNY, Buffalo, March 1978.

LITWAK, E. Agency and family linkages in providing neighborhood services. In D. Thurz & J. Vigilante (Eds.), *Reaching people: The structure of neighborhood services.* Beverly Hills, CA: Sage Publications, 1978.

LITWAK, E., & MEYER, H. J. *School, family and neighborhood: The theory and practice of school-community relations.* New York: Columbia University Press, 1974.

National Commission on Neighborhoods (NCN). *People, building neighborhoods.* Washington, DC: Government Printing Office. 1979.

PANCOAST, D., & CHAPMAN, N. Roles for informal helpers in the delivery of human services. In D. Biegel & A. Naparstek (Eds.), *Community support systems and mental health: Building linkages.* New York: Springer, forthcoming.

President's Commission on Mental Health (PCMH). *Task force report on community support systems,* Volume II, Appendix. Washington, DC: Government Printing Office, 1978.

RIESSMAN, F. How does self-help work? *Social Policy,* 1976, *7,* 41-45.

TUCKER, D. Coordination and citizen participation. *Social Service Review,* 1980, *54,* 13-30.

TURNER, J. C., & TENHOOR, W. J. The NIMH community support program: Pilot approach to a needed social reform. *Schizophrenia Bulletin,* 1978, *4,* 319-348.

WILENSKY, H. L., & LEBEAUX, C. N. *Individual society and social welfare.* New York: Russell Sage, 1958.

Wolfenden Report. *The future of voluntary organizations.* London: Croom Helm, 1978.

Chapter 11

COLLABORATION WITH NATURAL HELPING NETWORKS
Lessons from Studying Paraprofessionals

ROGER E. MITCHELL
DANIEL J. HURLEY, Jr.

Recently, there has been increased attention to the health protective effects of membership in a network of ongoing, reciprocal and supportive relationships. Researchers from a variety of fields have begun to investigate the role that support from one's social network may play in mediating the maladaptive effects of stress (Caplan, 1974; Cassel, 1974; Cobb, 1976; Dean & Lin, 1977; Wilcox, forthcoming). New appreciation of the unique supportive capabilities of indigenous helping networks has prompted a call for professionals to try to collaborate with these individuals and groups who represent resources in the promotion of mental health (Gottlieb, 1979; Rappaport, 1977). Consequently, there have been a variety of intervention efforts aimed at bolstering the resources of those "natural helpers" likely to come into contact with distressed individuals (Collins & Pancoast, 1976; Conter et al., 1980; Cowen et al., 1979; Leutz, 1976; Wiesenfeld & Weis, 1979).

Authors' Note: The authors wish to thank Ben Gottlieb and Bart Hirsch for their helpful comments on drafts of this chapter.

277

The current emphasis on working with natural helpers is reminiscent in many ways of past work with indigenous paraprofessionals. First, both efforts developed in reaction to perceived inadequacies of the formal service system. Proponents of both these approaches, for example, have cited the inadequate numbers of trained personnel, the inability (or unwillingness) of the service system to deal effectively with disadvantaged and underserved populations, and the failure of large numbers of people to rely on the formal service system as a primary source of help. Second, both efforts have viewed professional-citizen collaboration as a way of mobilizing community resources, and as a way of providing the community mental health field with a new technology for helping distressed and/or high-risk individuals and groups. Thus, indigenous paraprofessionals were recruited to serve as a bridge between the agency and the community, while natural helpers are now receiving consultation and training from professionals who hope thereby to enlarge the helpers' reach and to optimize the support they extend to local social networks. Finally, the scope and range of effort within each movement seem equally broad. The diversity of ranks from which paraprofessionals were drawn (e.g., students, housewives, individuals from underserved populations) is matched by the diversity of individuals who have been identified as natural helpers (e.g., attorneys, beauticians, Cub Scout den leaders, neighbors).

Given these similarities, the indigenous paraprofessional movement may provide some useful lessons for those currently attempting to collaborate with informal helpers. In particular, we will argue that the paraprofessional experience has highlighted the need for more critical attention to the individual, environmental, and situational characteristics that mediate the effectiveness of lay helping activities. For example, while recent studies suggest that paraprofessionals may be as effective as professionals in a number of areas (e.g., Durlak, 1979), there has been little information on the factors that contribute to their effectiveness. Anecdotal descriptions have mentioned the importance of the personal qualities of the paraprofessional, and his or her "connections" to the community being served. However, without more detailed understanding of how these factors operate and how they might be mediated by other variables (e.g., the particular task under consideration), our ability to enhance the helping process is limited, and criteria for selection and training of informal helpers remain ambiguous and subjective.

Similarly, as calls for collaboration with natural helpers increase, we are faced with unanswered questions about the informal helping process. While investigators have begun to document the specific helping responses used by various caregivers (Cowen et al., 1979; Felner et al., 1980), we have no understanding of how the effectiveness of helping efforts may be moderated by the *type* of problem, the *type* of help, or the *source* of the help. The availability of the informal caregiver through membership in the potential helpee's personal community has been cited as a critical factor (Collins & Pancoast, 1976), but it is unclear how the process and effectiveness of helping are influenced by the particular role of the informal caregiver (e.g., neighbor, hairdresser, bartender). We suggest that a more revealing assessment of the benefits of professional-natural helper collaboration can be achieved through more detailed specification of the variables mediating the occurrence and effectiveness of informal helping transactions.

The purpose of this chapter, then, is to look at some of the historical conceptual difficulties that limited the development of the indigenous paraprofessional movement, and to draw parallels with current attempts to develop professional-informal helper alliances. In particular, two issues are addressed: (1) There is a need for more detailed specification of the goals, processes, and outcomes of specific interventions. The rubric "informal helping" has been used to categorize a diverse group of individuals and activities. What is particularly helpful in one context or from one individual may not be as salient under different circumstances. (2) There is a need to view the interpersonal helping process within its broader environmental context, and to understand how systemic factors influence the pattern of relationships among professionals, indigenous personnel, and the targets of helping efforts. Researchers have focused on the personal characteristics of paraprofessionals and natural helpers, for example, and have tended to ignore the impact of environmental variables in facilitating or constraining particular types of helping activities.

INDIGENOUS PARAPROFESSIONAL MOVEMENT

Widespread utilization of paraprofessional personnel during the 1960s arose from a complex array of social, political, and scientific developments. While nonprofessional helping has a long history (Levine, et al., 1979) three types of legislative and political activity spurred its expansion. First, the antipoverty campaigns of the early 1960s drew upon indigenous paraprofessionals as a way of improving the quality of services to the poor, and increasing their input into, and control over, the decisions made about service delivery. Second, the passage of the Community Mental Health Act of 1963, and later approval of mental health center staffing grants, provided funds for bringing service delivery under the direction of those at the local level, and provided for the utilization of personnel with varying levels of training. Third, an expanding National Institute of Mental Health had begun to fund paraprofessional training grants and demonstration projects. At the same time, a number of studies appeared that suggested that paraprofessionals could be effective in producing client change and increasing the scope of the professional's work. These studies examined paraprofessionals from a wide range of populations: college students (Poser, 1966; Scheibe, 1969), middle-class housewives (Rioch, 1967), and members of underserved and minority populations (Goldberg, 1969; Grosser, 1969; Pearl & Riessman, 1965). These political and professional developments resulted in widespread acceptance of the utilization of paraprofessionals in mental health programming.

The purposes to be served by the employment of paraprofessionals were varied, often implicit, and sometimes contradictory. For example, paraprofessionals became embroiled in the controversies that arose during the 1960s when recognition of the inadequacies of the formal service system prompted calls for reform and alternative arrangements. As Lenrow and Cowden (1980: 479) note, those attempting to "perfect" the professional service system called for "ever more comprehensive, centralized, professionally managed, effectively coordinated, unified service systems," while more "populist proposals" called for decreasing professional and bureaucratic control of services by increasing the influence of the users of service. Paraprofessional utilization was viewed as a favored strategy within both schemes. Some saw utilization of indigenous paraprofessionals as a way of extending the reach of traditional services, while others saw such utilization as a way of changing the nature and orientation of the services delivered. The failure to specify the ultimate objectives within specific programs sometimes led to heightened conflict. In the Lincoln Hospital Project, for example, paraprofessionals' goals of creating social change within their community and agency conflicted with the organization's objectives of providing more traditional services (Shaw & Eagle, 1971).

Thus, agreement about the utility of paraprofessionals was not accompanied by consensus or clarity about the goals they were to achieve, or about the processes underlying paraprofessional effectiveness. In addition, there was very little information about how such processes were influenced by contextual and environmental variables. This latter issue will be discussed in more detail in the following paragraphs.

While the outcomes of paraprofessional helping have compared favorably with the work of professionals, there has been little evidence documenting the processes through which positive changes occurred. Descriptions of indigenous paraprofessional performance have typically focused on the paraprofessional's personal qualities, his or her indigenous community membership, and the type of training received. In terms of personal qualities, studies have focused on the traits of warmth, naiveté, motivation, informality, empathy, genuineness, enthusiasm, and "nonprofessional" approach (Carkhuff & Truax, 1965; Collins, 1971; Reiff & Riessman, 1965; Reiser, 1963; Rioch, 1967). The assets of indigenous paraprofessionals also typically included their membership in the community from which the agency's clients originated. In describing the basis for the effectiveness of paraprofessionals, Pearl and Riessman (1965: 85) state, "The most obvious variable is their (peer) status attributes — they are poor, are from the neighborhood, are often members of minority groups." It was because of these qualities that the indigenous paraprofessional was able to act as a "bridge" between the agency and the consumer.

In the wave of enthusiasm for indigenous paraprofessionals, there was a failure to specify how the resources they brought to community mental health work influenced specific helping transactions. In addition, the attention paid to the personal traits of the paraprofessional obscured specification of the task and contextual dimensions of their activities. Recent descriptions of paraprofessional programs (e.g., Alley et al., 1979) suggest that several levels of factors are involved in effective paraprofessional performance: the nature and scope of the tasks involved; the personal qualities and skills of the paraprofessional; and the ideology and organizational structure of the agency within which the paraprofessional is employed. To attribute paraprofessional effectiveness to vague personality traits and "nonprofessional" status is to oversimplify and "mystify" a series of very complex processes.

How, for example, might community membership increase the potential effectiveness of indigenous helpers? One might speculate that some indigenous helpers may be especially effective because (a) they may have an ability to develop and utilize ties with a variety of informal resources, and/or (b) their knowledge of the norms and values of a particular community may allow them to structure helping transactions in ways that are more comfortable and credible for consumers. Such skills are not likely to be distributed equally among indigenous helpers. Without specification of the nature of such skills or their relative importance for particular tasks, selection and training remained rather subjective endeavors. The response of some professionals was to fall back solely on traditional therapeutic models of training, and to run the risk of underutilizing the indigenous paraprofessionals' unique skills and resources.

Blurring of the complex processes influencing paraprofessional effectiveness led to neglect of both contextual and environmental issues. For example, an awareness of community resources and the ability to utilize a number of informal networks might be more crucial in a consultation and education position than in more direct service roles that paraprofessionals might assume. Even within clinical roles, such factors as the type of target population and the degree of structure of the treatment program may make a difference in the skills required.

Similarly, the emphasis on the personality traits of the paraprofessional has tended to obscure the professional's role in influencing the context within which the paraprofessional works. The Lincoln Hospital Project, for example, was a widely publicized program that utilized indigenous paraprofessionals in neighborhood storefront service centers to deal with a wide range of human service needs in a socioeconomically depressed inner-city urban area (Reiff & Riessman, 1965). The orientation of many of these paraprofessionals was social advocacy, and their ability to act as a "bridge" between the formal service system and the community was widely proclaimed. As funding patterns prompted reorganization of services along more centralized and traditional lines, indigenous paraprofessionals were faced with the task of accommodating themselves to a professionally dominated system that devalued their worth and curtailed their autonomy (Kaplan & Roman, 1973; Minuchin, 1969; Shaw & Eagle, 1971). The resulting conflict seriously affected the program. In less dramatic fashion, Hurley & Tyler (1976) found that the model of care adopted by mental health center teams (psychosocial learning versus traditional medical model) had effects on paraprofessionals' perceptions of job satisfaction, role flexibility, and team cohesiveness. Hence, professionals have an impact on paraprofessional effectiveness through the organizational structure and climate that they create.

Thus, the success of the outreach and "bridging" functions that were to be served by paraprofessional utilization was, to a large extent, a function of agency structure, organization and ideology. As Pattison et al. (1979: 253) state, "a community-involved service program must be constructed as a system-wide effort involving the total program. The use of mental health workers is the consequence of a system-wide, community-integrated program, not the cause." Thus, without institutional support, it was difficult for paraprofessionals to perform community outreach tasks for which they were presumably well suited.

One final result of the "mystification" of the roles that indigenous paraprofessionals could most capably assume in community mental health has been to limit the degree of impact they could have on the formal service system. Without specification of the particular skills unique to and effectively used by indigenous paraprofessionals, there was little impetus for professionals to discern which skills themselves might have learned and profitably used.

These experiences suggest that the effectiveness of indigenous personnel depends not only on their personal characteristics, but also on the nature of the tasks they are trying to accomplish, and the constraints imposed by the environment within which they are operating. The mere fact of membership in local social networks may help create opportunities for help-giving; in addition, the specific types of helping interactions that are likely to bring about specific outcomes must be examined. The following section will discuss these issues as they apply to efforts to work with informal caregivers.

INDIGENOUS HELPING NETWORKS

Similar confusion seems to exist about the factors underlying effective helping transactions among informal caregivers, and about the best ways for professionals to involve themselves in such processes. Attorneys, Cub Scout den leaders, hairdressers, neighbors, and shopkeepers, for example, have all been described as people whose roles include providing support, and who have the potential to increase their caregiving activities (Conter et al., 1980; Cowen et al., 1979; D'Augelli et al., forthcoming; Felner et al., 1980; Leutz, 1976;

Pancoast, 1980). However, not much information is available about who gets helped under what circumstances and with what effects. Our uncertainty about the most important factors in informal helping transactions has led to rather divergent approaches to consulting with informal caregivers. Wiesenfeld and Weis (1979: 789) for example, implemented a consultation program for hairdressers, which stressed "the strategies of empathic listening, reflecting clients' feelings and presenting behavioral alternatives." Such an approach seems geared toward taking advantage of accumulated knowledge of behaviors that are helpful in "therapeutic" transactions. In contrast, Collins and Pancoast (1976: 76) warn against "professionalizing" informal helpers. They state that natural neighbors' "style should be supported but in no respect altered by training or supervision." At present, we do not know the circumstances under which either of these approaches might be most useful.

We may be better able to address these issues once we gain a better understanding of processes of helping within different contexts. The following pages will discuss how the effectiveness of helping transactions can vary as a function of the type of outcome, the type of help, and the source of help being considered.

Specifying the Outcomes of Informal Helping Transactions

It is important for proponents of natural support systems to be more precise in specifying the goals they hope to achieve as a result of their efforts. Suggesting that social support should be provided for the sake of "health promotion" is not enough. Health, well-being, and adjustment are multidimensional concepts, and particular kinds of support may be related to specific categories of outcome. Specifying a range of outcome criteria gives one a basis for making more detailed evaluations of programs, and for developing more realistic expectations of their impact. In addition, specifying a range of possible outcome dimensions can provide a context for examining intended and unintended, adaptive and maladaptive consequences of such efforts.

An example of the need to specify outcomes explicitly is provided by programs designed to provide social support to couples who recently have made the transition to parenthood (McGuire & Gottlieb, 1979; Wandersman et al., 1980). Underlying these programs was the view that the birth of a first child is a considerably stressful event because of the readjustments in lifestyle as well as the added demands on the couple. Hence, McGuire and Gottlieb (1979) and Wandersman et al. (1980) implemented social support groups that focused on the sharing of experiences among couples as a way of improving their adjustment to their newly acquired parenting roles. The results seemed to indicate that these support groups, in comparison to control groups, had specific rather than general, effects. Wandersman et al. (1980), for example, found involvement in a support group generally to have no significant relationship to well-being, quality of marital interaction, and participants' sense of competence as parents. Similarly, McGuire and Gottlieb (1979) found their support groups to have no effect on stress, health, and well-being, but did find effects in more specific areas. Couples in the support group significantly increased the frequency and comfort with which they later discussed child-rearing matters with their informal network (relatives, friends, neighbors, and so on). Given the role of the parents' social network in reinforcing appropriate parenting behavior (Cochran & Brassard, 1979), such findings may represent important gains. Nonetheless, the failure to find a relationship between the support groups and more global measures of adjustment may mean that too much was expected too soon of a short-term intervention. At the very least, these studies highlight the need to evaluate helping transactions in terms of a range of outcomes.

Clarity about the range of possible outcomes may also be helpful in designing interventions that attempt to mobilize social support. Felner et al. (1980), for example, have argued that lawyers may play key caregiving roles in their dealings with clients who are in the process of divorce. In their survey, a majority of attorneys showed an awareness of clients' extralegal problems, viewed the provision of support and counseling as part of their role, and expressed an interest in consultation from mental health professionals. What outcomes could be expected as a result of a consultation program for such lawyers? As Hetherington et al. (1978) state, major tasks for the divorced individual include (a) practical problems related to the maintenance (or establishment) of one's household, occupational, and economic stability; (b) interpersonal problems in maintaining/reestablishing social relationships; and (c) management of the emotional distress associated with changes in self-concept and identity. Are interactions with attorneys (which in some cases tend to be brief) expected to have an impact on such outcomes? Or are the potential outcomes more modest? For example, one could also conceive of attorneys attempting (a) to reduce the level of client stress that is associated with the legal proceedings themselves; and (b) to provide information concerning a variety of resources that the parties to the divorce may need at this time and in the near future (e.g., child care, employment counseling, mental health counseling, support groups). If mental health professionals have a clear idea of the outcomes they think informal caregivers can accomplish, it may become easier to design programs focusing on particular skills. Similarly, if attorneys have a clearer idea of a range of reasonable outcomes, they may avoid developing unrealistic expectations of what they can do. Programs that focus on interpersonal skills but do not present any conception of their limits within an attorney-client relationship may cause some attorneys to develop too high expectations of their impact and then to become frustrated with the helping process.

Similarly, several possible objectives may be accomplished in work with neighborhood "central figures." One might aim at (a) increasing the number of people reached by natural helpers, without altering their process or criteria for selecting who will be "helpees"; (b) increasing the number of people reached from particular "at-risk" populations (e.g., families involved in child neglect); or (c) increasing the helping capacities of the network, so that other network members may be more willing and able to initiate helping exchanges without relying on the "central" figure. Depending on one's goals, one might use different consultation strategies with neighborhood central figures. For example, in order to build up the capacities of the network as a whole, one might encourage individuals to be more active in prompting other network members to respond to requests for aid.

Specifying Processes

Although evidence testifying to the connection between social support and adjustment has been accumulating (Andrews et al., 1978; Lin et al., 1979; Wilcox, forthcoming) it is still unclear which specific behaviors in which situations are most effective. A number of aspects of these processes are unclear. Are particular *types* of support, for example, more helpful than others in dealing with particular types of difficulties? Are some *sources* of help more potent than others, even when similar helping behaviors are elicited from each source? Does support have its salutary effects primarily in buffering those individuals experiencing stress, or does it serve more general health-promotive functions? Do coping styles influence one's ability to use support that is offered? Our implicit answers to these questions are important, because they influence our assessments of what interventions will be most helpful, and where we should best direct our energies.

The importance of clarifying these issues is illustrated in the following intervention program. Cowen et al. (1979) examined the helping transactions of hairdressers, whose caregiving potential arises out of their repeated contact with segments of the public, some of whom might be experiencing distress. Indeed, hairdressers reported that 33 percent of the dialogues they had with customers involved the discussion of moderate to serious problems. The four most frequent responses of these informal caregivers involved "support and sympathy, trying to be light-hearted, just listening, [and] presenting alternatives" (Cowen et al., 1979: 640). Wiesenfeld and Weis (1979), in fact, developed a consultation program for several of these individuals, which attempted to strengthen their interpersonal helping skills (i.e., empathic listening and behavioral alternatives) and to increase their knowledge of referral options in the community. After the program, participants reported significant changes toward such helping responses as "reflecting feelings" and away from such responses as "count your blessings" or "specific advice."

The *types* of interpersonal helping reinforced by Wiesenfeld and Weis (1979) may not have been the most effective for all problem areas. Depression, for example, was one of the more frequently occurring problem areas that hairdressers reported facing in their dealings with customers. In a prospective study of a sample of middle-aged community residents, Schaeffer et al. (forthcoming) examined the relationship of emotional, tangible, and informational support to a variety of measures of psychological functioning. The results showed that depression was most strongly related to tangible support, i.e., the degree to which subjects perceived that someone would be available to them for help in situations requiring material assistance. Thus, our attempts to make informal helping transactions resemble therapeutic encounters (emphasis on "reflecting feelings" and the like) may not necessarily result in the kinds of help that are most salient for the particular type of problem.

A second issue spotlighted by this example concerns the *source* of help. Weiss (1974), for example, has tried to specify the different "provisions" that individuals gain from different social relationships.

He suggests that people in different social roles are not wholly interchangeable in the types of "provisions" that they provide. Attachment, for example, "is provided by relationships from which participants gain a sense of security and place." Typically, this is provided by a "cross-sex, committed relationship" (1974: 23). Reassurance of worth is provided by relationships that attest to an individual's competence in a social role" (1974: 24), and often arises through one's work associates. Social integration is provided by a network of relationships that serve as a base for "shared interpretation of experience," "pooled information," "exchange of services," and "source of companionship" (1974: 23). A person lacking a network of peers, then, may feel a loss that no intimate relationship will adequately be able to satisfy. Similarly, a network of peer relationships may not be able to mitigate the need for an intimate relationship (e.g., for the divorced, widowed, or separated). Although the customer and hairdresser may have regular and positive transactions, the latter may not have an important enough place (or the appropriate roles) within the customer's network to satisfy his or her support needs. (Gottlieb elaborates on this issue in Chapter 8, this volume.)

A final issue involves the specification of the occasions when the provision of social support has its strongest effects. Does social support at any time enhance the well-being of the individual? Or does social support primarily play its role in helping those who are experiencing high levels of stress (i.e., the stress-buffering effect)? McGuire and Gottlieb (1979), for example, seem to take the latter view in explaining their failure to find more widespread health changes in the participants of their support groups for parents. They note that the participants had low absolute levels of stress at pretest, and suggest that more dramatic changes in health and well-being might have occurred if participants had been experiencing greater stress. The programmatic implications of such an assumption must be carefully considered. For example, interventions based on such a view would encourage natural helpers selectively to aid those persons experiencing the highest levels of stress. Yet because these persons might be least able to reciprocate this help, the natural caregiver's social field might become populated by larger proportions of asymmetrical, nonreciprocal relationships. Consequently, the caregiver may be more vulnerable to burnout.

In contrast, interventions to improve the interpersonal and/or helping skills of individuals without regard to their level of stress seem to assume direct effects or benefits of increased social support (Conter et al., 1980; D'Augelli et al., forthcoming). Although the evidence is still equivocal, Billings et al. (1980) review some findings of a direct effect of support on functioning. In addition, they suggest that support may have an indirect effect on functioning by reducing the level of stress that individuals are likely to experience in the first place. For example, persons with high levels of support consistently experienced fewer negative life events than persons with low levels of support (Billings & Moos, forthcoming).

Helping transactions, then, can vary along a variety of dimensions. The type of help, source of help and type of problem are factors that add to the complexity of the helping process. Are specific types of social support important (e.g., emotional support, tangible assistance, companionship, information)? or do they all merely signal to the individual that he or she is cared for? It is important that future work begin to look at helping processes in detail so that such questions can be answered.

Adopting a Systems Perspective

Just as the role of indigenous paraprofessionals is shaped by the structure and ideology of the organization within which they work, the activities of natural helpers are also shaped by the structure and prevailing norms of their immediate community settings. An awareness of the environmental context provides a better understanding of the constraints surrounding the helping process. It then becomes possible to design interventions aimed not only at individual's helping skills, but also at the ecology that shapes the development and use of such skills.

Efforts to understand the effectiveness of natural helpers have focused largely on the traits and characteristics of these individuals. In working with "natural neighbors," Collins and Pancoast (1976: 28) stated that "our experience leads us to believe that personal traits provide the most likely explanation for the development of central figures whose helping activities persist over long periods of time." Such persons were seen as being able to provide physical and emotional resources to others without fear of being "drained." Similarly, work with potential caregivers (bartenders, beauticians, and the like) has centered on an examination of the specific help-giving responses they are likely to express (Cowen et al., 1979; Felner et al., 1980). As experience with indigenous paraprofessionals has shown, a focus on the dyadic helper-helpee relationships can obscure the influence of the larger environmental system within which these relationships develop. The following paragraphs will discuss environmental variables within the neighborhood, and within the social network that shapes the informal helping process.

While the personal qualities of natural helpers are certainly important, the larger neighborhood context is likely to set conditions that influence the willingness of these individuals to help, the scope of their activities, and the readiness of others to engage in mutual relationships with "natural helpers." An example of the impact of neighborhood contexts is provided by Garbarino and Sherman (1980), who examined the differences between two socioeconomically matched neighborhoods that differed in their degrees of risk for child abuse. One community had a much higher rate of child abuse, and the other a much lower rate than would have been expected from their similar socioeconomic profile. Families in the "high-risk" neighborhood tended to be "socially impoverished," in that they tended to report fewer resources available for child-care arrangements as well as for more general helping exchanges within the neighborhood. These families were also more likely to be "ambivalent" about developing reciprocal helping relationships, given the degree to which "impoverished" neighbors might be likely to "drain" them of their own resources. In such a neighborhood context, residents might be less inclined to engage natural helpers, and those few natural helpers who are present might find it difficult to expand their helping role and still experience "freedom from drain."

Warren (1980) has undertaken a broader examination of the social-structural characteristics of neighborhoods and their influence on help-seeking and help-giving behavior. He identified and described six neighborhood "types" (integral, parochial, diffuse, stepping-stone, transitory, anomic) as a result of neighborhood communities' scores along three dimensions: identity (a feeling of belongingness to the neighborhood community), interactions (frequency and types of contacts with neighbors), and linkages (associations and contacts with individuals and groups outside the immediate local neighborhood). The integral neighborhood (high identity, high interaction, high linkage) is one in which there is a strong community identity, people are likely to know one another, and a large number of residents are likely to have contacts with institutions in the larger community that can have an influence on neighborhood life. The parochial neighborhood (high identity, high interaction, low linkage) is one in which there is also a strong sense of neighborhood identity and contact, but much less contact with institutional and community life outside the neighborhood. Persons in need of help or exhibiting deviant behavior are likely to be recognized and dealt with, although the resources and some of the values of the larger community may be ignored in this process. The diffuse neighborhood (high identity, low interaction, low linkage) "tends to provide a rather homogeneous setting (for example, subdivision in suburban areas or public housing projects in urban locations)" in which individuals share a sense of community identity, but do not focus their social networks around their neighborhoods (Warren, 1980: 75-76). This follows a pattern described by Craven and Wellman (1973), in which individuals' network relationships become more geographically dispersed.

As Warren (1980) indicates, these neighborhood differences have important implications for the patterns of helping that take place, and for interventions that attempt to influence these processes. The integral neighborhood is one that is most likely to have numerous "central figures," most likely to use both informal and formal helping resources effectively, and less likely to resist the consultative advances of professionals. Such neighborhoods are also the ones that are perhaps least in need of such help. While parochial neighborhoods may be set off from both the institutional resources and values of the larger community, they do have an active informal helping community. If resistance to "outsiders" could be overcome, consultants could promote access to communitywide resources. Finally, the diffuse neighborhood provides a different set of problems for the professional. Networks within the neighborhood are likely to be limited, so that those persons potentially capable of being "natural neighbors" have a more difficult time of creating links to those in need as well as to resources. Thus, the neighborhood setting, both in its values and social participation patterns, facilitates and constrains natural helping networks in ways that the change agent must understand. If we want to use community resources, we need to be aware of how the community context shapes the availability and distribution of these resources.

A more systems-oriented perspective can also provide the professional with a better understanding of the operation of particular locality-based networks and their potential for including new individuals. Relationships within natural networks have been described as displaying mutuality, reciprocity, and ongoing contact. Individuals are likely to develop networks of people with whom they feel comfortable (Collins & Pancoast, 1976: 76). They are also likely to be most receptive to individuals who have the potential to provide resources for future exchanges (Politser, 1980), even if these individuals are currently in need (e.g., a family just moving into the neighborhood). Individuals are not equally attractive to the network as potential members. Those who show disturbing behaviors and/or low levels of functioning may not receive the same invitations to engage in reciprocal exchanges that more "normal" individuals might receive. Some empirical evidence suggests this might be the case. In a study of experimentally structured telephone conversations between strangers, for example, depressed persons were more likely to elicit hostile and rejecting responses than were "control" individuals (Coyne, 1976). Similarly, Mitchell (forthcoming) found that high psychopathology in chronic psychiatric clients was associated with decreased support from peers, as well as with environmental conditions unlikely to encourage social interaction. Thus, established natural networks may be just as selective as the formal service system in preferring people who are functioning relatively well and who are likely to be the most responsive to assistance (i.e., providing the most payoff for the helper's investment of time and energy). It would be ironic if the populations underserved by the formal service system (chronic psychiatric clients, families engaging in domestic violence, and so on) were also those that were least readily accepted into some indigenous helping networks. Providing support to "at-risk" and "resource-deficient" populations seems to remain a formidable task, whether undertaken in the service system or in the community.

Assessing the Impact of Collaborative Interventions

Much of this chapter has focused on the context of helping activities, and how various factors influence the ultimate effectiveness of helping transactions upon the target individual. We believe that collaborative interventions have consequences in other areas as well, and that these must also be considered in evaluating the impact of such efforts. One can examine the effects in the following areas: (a) whether the intervention has improved the target individual's ability to deal with the immediate task or situation at hand; (b) the impact on the indigenous helpers, in terms of both their skills and the way they relate to their indigenous networks; (c) the impact on professionals' knowledge, values, and skills, and the manner in which they relate to their organizational or professional bases; (d) changes in the indigenous network itself; and (e) changes in the professional service system. Particular interventions are likely to have multiple effects.

Focusing at only one level of outcome is likely to obscure effects in other areas. In both the indigenous paraprofessional and the natural helper movements, for example, there has been concern about the impact of collaboration on indigenous personnel themselves. Professionals have urged that caution be exercised in dealing with indigenous helpers, for fear that these individuals may be "colonized" by, and "coopted" into, the professional establishment, and away from "natural" helping styles (Gottlieb, 1974). However, such thinking sometimes had negative consequences for paraprofessionals. Concerns about "cooptation" became a convenient excuse for creating roles for indigenous paraprofessionals that were peripheral and that provided little power for challenging the assumptions underlying service system operations. Paradoxically, when indigenous paraprofessionals did try to gain more influence on decision-making within the service system, they were accused of aspiring to professional roles and distancing themselves from the host community. In short, the professionals' attempts to "protect" paraprofessionals from cooptation and the community's fear that its interests would be lost as paraprofessionals gained power within the agency both tended to restrict meaningful input from paraprofessionals.

Similarly, a broader perspective on the effects of indigenous helping interventions is likely to expand more quickly our knowledge of adaptive and maladaptive, intended and unintended consequences. For example, while central neighborhood figures have been a focus of attention (Collins & Pancoast, 1976), it may be important to look at how norms and behaviors of the network *as a whole* may be changed. If the central figure becomes more involved in new helping relationships, does this change the nature of the helping processes as a whole? Do other individuals become more likely to initiate helping exchanges without the prompting of central figures? Perhaps intervention strategies could be more explicitly aimed at changing the help-giving capacities of the network as a whole (e.g., using central figures to try to change norms concerning who are acceptable recipients of help). The important task may be to discover how the network supports or constrains individuals in particular help-exchanging situations.

Focusing solely on central figures may divert attention from the operation of, and the possibility for change in, the network as a whole. In any case, it seems important to be aware that effects can occur at multiple levels.

CONCLUSION

This chapter has tried to draw some parallels between past experiences in utilizing indigenous paraprofessionals and current efforts to collaborate with informal community caregivers. Past experience suggests that the effectiveness of indigenous helping transactions depends on contextual, personal, and environmental factors. Specification of these factors highlights the complexity of understanding helping transactions, let alone influencing them. Nonetheless, we feel that there are several benefits to be derived from attention to the issues discussed in this chapter.

First, a more detailed specification of the particular processes involved in specific helping encounters may give us a better idea of the strengths and limits of various intervention strategies, and a more realistic set of expectations concerning the possibilities of such efforts. This chapter has outlined some of the difficulties involved in designing preventive interventions using social support. The optimism surrounding work with "natural support systems" in the community can fade quickly in the face of such complexities, with the danger that interventions in natural helping networks may be prematurely abandoned before they are adequately implemented and evaluated. To quote Levine and Perkins (1980: 148): "The history of human services is littered with programs which began by overpromising their benefits, and later collapsed amid public disillusionment when the overpromise was not fulfilled. . . . Even though it is exciting to hold out for a bold vision of the future, we are obliged to promise or to contract for that which can be delivered given a reasonable level of resources and a reasonable amount of time." Thus, a realization of the limits of our ability to increase and/or redistribute social support in the community should not lead to disillusionment. Instead, such information should allow us to make more informed choices about the costs and benefits involved in undertaking particular projects, and strengthen our ability to defend more modest but significant gains that work with informal helpers can achieve.

Second, the experience of indigenous paraprofessionals suggests the need to go beyond the examination of the characteristics of the helper-helpee dyad and attend to the environmental context within which such helping transactions occur. This emphasis is particularly crucial for the social support "movement" at this time. While an examination of the particular supportive behaviors of indigenous helpers is necessary (see Cowen et al., 1979), it is important that we not forget to examine the links between social structures and the supportive capacities of individuals within them. Stress and social support are not randomly distributed among social settings, and interventions at the system level may in some cases facilitate the emergence of supportive behaviors. In a study of elderly in sheltered-care facilities, for example, David et al. (forthcoming) found that facilities with an emphasis on independence in their program policies tended to have greater levels of resident socialization within the facility, and greater participation by residents in activities in the community. Similarly, Segal et al. (1980) describe how community reaction to the mentally ill can influence the integration of the board and care residents in their communities. It is important that our ambitions to bolster the support of "network-deficient" individuals not lead us solely into the mode of individual-focused interventions. An important area for future research is how various social settings influence the development of helping networks and supportive transactions within them.

REFERENCES

ALLEY, S., BLANTON, J., & FELDMAN, R. (Eds.). *Paraprofessionals in mental health: Theory and practice.* New York: Human Sciences Press. 1979.

ANDREWS, G., TENNANT, C., HEWSON, D., & VAILLANT, G. Life event stress, social support, coping style, and risk of psychological impairment. *Journal of Nervous and Mental Disease,* 1978, *166,* 307-316.

BILLINGS, A., MITCHELL, R., & MOOS, R. *Social support and wellbeing: Research implications for prevention programs.* Unpublished manuscript, Social Ecology Laboratory, Department of Psychiatry, Stanford University Medical Center, Stanford, California, 1980.

BILLINGS, A., & MOOS, R. The role of coping responses and social resources in attenuating the stress of life events. *Journal of Behavioral Medicine,* forthcoming.

CAPLAN, G. *Social support and community mental health.* New York: Basic Books, 1974.

CARKHUFF, R., & TRUAX, C. Lay mental health counseling: The effects of lay group counseling. *Journal of Consulting Psychology*, 1965, *39*(5), 426-431.

CASSEL, J. Psychosocial processes and "stress": Theoretical formulation. *International Journal of Health Services*, 1974, *4*(3), 471-482.

COBB, S. Social support as a moderator of life stress. *Psychosomatic Medicine*, 1976, *38*, 300-314.

COCHRAN, M., & BRASSARD, J. Child development and personal social networks. *Child Development*, 1979, *50*, 601-616.

COLLINS, J. Manpower issues in the mental health field. *Hospital and Community Psychiatry*, 1971, *22*, 362-367.

COLLINS, A., & PANCOAST, D. *Natural helping networks*. Washington, DC: National Association of Social Workers, 1976.

CONTER, K., HATCH, D., & D'AUGELLI, A. Enhancing the skills of Cub Scout den leaders. *American Journal of Community Psychology*, 1980, *8*(1), 77-85.

COWEN, E., GESTEN, E., BOIKE, M., NORTON, P., WILSON, A., & DeSTEFANO, M. Hairdressers as caregivers: 1. A descriptive profile of interpersonal helpgiving involvements. *American Journal of Community Psychology*, 1979, *7*(6), 633-648.

COYNE, J. C. Depression and the response of others. *Journal of Abnormal Psychology*, 1976, *85*(2), 186-193.

CRAVEN, P., & WELLMAN, B. The network city. *Sociological Inquiry*, 1973, *43*, 57-88.

D'AUGELLI, A., VALLANCE, T., DANISH, S., YOUNG, C., & GERDES, J. The Community Helpers Project: A description of a prevention strategy for rural communities. *Journal of Prevention*, forthcoming.

DAVID, T., MOOS, R., & KAHN, J. Community integration among elderly residents of sheltered care settings. *American Journal of Community Psychology*, forthcoming.

DEAN, A., & LIN, N. The stress-buffering role of social support: Problems and prospects for systematic investigation. *Journal of Nervous and Mental Disease*, 1977, *165*, 403-417.

DURLAK, J. A. Comparative effectiveness of paraprofessional and professional helpers. *Psychological Bulletin*, 1979, *86*(1), 80-92.

FELNER, R., PRIMAVERA, J., FARBER, J., & BISHOP, J. *Attorneys as caregivers during divorce*. Paper presented at the 88th Annual Meeting of the American Psychological Association, Toronto, September 1980.

GARBARINO, J., & SHERMAN, D. High-risk neighborhoods and high-risk families: The human ecology of child maltreatment. *Child Development*, 1980, *51*, 188-198.

GOLDBERG, G.S. Nonprofessionals in human services. In C. Grosser, W. E. Henry, & J. Kelly (Eds.), *Nonprofessionals in the human services*. San Francisco: Jossey-Bass, 1969.

GOTTLIEB, B. H. Re-examining the preventive potential of mental health consultation. *Canada's Mental Health*, 1974, *22*, 8-11.

GOTTLIEB, B. H. The primary group as supportive milieu: Applications to community psychology. *American Journal of Community Psychology*, 1979, *7*(5), 469-480.

GROSSER, C. Manpower development programs. In C. Grosser, W. E. Henry, & J. Kelly (Eds.), *Nonprofessionals in the human services.* San Francisco: Jossey-Bass, 1969.

HETHERINGTON, E., COX, M., & COX, R. Stress and coping in divorce: A focus on women. In J. Gullahorn (Ed.), *Psychology and transition.* New York: B. H. Winston, 1978.

HURLEY, D., & TYLER, F. *Relationship between mental health systems' paradigm and personpower utilization.* Paper presented at the Annual Meeting of the Eastern Psychological Association, New York, August 1976.

KAPLAN, S., & ROMAN, M. *Organization and delivery of mental health services in the ghetto: Lincoln Hospital experience.* New York: Praeger, 1973.

LENROW, P., & COWDEN, P. Human services, professionals, and the paradox of institutional reform. *American Journal of Community Psychology,* 1980, *8*(4), 463-484.

LEUTZ, W. The informal community caregiver: A link between the health care system and local residents. *American Journal of Orthopsychiatry,* 1976, *46*(4), 678-688.

LEVINE, M., & PERKINS, D. Social setting intervention and primary prevention: Comments on the Report of the Task Panel on Prevention to the President's Commission on Mental Health. *American Journal of Community Psychology,* 1980, *8*(2), 147-157.

LEVINE, M., TULKIN, S., INTAGLIATA, J., PERRY, J., & WHITSON, E. The paraprofessional: A brief social history. In S. Alley, J. Blanton, & R. Feldman (Eds.), *Paraprofessionals in mental health: Theory and practice.* New York: Human Sciences Press, 1979.

LIN, N., SIMEONE, R., ENSEL, W., & KUO, W. Social support, stressful life events, and illness: A model and an empirical test. *Journal of Health and Social Behavior,* 1979, *20,* 108-119.

McGUIRE, J., & GOTTLIEB, B. Social support groups among new parents: An experimental study in primary prevention. *Journal of Clinical Child Psychology,* 1979, *8*(2), 111-116.

MINUCHIN, S. The paraprofessional and the use of confrontation in the mental health field. *American Journal of Orthopsychiatry,* 1969, *30,* 722-729.

MITCHELL, R. Social networks and psychiatric clients: The personal and environmental context. *American Journal of Community Psychology,* forthcoming.

MITCHELL, R., & TRICKETT, E. Social network research and psychosocial adaptation: Implications for community mental health practice. In P. Insel (Ed.), *Environmental variables and the prevention of mental illness.* Lexington, MA: D. C. Heath, 1980.

PANCOAST, D. Finding and enlisting neighbors to support families. In J. Garbarino & H. Stocking (Eds.), *Protecting children from abuse and neglect.* San Francisco: Jossey-Bass, 1980.

PATTISON, E., KUNCEL, E., MURILLO, F., & MADENLIAN, R. A system-wide program for mental health worker utilization. In S. Alley, J. Blanton, & R. Feldman (Eds.), *Paraprofessionals in mental health: Theory and practice.* New York: Human Sciences Press, 1979.

PEARL, A., & RIESSMAN, F. *New careers for the poor: The nonprofessionals in human service.* New York: Free Press, 1965.

POLITSER, P. Network analysis and the logic of social support. In R. Price &
P. Politser (Eds.), *Evaluation and action in the social environment*. New York:
Academic Press, 1980.

POSER, E. The effects of therapists' training on group therapeutic outcome. *Journal
of Consulting Psychology*, 1966, *30*, 283-289.

RAPPAPORT, J. *Community psychology: Values, research and action*. New York:
Holt, Rinehart & Winston, 1977.

REIFF, R., & RIESSMAN, F. The indigenous paraprofessional. *Community Mental Health Journal*, 1965, Monograph No. 1.

REISER, M. Utilizing non-professional case aides in the treatment of psychotic
children at an outpatient clinic. *American Journal of Orthopsychiatry*, 1963, *33*,
544-546.

RIOCH, M. Pilot projects in training mental health counselors. In E. Cowen,
E. Gardner, & M. Zax (Eds.), *Emergent approaches to mental health problems*.
New York: Appleton-Century-Crofts, 1967.

SCHAEFFER, C., COYNE, J., & LAZARUS, R. The health-related functions of
social support. *Journal of Behavioral Medicine*, forthcoming.

SCHEIBE, K., KULICK, T., HERSCH, P., & La MACCHIA, S. College students on chronic wards. *Community Mental Health Journal*, 1969, Monograph
No. 5.

SEGAL, S., BAUMOHL, J., & MOYLES, E. Neighborhood types and community reaction to the mentally ill: A paradox of intensity. *Journal of Health and
Social Behavior*, 1980, *21*, 345-359.

SHAW, R., & EAGLE, C. Programmed failure: The Lincoln Hospital story. *Community Mental Health Journal*, 1971, *7*(4), 256-264.

WANDERSMAN, L., WANDERSMAN, A., & KAHN, S. Social support in the
transition to parenthood, *Journal of Community Psychology*, 1980, *8*(4), 332-342.

WARREN, D. Assessing community support systems in different types of
neighborhoods. In J. Garbarino & H. Stocking (Eds.), *Protecting children from
abuse and neglect*. San Francisco: Jossey-Bass, 1980.

WEISS, R. The provisions of social relationships. In S. Rubin (Ed.), *Doing unto
others*. Englewood Cliffs, NJ: Prentice-Hall, 1974.

WIESENFELD, A., & WEIS, H. Hairdressers and helping: Influencing the behavior of informal caregivers. *Professional Psychology*, 1979, *10*(6), 786-792.

WILCOX, B. Social support, life stress, and psychological adjustment: A test of the
buffering hypothesis. *American Journal of Community Psychology*, forthcoming.

ABOUT THE EDITOR

Benjamin H. Gottlieb is Associate Professor in the Department of Psychology of the University of Guelph in Guelph, Ontario, Canada. He completed his undergraduate work in psychology, earned a master's degree in social work, and received a joint Ph. D. in social work and psychology at the University of Michigan in Ann Arbor. During his graduate training he worked as a group therapist with emotionally disturbed children, as an aftercare counselor in a program aimed at deinstitutionalizing care of the mentally ill, and as a staff trainer and program planner in a project that diverted young offenders from training schools in Michigan. Since coming to Guelph, Gottlieb has been active in helping to establish a master's-level program in applied social and community psychology, and he has focused his research and writing on the nature and role of social support in health maintenance and health promotion. He is a member of the editorial boards of the *American Journal of Community Psychology,* the *Journal of Prevention,* and the newly established *Canadian Journal of Community Mental Health.* He recently edited a special issue of *Canada's Mental Health* devoted to the topic of informal support systems, and is also an active member of the board of the Council of Community Psychology Program Directors.

ABOUT THE CONTRIBUTORS

Manuel Barrera, Jr., received his Ph. D. in clinical psychology from the University of Oregon in 1977. Currently he is Assistant Professor in the Department of Psychology at Arizona State University. The topics of Barrera's previous publications and ongoing research interests include mental health service utilization, self-help psychotherapies, and depression.

Rosemary W. Burch is a registered nurse and health educator. She has developed a health education curriculum for children from preschool through grade twelve at Lincoln School, Providence, Rhode Island. A graduate of the University of Rochester School of Nursing, she has had research and health-care responsibilities in the obstetrics and gynecology service, Strong Memorial Hospital, Rochester, a problem-pregnancy clinic in Rochester, the pediatric service, Boston Floating Hospital, the Navy Medical Research Unit, Taiwan, an adolescent walk-in clinic on Taiwan, and community health nursing in Providence. Her interests include the development of collaboration among professionals, parents, and children to promote health-related decision-making skills.

Nancy J. Chapman is Associate Professor in the School of Urban Affairs at Portland State University, and co-principal investigator of the Natural Helping Networks and Service Delivery grant. She is an environmental and social psychologist, and has written in the areas of social networks, privacy, and assessing the environmental needs of specific populations such as the elderly and families living in public housing.

M. Robin DiMatteo is Associate Professor of Psychology at the University of California, Riverside. She received her Ph.D. in 1976 from Harvard University. In her dissertation, *The Sensitive Physician,* she sought to define the art of medicine. In 1976-1977 DiMatteo received a fellowship in health care from the Kellogg Foundation, and in 1977-1978 a research grant from the National Institute of Mental Health for further investigation of the factors in physician behavior that predict rapport with patients. She has published in such journals as *Medical Care* and *The Journal of Social Issues* (for which she co-edited a special issue on health care). Her research interests focus on social psychology and behavioral medicine, preventive and rehabilitative health behavior, and family therapy in medical settings.

John Eckenrode is a Research Associate and Lecturer in the Department of Behavioral Sciences of the Harvard School of Public Health (677 Huntington Avenue, Boston, Massachusetts 02115). He is a social psychologist whose current research concerns the impact of stress and social supports on the utilization of primary-care health services. His broader interests include the role of health care settings in addressing the psychosocial needs of their clientele.

Charles Froland is Assistant Professor at the School of Social Work and the Regional Research Institute for Human Services, Portland State University, Portland, Oregon. He is the project director of a national study for DHHS's Office of Human Development Services on agencies working to develop natural helping systems, self-help efforts, or informal networks of social support. His other interests include mental health, program evaluation, and income maintenance programs.

Susan Gore is Associate Professor of Sociology at the University of Massachusetts, Boston, Harbor Campus. She is interested in the mental and physical health consequences of life stress and in the dynamics through which support systems influence health status and utilization behaviors.

Ron Hays, M.A. (psychology), is a Ph.D. candidate in the social/personality program at the University of California, Riverside, and is presently a National Institute of Mental Health Trainee in Social Ecology. He is primarily concerned with studying problem or "deviant" behavior, and he has also been involved in research on the physician-patient relationship, alienation in young adulthood, authoritarianism and presidential candidate preference, and self-initiated honesty. His present interest in the role of social support in health care developed from training he received in the treatment of alcoholism while doing volunteer work at the Boulder Alcohol Recovery Center (Boulder, Colorado) during 1979-1980.

Barton J. Hirsch is Assistant Professor of Psychology at the University of Illinois, Urbana-Champaign. He received his B.A. in philosophy from the University of Wisconsin, did a year of graduate work in philosophy at the University of Michigan, and went on to receive his M.A. and Ph.D. in clinical psychology from the University of Oregon. He has been a postdoctoral research fellow at the Stanford University Social Ecology Laboratory. His research focuses on the study of social networks, coping strategies, and prevention among adolescents and adults, and he has consulted and authored several articles in these areas.

Daniel J. Hurley, Jr., Ph.D., is a Community-Clinical Psychologist who received his degree in 1977 from the University of Maryland Clinical Psychology Training Program. He is Assistant Professor in the Department of Psychology at the University of Rhode Island and the Executive Director of the Center for Community Cooperation, an action research institute committed to developing and studying the dynamics of cooperation at individual and community levels. Through the Center, he is involved in developing and evaluating the impact of resource exchange/bartering systems in urban and rural neighborhoods in Rhode Island. His experiences include work with community mental health, delinquent adolescents and their families, and paraprofessional/indigenous helpers.

Priscilla J. Kimboko is an urban anthropologist and a research assistant at the Regional Research Institute for Human Services, Portland State University. She has been involved in research in the areas of social networks, natural helping networks, family and personal adjustment to change (in divorce and in remarriage), and organizational responses to innovation. She has also worked in local government as a land use and development planner, with emphasis on issues of housing needs and community and economic development.

Peter B. Lenrow is Lecturer on Psychology, Harvard Medical School, and Associate Director for Research and Evaluation. Institute for School Consultation, McLean Hospital, Belmont, Massachusetts. He received his graduate training in the Harvard Department of Social Relations and at the Children's Hospital, Boston. His teaching, research, and consulting are concerned with the development of social settings in which the widest diversity of individuals can thrive. This involves promoting collaboration among professionals and laypeople to make more effective use of their resources. Toward this end, he trains consultants for work in schools, health services, and informal support systems.

Roger E. Mitchell is a Postdoctoral Fellow at the Social Ecology Laboratory, Department of Psychiatry and Behavioral Sciences, Stanford University Medical Center, Stanford, California 94305. Dr. Mitchell received his Ph.D. in 1980 from the Clinical Psychology Training Program at the University of Maryland. Dr. Mitchell's research interests have centered on the areas of program evaluation, indigenous helping networks, and social support. He is currently investigating the determinants and effects of social networks among individuals being treated for depression.

Diane L. Pancoast is a social worker and a Research Associate at the Regional Research Institute for Human Services, Portland State University. She has written and taught extensively on natural helping networks. She was principal investigator of the Natural Helping Networks and Service Delivery Project.

Barry Wellman has been studying social networks for a decade at the Centre for Urban and Community Studies, University of Toronto. His principal interest is in analyzing the effects of such large-scale phenomena as bureaucratization and capitalism on the structure and content of urban social networks. He currently directs the Department of Sociology's Structural Analysis Program, a collaborative research group using network analysis to study a broad range of sociological issues. He also coordinates the 350-member International Network for Social Network Analysis (INSNA) and edits its informal journal, *Connections*.

Brian L. Wilcox is an Assistant Professor at the University of Virginia, associated with the Community Psychology and Social Ecology and

Development Programs. He received his Ph.D. in community psychology from the University of Texas at Austin. His research interests include social support and social networks, coping in families at risk, environmental assessment, and environmental psychology.